Decisions for successful living

Decisions for successful living

by
President Harold B. Lee

Formerly **Youth and the Church**

Published by
DESERET BOOK COMPANY
Salt Lake City, Utah
1973

ISBN No. 0-87747-348-X
Library of Congress Number: 79-130323

Printed in
U.S.A.

FOREWORD

"Blessed are they which do hunger and thirst after righteousness: for they shall be filled." Such is the promise of the Lord spoken on the Mount.

Both in and out of the Church today are tens of thousands of young adults and good people everywhere, many of them perplexed and frustrated, who hunger and thirst after righteousness, some knowing not where to turn. In this volume written by President Harold B. Lee, they will find answers to their problems; they will find wisdom, strength, and inspiration.

Those who counsel others usually do so from two sources of knowledge—their own experiences, and the learning and observations of others.

President Lee speaks wisely from both such sources. In the three-quarters of a century of his life, his experiences have afforded him firsthand knowledge of the problems of people. He has known adversity. He has known sorrow and heartbreak. He has seen his dreams collapse. He has tasted disappointment. He has been acquainted with loneliness. He has witnessed at close range the tragedies of those who have stumbled in sin. And he has known the sweet taste of achievement and recognition after hard and discouraging effort.

He was born in an inconspicuous Idaho farm community where life was an unremitting, and all too often an unrewarding, struggle with the elements. At the age of seventeen he became a school teacher, an experience which tested his talents and strengthened his resolution to secure further education and move on into a wider and more challenging world.

But in the microcosm of that Idaho farm community he saw life as men live it, some with indifference, some with carelessness, some with ambition, some with great faith, some with frustration. He has never lost his feeling for the poor, for the struggling, for those who work so hard to keep afloat in adverse seas that would overwhelm them.

He responded without hesitation or question to serve a mission in the Western States. His call was not to one of those "far-away places with the strange-sounding names," but just over the mountains to Denver. But in his faith he knew that it was the Lord who had called him. And it was the Lord who rewarded that faith with a sweet harvest, and later the companionship of a talented and beautiful young woman whom he met while she also was serving in the same mission and who later became his wife.

There followed years of struggle for further education, in teaching school, and serving as a principal, as a businessman, and as City Commissioner in Salt Lake City.

Concurrent with all of this were calls to various Church responsibilities, including stake president at the age of thirty-one. Then in 1936, with organization of the Church Welfare Program, he was called to serve as Managing Director. The nation and the world were in the grip of a paralyzing economic depression. His great service in handling difficult problems commended him to the leaders of the Church. In 1941 he was called to the Council of the Twelve. In this capacity he traveled widely over the earth, developing understanding out of observation, sympathy as he walked among the poor, love as he mingled with the faithful, resolution to act fearlessly against those in transgression, and the capacity to sorrow with them and to extend the hand of helpfulness to assist with their restoration.

In business and in public affairs he was served with men of stature over the nation and won their respect.

His home has been an exemplary one with a gracious and able companion, their example before the Church and the world standing as one worthy of emulation.

Out of such varied experiences over many years has been molded a man with appreciation for the problems, the struggles, the frustrations of his fellows, and particularly those of young people.

Added to all of this is the wisdom of others acquired through wide reading and intensive study. His knowledge of the scriptures is profound. He knows them to be the word of God. He has drunk deeply of their wisdom and inspiration. The reader of this book will sense the breadth of this knowledge as he notes the many quotations of scriptural texts on a great variety of subjects. President Lee constantly fortifies his themes with the revealed word of the Lord.

Here for the reader is wisdom—divine wisdom, spoken in various dispensations, and preserved and "brought forth by the gift and power of God." The man or woman, young or old, who reads this volume will drink from this spring of scriptural truth and will find new understanding of and added appreciation for these sacred records.

President Lee, out of his cultivated acquaintance with these volumes, uses with ease and facility, words of sacred writ to give authority to the many themes with which he deals.

And in addition, he reveals his broad acquaintance with the writings of the literary masters of the past as well as with contemporary authors.

He therefore counsels from the wisdom of his own broad experience, and the learning and observations of others. But beyond all of this is an even greater wisdom. It is the wisdom that comes of revelation. Most of the material in this book was prepared some years ago as a series of radio addresses to youth. Elder Lee was then a member of the Council of Twelve. He prepared only after seeking the direction of the Holy Spirit. The original text breathes that influence.

Now he stands as the President of the Church, sustained as Prophet, Seer, and Revelator. The original text has been updated and added to.

To what source might youth, and Church members generally, more hopefully and expectantly turn for strength, for insight, for inspiration in dealing with the complex problems of their lives? They will find within these pages truths of timeless value expressed in a contemporary setting. And those who hunger and thirst after righteousness will be filled with that wisdom which comes of experience and

learning, and, more importantly, with the light of truth
which comes of divine revelation.

—Gordon B. Hinckley

PREFACE

In offering this volume under the title *Decisions For Successful Living*, it seems appropriate to explain the contents and background of this book.

The writings contained herein are based, for the most part, on a series of radio talks delivered over radio station KSL in Salt Lake City from January 1 to June 24, 1945. The radio series bore the title "Youth and the Church." At that time America was in the final stages of World War II, and the youth of the Church were faced with tremendous challenges in combatting the evils that surround war. The talks were ultimately compiled in a book under the title *Youth and the Church*.

It has been gratifying to me to reflect on the thoughts presented at that time and realize how vital the principles of the gospel are to any age, under any circumstance.

This new volume, like its predecessor, is presented as an answer to some of the many problems with which any generation may be confronted. My hope is that all who read this book will be led to the sure conclusion that within the revealed gospel of Jesus Christ, and from the teachings of our Church leaders, may be found the answer to every question and the solution of every problem essential to the social, temporal, and spiritual welfare of human beings who are all the children of God, our Eternal Father.

The matters discussed, both from the former volume, and the new material which has been added, are on subjects that concern every soul in the never-ending contest between truth and error, righteousness and wickedness, hence I have chosen to address these writings to each one who may read in such a way as to try to impress the reader with the fact that these subjects do have a personal application to each one of us. If, by a reading of my humble offerings, the reader creates a desire for a deeper study of the scriptures wherein may be found the sure guide to eternal happiness through an abiding testimony in the mission of the Lord Jesus Christ, I will have accomplished my purpose.

When this material was first prepared my own daughters, Maurine and Helen, served as representatives of the modern youth of the day, and were my chief critics and consultants in the preparation of these chapters.

Ever praying that the blessings of the Lord may be upon all mankind today to the end that they might, by prayerful study and learning, come to an understanding of all things necessary to combat the evils of the world, I am,

Faithfully, your brother,
HAROLD B. LEE

Contents

Decisions for Successful Living
_____ *1* _____

Decisions. Decisions.

Life seemingly is one decision after another, and often the weightiest problems of life revolve around the decision-making process.

Yet this freedom to decide for ourselves is the greatest blessing we could have in our lives. Growth and development could never be achieved if everything was forced upon us and all we had to do was blindly follow a monotonous course of meaningless routine.

The freedom to choose was a basic issue in the grand council of heaven before we ever came to earth, and had to be defended there by a war in heaven. The forces of truth have been defending this right ever since, and the struggle gets no easier.

Fortunately, a loving Father in Heaven has provided counsel and direction for us in making the decisions of life. His direction to us is embodied in the gospel of his Son, Jesus Christ. As I study the gospel plan, it becomes more evident to me every day that the basis for every correct decision in life can be found in the gospel. Every need of man has been thought of by a loving Father but what we must do is decide to follow this path of truth. The best decision for successful living is the decision to keep the commandments of God.

We all desire success. We desire to be well thought of by our associates. We want to feel needed and wanted in the presence of others. Born into us is that desire to feel

comfortable with others. Success is many things to many
people, but to every child of God it ultimately will be to
inherit his presence and there be comfortable with him.

The path to this exalted condition is rugged and steep.
Many stumble and fall, and through discouragement never
pick themselves up to start again. The forces of evil cloud
the path with many foggy deterrents, often trying to detour
us in mis-leading trails. But through all this journey there is
the calming assurance that if we choose the right, success
will be ours, and the achievement of it will have molded
and formed and created us into the kind of person qualified
to be accepted into the presence of God. What greater success could there be than to have all that God has.

What now follows in the remaining chapters of this
book is an effort to portray the gospel plan in relationship
to the decisions of life. Successful living is born of gospel
living. Keep the commandments taught herein, search the
scriptures, pray always, and be obedient, and eternal success will be yours.

Choose The Right

I desire to relate a brief narrative of some of the experiences of our ancestors, the ancient Israelites, and the lessons that they learned from those experiences. All students of the scriptures are familiar with this story. Through a train of interesting circumstances related in the Bible, the children of Israel, or in other words the families of Jacob, were residing in the land of Egypt among the idolatrous Egyptians whose religious ideals and practices were in contradiction of the Gospel which they had received from the teachings of their fathers. The Prophet Moses was raised up from among them and commissioned by the Lord to lead them from bondage, which he was able to do by aid of miraculous interventions demonstrating the power that had been given him as a servant of the Lord. After the Israelites departed from Egypt they journeyed for forty years in the wilderness where they underwent the most severe trials that tested not only their powers of physical endurance but their faith and faithfulness. When they lived righteously they were given strength to successfully compete against their foes. The Lord finally sent hornets as a scourge to drive out the Amorites who possessed the promised land over the River Jordan that was to become the abode of the Israelites, now under the leadership of Joshua, who had succeeded Moses as the leader of the people. Joshua received a revelation from the Lord in which Israel was reminded of the many blessings they had received. This impressive revelation concluded with these words:

"And I sent the hornet before you, which drave them out from before you, even the two kings of the Amorites; but not with thy sword, nor with thy bow.

"And I have given you a land for which ye did not labour, and cities which ye built not, and ye dwell in them; of the vineyards and oliveyards which ye planted not do ye eat." (Joshua 24:12-13.)

Then follows the admonition of Joshua which has been the text for many a sermon:

"Now therefore fear the Lord, and serve him in sincerity and in truth: and put away the gods which your fathers served on the other side of the flood, and in Egypt; and serve ye the Lord.

"And if it seem evil unto you to serve the Lord, *choose you this day whom ye will serve;* whether the gods which your fathers served that were on the other side of the flood, or the gods of the Amorites, in whose land ye dwell: *but as for me and my house, we will serve the Lord.*

"And the people answered and said, God forbid that we should forsake the Lord, to serve other gods. . . .

"If ye forsake the Lord (Joshua replied) and serve strange gods, then he will turn and do you hurt, and consume you, after that he hath done you good.

"And the people said unto Joshua, Nay; but we will serve the Lord." (Joshua 24:14-16, 20-21.)

Thus concludes the brief narrative of this ancient people.

Now I should like to relate another story of God's dealings with modern Israel which presents a striking parallel to that which I have just related, a story which cannot be completely told because we today are a part of it and are helping to write it. That the Lord had designated another promised land on another continent besides the land over Jordan is evidenced in the inspired blessings of Father Jacob to his son Joseph, and also in the revelations of the Lord to the early inhabitants of the land of America as related in the Book of Mormon, that here in America was a land choice above all other lands and that the descendants of the children of Israel who came here would "dwell in prosperity long upon the face of this land; and nothing, save it shall be iniquity among them, shall harm or disturb their prosperity upon . . . this land forever. Wherefore, if ye shall keep the commandments of the Lord, the Lord hath consecrated this land for the security of thy seed." (2 Nephi 1:31-32.)

Fulfillment of Prophecies

The early discoverers and settlers of this land America came not by chance, but according to the prophecies of the scriptures, they were moved upon by the Spirit of the Lord to explore, to colonize and to make their homes here. Many of them, including our own progenitors, we know from inspired pronouncements, were of the scattered sheep of the House of Israel spoken of in the scriptures. For the most part their primary purpose in coming was to seek religious freedom from old world oppressions. Inspired men were raised up as the founders of this nation, the government of "which should be maintained for the rights and protection of all flesh, according to just and holy principles; that every man may act in doctrine and principle pertaining to futurity, according to the moral agency which" . . . (the Lord) "has given unto him, that every man may be accountable for his own sins in the day of judgment. Therefore, it is not right that any man should be in bondage one to another." (Doc. & Cov. 101:77-79.) Bloody wars have been fought to preserve those liberties. The pioneers of this western land sacrificed their homes, their possessions, comforts and luxuries that here in the tops of the mountains the Lord's House should be established.

A Parallel Drawn

To us, the citizens of this great country, as the descendants of these modern Israelites in this promised land of America, it might as well be said as was said by Joshua to the Israelites of ancient times: "We too have been given a land for which we did not labor, and cities which we built not, and we dwell in them; of the vineyards and oliveyards which we planted not, do we eat." We are reaping the bounteous harvest of luxuries, opportunities and privileges from the seeds planted by the sweat and blood and tears of our forebears. This land of our inheritance is a land blessed above all other lands and we have been blessed thereon. It is a land of liberty and no king has been upon it to become its ruler, for the Lord, the King of heaven, only shall be the king to those that hearken unto his words. It has been fortified against all other nations and he that fighteth against Zion shall perish as will those who attempt to raise up a king here. All this was foretold by prophecy and thus far we have seen it fulfilled. (II Nephi 10:10-19.)

As we contemplate the blessings of all these things that we have as a rich legacy, it would be well to heed the counsel of James Truslow Adams, the American historian, who wrote this: "Perhaps it would be a good idea, fantastic as it sounds, to muffle every telephone, halt every motor and stop all activity some day to give people a chance to ponder for a few minutes on what it is all about, why they are living and what they really want."

Questions of Youth

By medium of this writing I would send those questions far beyond the range of my voice in the hope that they might cause the youth of today, and indeed all who may read, to halt in their mad scramble for pleasure, for education, for wealth, for opportunity, for honors, for special privileges, and to consider seriously the questions: What is it all about? Why are you living and what do you really want?

The answers to these questions involve the determination of ideals for you to follow or, in other words, "gods" for you to worship. It seems logical that if we are to preserve the freedom and liberty vouchsafed to us by our pioneer fathers we must pursue likewise their lofty ideals. Now to discover those ideals: In a published statement by John Collier, former United States Commissioner of Indian Affairs, is found the declaration of a great ideal that has given strength to the pioneers of this land. I quote his words:

"At a recent Congressional hearing, a committee member thought that for Indians to become organized, to conduct their enterprises by cooperative methods and to preserve their own life motives and beliefs might be contrary to the American idea. Replying I used the Mormon pioneer people as an example, a people with strong religious tradition, a strong tradition of cooperating and bearing each other's burdens, a persevering ideal which can maintain itself anywhere in the United States or indeed anywhere in the world. Such group cooperativeness, such perseverance of ideal and aim, such loyalty to heritage is not in conflict with the American idea but is the very heart and soul of the American idea."

The loftiest concepts of life are embodied in what Mr. Collier calls "religious tradition," the complete embodiment of which is the fulness of the Gospel of Jesus Christ. The Church is the treasure house in which these sacred concepts are preserved. All morality must have a religious base. If we are to accept the thesis as proposed by some "that morals are relative as to time and place, that what is good in one society is bad in another," we are accepting a teaching that is separated only by a hair's breadth from the thought that there is no such thing as sin. If tonight you are faced with a moral crisis and the making of a wrong decision involves the loss of your virtue, what shall guide you from a secret immoral sin unless you have faith in the divine commandments thundered from Mount Sinai, "Thou shalt not!"? Why should you not rob the rich or kidnap to get gain, if you are poor? Property, virtue and life itself are safe only in that land where lawmakers are influenced by and laws are made and enforced and obeyed in conformity with the basic moral standards found in the holy scriptures. The Nazi fuehrer of yesterday was once quoted as describing the Nazi movement as "a great battle for humanity's liberation from the curse of Mount Sinai," (meaning the Ten Commandments). Anyway the Nazis have shown us what a world devoted to the breaking of the Ten Commandments looks like, with murder, immorality, robbery, covetousness and lying running rampant throughout the world and unquestionably with the official sanction of the governments that have fostered these well-nigh unbelievable crimes in disobedience of divine laws. God forbid a civilization that wages successful battle for the liberation of humanity from the commandments of Mount Sinai!

Youth Needs the Church

Any youth without religious convictions and lacking a faith in eternal values is as a sailor without a compass or as a traveler without a guide. Youth today needs the Church as the world reels drunkenly under the impact of bloody conflict induced by men unguided by religious influence.

The gospel is not merely a code of ethics or a social program, although "living upon the earth involves a plan of living together in order to cast out greed and avarice, selfishness, vice and wickedness, self-seeking for earthly power and dominion." The gospel is the plan of our Heavenly Father to guide mankind in their associations together in mortality to the end that eventually they shall be saved and exalted in the world to come. The gospel is divine truth, "it is all truth existent from eternity to eternity." The laws contained in the gospel are God's laws. They are not to be changed or modified to suit the whims of individuals and are designed to develop our inward souls through proper observance of and respect therefor. Any conduct on the part of an individual that does not advance him toward the goal of eternal life is not only wasted energy but actually becomes the basis of sin. We must never forget the injunction of the Savior: "Lay not up for yourselves treasures upon earth, where moth and rust doth corrupt, and where thieves break through and steal: But lay up for yourselves treasures in heaven, where neither moth nor rust doth corrupt, and where thieves do not break through nor steal." (Matt. 6:19-20.)

Kingdom of God

The Church is the Kingdom of God established upon the earth with authority from the Lord to administer the laws and the ordinances of the gospel in accordance with the plan of salvation. The Church of Jesus Christ of Latter-day Saints stands today as it has always stood, as a continuing revolution against the norms of a society that fall below the standards of the Gospel. The failure of the Church to take such a stand would make it unworthy of the sacred name given it by the Lord himself. For that very purpose the Lord declared he had sent his "everlasting covenant into the world, to be a light to the world, and to be a standard for my people and for the Gentiles to seek to it, and to be a messenger before my face to prepare the way before me." (Doc. & Cov. 45:9.)

The conviction grows on me as new experiences multiply that the safety of youth today and the perpetuation of the fundamental ideals of the founders of this nation and the pioneers of this land lie in the ability of the Church to instill gospel principles into the minds and hearts and souls of youth and their parents, that these principles might become the guiding ideals of their lives. The only hope I can see for their salvation in the midst of overwhelming temptations in this day predicted when the Devil should have power over his own dominion, is that each one shall have in his heart a firm conviction of right and wrong and a determination to live righteously.

My sole purpose will be to aid every honest soul to choose this day whom he would serve, whether the God served by our fathers or the false gods being worshipped at shrines built by false teachers among us. All this to the end that each will be led to say in his heart, "Nay, but we will serve the Lord."

A few years ago I was invited to give some talks to a group of young people and had been requested to select a subject heading under which these talks could be announced. In the laboratory of my home that night I experimented with several suggested subject titles. One suggestion that I title my talks "The Problems of Youth" brought forth a significant remark from a young university student who sat across the table. "Youth and older folks," she said, "don't agree as to what constitute the problems of youth. What to parents and grandparents is an abnormal and difficult period is for youth the only period of time they have known."

As I think about that remark I am made aware that you as the youth of today, as judged by fathers and mothers of middle age, have lived your entire lives during a period that has been marked by a series of circumstances that are quite different from those experienced by the youth of yesterday. Your most serious problems are, therefore, not readily apparent and are often overshadowed in your own thinking by those of less consequence.

An Unusual Period

The Second World War ended in 1945. Therefore it might be said that every person living today under thirty years of age has lived during an unusual period in the world's history. Let us analyze for a few moments some of these conditions. Following the close of the First World War there was a reconstruction period that saw the prices of farm products decrease fifty per cent in one year and drastic reduction in wages for those in urban industrial areas. But following the Second World War there seemed to be a boom in the economy, with some intermittent recessions, but ever increasing periods of prosperity and inflation. Living "on terms" became the way of life. Homes, furniture, automobiles, clothes, appliances, and a burgeoning amount of luxuries could all be bought on credit. Many lived as though they thought the day of reckoning would never come.

But most significant was the change in the mobility of the people. Families started moving around. Employment transfers from one state to another or across the nation became commonplace. The improvement of technology in automobile production made more and more cars available, and people traveled away from home for practically all of their social life. In earlier days fathers and mothers and their children attended dancing parties most usually held under Church auspices, where constant parental chaperonage was always in evidence and where mother's acquaintance with her daughter's escort was most intimate. The speed and the license in this age of the automobile made possible a radical change in those previous contacts. An eminent astronomer is reputed to have lamented about this condition to the effect that by his science he was able to predict for years in advance the exact times an eclipse or starry phenomena would occur, but for the life of him he could not predict where his daughter would be at eleven o'clock that night.

Educational Theories and Philosophies

Recent years have ushered in educational theories and philosophies that have questioned all the old standards of religion, morality and family relationships. Modern iconoclasts have been at work under guise of what we have come mistakenly to call "higher criticism" to destroy faith in the old and trusted authoritative teachings of the scriptures and to supplant therefore the uninspired, man-made ethical doctrines that change with time and place.

With the coming of the radio and television much of good and some of bad have resulted. Every few years we have a spirited election campaign. In former generations the discussion of campaign issues was largely limited to newspapers, with occasional opportunities to meet and hear a campaign orator at a political party rally. In contrast, during our last political campaign, we have listened to all and sundry who had enough money to purchase the necessary radio and television time. If youth have listened to many of these broadcasts, they may well have had some doubts raised in their minds as to the importance of giving due respect to those who are to make and to administer the law because of false impressions fostered by careless politicians who overlooked the probable ill effects of their unwisdom. That type of broadcast, together with those coming in to every home that literally try to make vice a virtue and evil a desirable thing can hardly be expected to be an improvement over the generation just past, where respect for law and governmental authority and abstinence were urged from home and school and pulpit. Vivid recitals of gangster and crime scenes or dramatic portrayals of unnatural social relationships likewise do not conduce to an advancement of our interests or an increase of our happiness.

Rural Discipline

I have thought of the discipline of the boy and girl of my youthful days in a rural community. We began to "do chores" shortly after daybreak so we could "start" with the day's work by sun-up. When the day's work was finished, we had yet to do our evening "chores," usually by aid of a lantern. Despite the fact that there were no wages and hours regulations or child labor laws, we did not seem to be stunted from our exertions. Sleep requirements did not admit of too frequent frivolities. Returns from our labors were small and usually came on a once-a-year basis at harvest time. Homes of that day went throughout the summer with but very little ready money but from our cows we were provided milk, butter and cheese; in our granaries there was usually sufficient wheat to be taken to the mill for flour and cereals. We had our own chickens and garden and fruits in season. Large families required mother to remodel the suits and dresses of the eldest to meet the needs of the youngest who rarely had a "boughten" suit from the store. I do not know how we would have managed with the advanced teachings we have today about vitamins, diets and minimum food budgets that require food items as though they were a necessity that then were only available as luxuries at Christmas time or on other like gala occasions. Education was provided and was within the reach of all who were willing to work, although it involved saving in the summer and "batching" and working one's way through school by part-time employment in the winter.

I have contrasted the experiences of my youth with the conditions under which many of the youth of today are living. Much of the work on the farm has now been mechanized and the drudgery of yesterday on the farm as well as in the home and in the factory has been reduced to a minimum by labor-saving devices. You have had provided for you today a farm subsidy program intended to remove the anxieties concerning market conditions and to make possible payments even for crops that are not planted, although you must expect to repay your subsidy income indirectly by increased taxes; a government home and farm loan program that makes possible loans at low interest rates, that in case of unavoidable failure may be refinanced by other existing loan agencies; a social security and medicare plan, plus other government subsidy plans for schools, highways and most activities of life. All this and other similar programs are in the nature of so-called social planning and uplift, and I will not say that in all this there may not be some good, but I call these things to your attention that you may seriously speculate as to possible effects of some of these changed conditions upon the generation of which you are a part. There are some who think of the conditions of the youth of past generations and thank the

Lord that a brighter day has dawned for their children in this generation, that living for them will be much easier than in the past through these modern social developments.

Upon you, the youth of today, may I urge that before you decry all that is past and applaud all that is present that you search the lives of the men and women of your community who have achieved in the business world, in education, in the Church. You will learn that in almost every instance the foundation stone of their success was a true sense of values born out of stern necessity.

Youth Have Faced Problems Before

The youth of every generation have faced problems just as stern in their nature as are the problems facing youth today. There were the days of poverty and hardships. The weak fell by the wayside; the strong triumphed. There followed times of persecution and mobbings when only the stout-hearted thought the struggle was worthwhile. Then came the flood of slander and dissension, when traitors from within tested the best fiber of their generation. The so-called age of sophistication ushered in the mental conflicts when a "little learning" in some proved to be a "dangerous thing." What shall we say of your day? Is yours the test, as someone has said, of "gold, luxuries and indulgence"? Who of you will say that yours may not be the severest tests? Youth who met the challenge of their day withstood the trials and temptations and passed to you the torch of their civilization. Will you too become strong through the climb up the mountains of your life's experience?

Builds Character

The overcoming of obstacles and the solution of problems involve the expenditure of energy that builds character, that increases the capacity of the individual. It was said by Benjamin Franklin "that to be thrown on one's own resources is to be cast in the very lap of fortune, for our faculties undergo a development and a display of energy of which they were previously unsusceptible." Remember it is the pursuit of easy things that makes men weak. Our ancestors become a strong, virile people because they braved dangers, overcame and triumphed in the face of seeming impossibilities. We must realize that in reality the only thing we have inherited from them is the "capacity to produce and to preserve the estate by remaking it." I well recall that of my boyhood associates in high school days two among them achieved greatest distinction. One of these, impelled to rigorous daily toil by the insistent demands of his boyhood days, became a leader of the farming interests in our nation. The other, totally blinded in his childhood became an attorney of high stand ing in his own state. Some others who learned easily and attained high scholastic honors with little effort are not those who held their places as leaders in the affairs of men. As cruel as were the exactions of a terrible war upon our youth in the armed services, those who overcame and remained "captains of their own souls" are the ones to whom the next generation will look for leadership.

Your elders think of these changed conditions as problems of modern youth and they bid you remember the lessons of the generations that have gone before you and the wisdom of the old adage, "To follow the course of least resistance makes men and rivers crooked." The darkest day in the life of a youth is that day when he sits down to contemplate how he can get something for nothing.

Someone commenting on this kind of attitude expressed the opinion that the political parties of tomorrow might well be made up of major pressure groups vying with each other to get what they could by way of government gratuities. If such a condition should come, what would happen to our democracy founded on the theory that each citizen must strive for that which is best for the entire nation? All this, together with the spirit of hatred and destruction and the loneliness of young men and women for social relations denied by the exigencies of war with the attending

frustration and feeling of defeatism, has all too often resulted in a wild orgy of immoral conduct and debauchery,
bringing in its wake remorse, bitterness and blighted hopes.

Standards Not Changed

As you analyze these conditions I have referred to, I
would impress upon you that despite changed conditions
and the abnormal times during which you have lived and
are now living, the standards of right and wrong have
not changed, but are as eternal and as unchanging as the
stars in the heavens. The youth of all generations have
faced tests just as severe as those you are facing. Their
strength to overcome great odds came from an abiding faith
in themselves and faith in the ultimate triumph of truth.
The same powers and influences that guided your parents
through their youthful days are with us today and will be
efficacious in your behalf to just the extent that you heed
the counsel of the Church and live as the Gospel teaches.

The harder the climb up the mountains, the greater
the thrill of triumph in the achievement. The first step
towards independence and a successful life is taken when
an individual resolves in his heart to live by his own exertions. What is that success after all for which you strive?
Hear the wise counsel of President Heber J. Grant, formerly
a president of the Church and a prophet and leader of our
own day. These are his words:

"Not he who merely succeeds in making a fortune, and
in so doing blunts the natural affections of the heart and
chases therefrom the love of his fellows, can be said to be
truly successful; but he who so lives that those who know
him best shall love him most; and that God, who knows not
only his deeds but also the inmost sentiments of his heart,
shall love him; of such a one only, notwithstanding he may
die in poverty, can be said indeed and of a truth, he should
be crowned with the wealth of success." (Gospel Standards,
p. 181.)

Parents of Tomorrow's Youth

4

As we have discussed the problems confronting youth today, you might well wonder if this fateful prophecy uttered by a prophet sixty-five years after the death of Jesus may not have foretold our own day: "This know also, that in the last days perilous times shall come." And then there follows a description of these predicted perilous times that accurately summarize conditions under which we now live:

"For men shall be lovers of their own selves, covetous, boasters, proud, blasphemers, disobedient to parents, unthankful, unholy,

"Without natural affection, truce-breakers, false accusers, incontinent, fierce, despisers of those that are good,

"Traitors, heady, highminded, lovers of pleasures more than lovers of God;

"Having a form of godliness, but denying the power thereof: from such turn away.

"For of this sort are they which creep into houses, and lead captive silly women laden with sins, led away with divers lusts,

"Ever learning, and never able to come to the knowledge of the truth." (II Timothy 3:1-7.)

In the midst of all our present living, you have asked, "How are youth to save themselves from the pitfalls from which they may not soon be retrieved?" Perhaps the approach to the solution of this problem is suggested by the writer of homely verse of another generation. I should

like to introduce the discussion of this chapter by reading
this poem, which was well-known to everyone in that day.
It is entitled "A Fence or an Ambulance" and its author is
Joseph Malius:

'Twas a dangerous cliff, as they freely confessed
Though to walk near its crest was so pleasant.
But over its terrible edge there had slipped,
A duke and full many a peasant.
So the people said something would have to be done
But their projects did not at all tally.
Some said, "Put a fence around the edge of the cliff."
Some, "An ambulance down in the valley."

But the cry for the ambulance carried the day,
For it spread through the neighboring city.
A fence may be useful or not, it is true,
But each heart became brimful of pity,
For those who slipped over that dangerous cliff;
And the dwellers in highway and alley
Gave pounds or gave pence, not to put up a fence
But an ambulance down in the valley.

"For the cliff is all right if you're careful," they said,
And if folk's even slip or are dropping,
It isn't the slipping that hurts them so much,
As the shock down below when they're stopping.
So day after day, as these mishaps occurred,
Quick forth would their rescuers sally,
To pick up the victims who fell off the cliff
With their ambulance down in the valley.

Then an old sage remarked, "It's a marvel to me
That people give far more attention
To repairing results than to stopping the cause
When they'd much better aim at prevention.
Let us stop at its source all the mischief," he cried.
"Come neighbors and friends let us rally.
If the cliff we will fence, we might almost dispense
With the ambulance down in the valley."

"Oh, he's a fanatic," the others rejoined,
"Dispense with the ambulance? Never.
He'd dispense with all charities, too, if he could,
No, no, we'll support them forever.
Aren't we picking up folks just as fast as they fall
And shall this man dictate to us? Shall he?

Why should people of sense stop to put up a fence
While the ambulance works in the valley?"

But a sensible few who are practical, too,
Will not bear with such nonsense much longer.
They believe that prevention is better than cure,
And their party will still be the stronger.
Encourage them then with your purse, voice and pen,
And while other philanthropists dally
They will scorn all pretense and put up a fence
On the cliff that hangs over the valley.

Better guide well the young than reclaim them when old,
For the voice of true wisdom is calling.
To rescue the fallen is good but 'tis best
To prevent other people from falling.
Better close up the source of temptation and crime,
Than deliver from dungeon and galley.
Better put a strong fence round the top of the cliff
Than an ambulance down in the valley.

The moral of that story in rhyme is so clear that it
hardly needs further comment or explanation. The home,
the school and the church must bend their energies toward
ways of prevention and constructive building rather than
to be merely detectives of crime after the act has been
committed.

Why do radio and television operators permit programs
that bring questionable propaganda daily into our homes, or
movie producers picture sensational stories that are destructive of moral standards? What brings the dispenser of beer
and the keeper of brothels and dens of vice to your neigh-
borhood? Why do dance hall managers permit smoking
and the sale of beer in their places of business? The
answer is simple. These people are in the business for profit. They are selling you the kind of commodity your
patronage demands. I gloried in the report of a foreign
military contingent of our American boys who greeted with
boos and expressions of disgust the filthy stories and suggestive remarks of a would-be entertainer of movie fame
who apparently had been misinformed as to the moral
stamina of this group of soldiers.

Program of Prevention

Now let us examine some of the factors that enter into this program of prevention. The director of personnel of the Chase National Bank of New York City, relates the story of his appointment and the counsel given him by the president of the bank, in which he was instructed in his new duties that consisted of selecting suitable employes for the institution. "Almost any person, Al," said the president, "can judge an animal when it has reached its peak at the county fair by measuring, weighing and counting up the points; but it takes a real expert to see a young colt in the pasture and judge how fast it will run as a three-year-old on the race track or to pick a blue-ribbon winner from a litter of two-weeks-old pigs. If you want to make money on steers, don't buy them at their peak. By that time the other fellow is making the profit. Always try to catch them on their way up."

Youth are the children of yesterday, and the parents of the children of tomorrow. What a youth is today depends largely upon what he learned as a child, and the lessons of today become the deeds of tomorrow. The glory of the work of those who touch the lives of youth is profoundly declared by Daniel Webster in these words: "If we work upon marble, it will perish; if we work upon brass, time will efface it; if we rear temples they will crumble to the dust; but if we work upon immortal souls, if we imbue them with principles, with the fear of God and the love of fellowmen, we engrave on those tablets something which brightens all eternity."

Children Well-Born

Someone has rightly said that the education and training of a child should begin a hundred years before he is born. We must not over look the importance of having our children well-born. I would hope for the day when you young people as the parents of tomorrow would be concerned with the pedigrees of the companions of your daughter, knowing as you do that from among her companions, she will one day choose her husband. I was somewhat concerned the other day when a mother could not be sure as to the spelling of the name of the young man her daughter is to marry. How well will you know your daughter's escort? You young men would do well to scan carefully the family background of the girl that may one day be the mother of your children. Can you catch the beauty and wisdom in the remark of the old Irish mother who was being chided by her grown son for being too greatly concerned about him? Said she, "Bless your soul. I've been concerned about you ever since you were but a mere twinkle in your 'father's eye.'" Likewise, you young men and young women must not forget that if the fountains of life are polluted at their source, children of such unions enter life with a great handicap to overcome.

A Noble Heritage

The Apostle Paul emphasized the great value of a good name and a noble heritage in his letter to Timothy whom he addressed as "My dearly beloved son." He said, "When I call to remembrance the unfeigned faith that is in thee, which dwelt first in thy grandmother Lois, and thy mother Eunice, and I am persuaded that in thee also." (II Timothy 1:5.) It has been said that if you train a boy, you are training only an individual but if you train a girl you are training an entire family. As a youth one may become divorced from the influence of a good home and he may become careless and wayward, but if the good mother's teachings of his childhood have been impressed upon his heart, he will return to them for safety, as does a ship to safe anchorage in a storm. The slogan of the soldier, "There are no atheists in a foxhole," is an expressed testimony of that truth revealed in the lives of hundreds of thousands of our servicemen, who except for their early teachings would have nothing on which to anchor their faith.

If you young women were one day to be the mother

of a son, would not your heart burn within you to have
him write this about his mother that I copied from a
letter written by one of our soldiers in the South Pacific
during World War II:

"The one who has had the greatest influence on my life
for good is my mother. The love of the gospel which she
instilled in me by the things she said and did has helped
me more than anything else to withstand the many temptations there are in the army. . . . I know that as long as
I keep the commandments of God that all the stratagems
of Satan will be unable to break through the armour of
righteousness which fortifies us against sin." The man of
wisdom has said, "Train up a child in the way he should
go: and when he is old, he will not depart from it." (Proverbs 22:6.)

We are living in a scientific age when some modern
mothers have adopted theories of training their children
that forbid sharp corrections and stern discipline lest the
initiative and personality of the little child be curbed to
his own hurt. I have often wondered just who these teachers
are who are masters of the techniques of bringing up children in this age of license and indulgence. Are they always
successful parents of successful children who are giving us
lessons from their own books of life? Constantly before
us are magazine articles and editorials urging strong parental authority as a cure for juvenile delinquency and commenting on the claim that the education of parents is the
only solution of juvenile delinquency. From one of these
editorials is this statement:

"We might as well argue that the ten commandments
given to ancient Israel and the measures Moses adopted to
compel observance thereof were not necessary, inasmuch
as church leaders could have taught the people to behave
without the authority of the law. But of this I am certain
that unless some action is taken to induce parents to keep
their children within the law there is no other point from
which to start development of strong character and good
citizenship."

In the meantime, while we are discussing this issue, millions of pampered or neglected youngsters are being apprehended, lectured, mildly disciplined and, as these children apparently believe, "interfered with in asserting their independence and exercising their budding individuality."

Product of Teachings

Remember that our grandparents and parents didn't do such a poor job in raising their children and as the products of their teachings, you and I may think, we have not turned out so badly. If they failed it wasn't because of their discipline in requiring respect for parents and for the rights of other members of the family. It wasn't because we were assigned daily chores that made us sense the value of teamwork and a feeling of responsibility in the home, and that put a realization of duty to parents and family before selfish desire and personal comfort. Neither was it because they taught us to make work our pleasure and that home entertainments provided most satisfactory diversions, where father and mother joined with son and daughter in a comradeship that invited intimacies of lasting benefit to both parent and child. They failed when constant parental care was lacking and where attendance at church and punctuality at school was not expected. They failed if they did not teach their children to hold sacred the names of our Father in Heaven and his Son and to be reverent in temples of God and places of worship. They failed if the father did not hold his wife in highest esteem before the children or when the mother became a scold or cast insults toward her husband in their presence. Mutual respect of father and mother breeds respect for parental authority in the home. Old-fashioned fathers and mothers who live for and with their children and who value a successful home above clubs or teas or lodges will have the reward of "a wise son" who "maketh a glad father," instead of "a foolish son" who "is the heaviness of his mother." (Proverbs 10:1.)

Comradeship Ripens With Maturity

If a father's love for his sons is strong, and from their infancy he has taken them into his arms in loving embrace and let them feel the warmth of his affection for them, I believe that such comradeship will ripen with maturity and keep them near when a crisis in the boy's life requires the steadying hand of a father who understands. The mother who awaits with anticipation the return of her daughter from a late dancing party to receive the goodnight kiss, together with treasured confidences expressed at the height of girlish bliss, will be richly rewarded with the daughter's undying love that will be an eternal bulwark against sin because mother trusts her.

Parents who are too busy or too tired to be troubled with the innocent disturbances of children and push them aside or out of the home for fear of their disturbing the orderliness of immaculate housekeeping may be driving them, because of loneliness, into a society where sin, crimes and infidelity are fostered. What will it profit a father, otherwise worthy of the Celestial Kingdom, if he has lost his son or daughter in sin because of his neglect? All the pleasurable uplift societies in the world, social or religious, will never compensate the mother for the souls lost in her own home while she is trying to save humanity or a cause, no matter how worthy, outside of her home.

Again the Lord himself has spoken plainly about this preparation for the safeguarding of youth from the dangerous pitfalls that would destroy them. He has placed a serious charge upon the homes of this land. Here are his words:

"And again, inasmuch as parents have children in Zion, or in any of her stakes which are organized, that teach them not to understand the doctrine of repentance, faith in Christ the Son of the living God, and of baptism and the gift of the Holy Ghost by the laying on of the hands, when eight years old, the sin be upon the heads of the parents. . . .

"And they shall also teach their children to pray, and to walk uprightly before the Lord.

"And the inhabitants of Zion shall also observe the Sabbath day to keep it holy.

"And the inhabitants of Zion also shall remember their labors, inasmuch as they are appointed to labor, in all faithfulness; for the idler shall be had in remembrance before the Lord.

"Now, I, the Lord, am not well pleased with the inhabitants of Zion, for there are idlers among them; and their children are also growing up in wickedness; they also seek not earnestly the riches of eternity, but their eyes are full of greediness.

"These things ought not to be, and must be done away from among them." (Doc. and Cov. 68:25, 28-32.)

It is the responsibility of the Church, in the language of the Prophet Joseph Smith, to "teach correct principles." Parents and youth must learn to govern themselves.

I am writing this to you, the youth of this land, because you are the parents of tomorrow's youth, and so I invite you to join in the building of a "fence round the edge of the cliff," by choosing materials for this building from the Church, a heaven-sent institution which the Lord declared was to be for "a defense and for a refuge from the storm and from wrath when it shall be poured out without mixture upon the whole earth." (Doc. & Cov. 115:6.)

The Importance of Ourselves

5

Your name either spoken or written is the most appealing word to you in the English language. If you are shown a picture of a group where you are present, the first face you look for is your own and whether or not the picture meets your approval depends largely upon reaction to your own likeness. Do you remember the interest you had in hearing your own voice after a transcription had been made? I remember a party being held by a Church organization honoring the retiring clerk who had served since the beginning of the organization. The clerk had brought to the party bound volumes of the minutes he had kept of all the meetings for over thirty years. I observed each member of the group as he scanned these interesting records. In which part of the record do you think each member had the most interest? Yes, you are right. Each one turned immediately to the minutes of the meetings he attended when he first became a member. All other information was of secondary importance to the record of happenings where he had been a participant and where his name appeared in connection therewith. So we might multiply examples that suggest the importance of ourselves in our own sight.

To Win Approval

What will one not do to win the approval of the crowd! The family that unwisely pampers the tiny babe soon finds it almost impossible to distinguish between a cry of pain and one of demand for more attention. The rowdiness of children and the incorrigibility of early adolescence are more often than not a bid for a kind of popularity that physical or mental endowments do not invite. The blase girl of our acquaintance who is overpainted and underdressed may be only the picture of the unhappy girl whose social appetites, not being satisfied by the appeal of her natural self, seeks by superficial adornments and abnormal conduct to supply that indefinable quality called charm. The first smoke and the first drink most often were taken to be a good fellow with the gang, whose scorn at non-conformity was more to be feared than the disapproval of parents or church.

Did you ever have the experience of expecting a word of commendation for some worthy effort from a leader in whom you had great confidence only to have him completely ignore you, or to have him find only that to criticize rather than to commend? If you do remember, then let your remembrance prompt you to be thoughtful and appreciative of the best efforts of your associates lest you risk the loss of your friends' confidence in you and what is worse, the loss of your friend's confidence in himself. One of the marks of true leadership in yourself is the ability to generously approve the good and to constructively criticize the bad in those whom you expect to follow your leadership.

At Expense of Youth

I have great anxiety when our newspapers placard their pages with vivid word pictures of the obscenity and immoral escapades of pseudo film luminaries and notorious gangsters. Why thus inflate their ego and encourage others of similar tendencies to seek notoriety at the expense of innocent youth who are readers of such filth? How long will it be before the church and decent thinking people will demand that we give greater publicity to men's virtues instead of an organized parade to their vices, and when the only publicity a criminal will get will be the notice of his sentence by the court?

It was the prayer of the old Edinburgh weaver, "O God, help me to hold a high opinion of myself." That should be the prayer of every soul; not an abnormally developed self-esteem that becomes haughtiness, conceit or arrogance, but a righteous self-respect that might be defined for the purpose of this discussion as "a belief in one's own worth, worth to God and worth to man."

Everyone can understand the feelings of the person that wrote:

> I have to live with myself and so
> I want to be fit for myself to know.
> I want to go out with my head erect,
> I want to demand all men's respect.
> I never can hide myself from me;
> I see what others may never see;
> I never can fool myself, and so,
> Whatever happens, I want to be
> Self-respecting and conscience free.

Self-respect is that quality of feeling, having which we consciously strive to improve but lacking which we grovel in the muck and mire of animal existence. To preserve that self-respect in man then should be our constant concern. How may one's self-respect be preserved and developed? In the twice daily exercise of family prayers the little child, as soon as he can lisp a prayer, becomes an important part of the family circle. Wise parents see that he takes his turn in prayer, and perhaps until he has been properly schooled, the family prayer might consist of one leading and the others repeating sentence by sentence, even though the prayer of the child be ever so simple and unschooled. Think of the feelings of a child so privileged to be so respected by his family. How did you help your child when he suffered his failures in public performances at school or in church or in his private conduct? Ridicule, sarcasm, scorn or contempt would produce a sense of inferiority that questions his ability to ever amount to anything in life.

Family Solidarity Fostered

Some time ago in a rural community, I was a guest in the home of young growing boys. In the morning I went to the barn where the oldest sons were getting the team ready for the day's work. Although this was a prosperous farm and the father was a kindly man, I was surprised to learn that neither of the sons desired to remain on the farm but already were planning to leave as soon as possible. On another occasion I visited with another family where also there were growing sons but here I found just the opposite attitude. The boys were contented and happy, with no thought of leaving the farm, but instead were planning and working for improvement and expansion. Upon inquiry I learned that in the first family the sons were hardly as fortunate as hired help, that spending money or personal ownership were possible only when they worked out for hire to other farmers. In the second family the father early in his family life had formed what he called a "corporation" consisting of himself and his wife, which owned the farm. This "corporation" had in turn rented to a partnership consisting of himself also and his sons on a strictly business basis. When the sons matured, the corporation went out of existence and there was a partnership of father and sons, while the mother and daughters received just rewards according to their stations in the family organization. Each member was a part of the family team and was given a sense of responsibility. There was a mutual respect for each other. Family solidarity was fostered through their common interest in the welfare of the family farm unit in which each was a share-holder.

We Learn To Do By Doing

That club, church organization, priesthood or auxiliary group is best supported by its members when they have participated together on some project or

activity and where their membership has been made to
mean more to them than merely the obligation of attendance at a class or a luncheon and social. We learn
to do by doing. Through successful service in school
or church or in the community, and by the assumption
of responsibilities as a leader, a sweetheart or as a
father, for example, an individual finds his way to
strength, self-confidence and respect. To feel that
someone is depending on you or has belief in or regard
and affection for you is to have a rebirth of resolution
and desire.

In one of our military hospitals two men were
lying badly wounded. Their beds were side by side.
One said, "I don't care whether I come through or not.
I am sick of war, of the world, of everything and everybody."

"I feel rather like that myself," said the other,
"and yet there is a girl somewhere in Scotland; she
cares."

Just so, mutual regard for each other in a happy
home is a powerful influence in developing those qualities in self that measure up to the high standards of
the family name.

To publicly humiliate a person before his friends,
to cause him to become an object of charitable gratuities for which he has not labored, or to act in any way
to diminish one's respect for and confidence in himself
is to become a party to moral sabotage.

Some time ago I received a letter from a young
man overseas that will serve to illustrate an experience
from which great harm may come to our boys who
were in military service or away from home, although
I for one would not wish to pass judgment upon the girl
in the story until I had heard her side of it. Here is a
part of the letter:

"Yesterday afternoon when the mail came we
were all gathered around getting letters when a young
fellow from Ogden opened a letter and turned pale to

almost faint. Everyone noticed and began to ask what was the matter. As soon as he could gather his wits he asked me to come aside with him. Then he handed me a letter from his wife. This is how it began: 'Dear _____: At last I have found someone I love more than you. I want a divorce. All I ask is for the baby.' Imagine how you would feel. I understand that very thing is happening to thousands of our fellows. This is an example of what happens to those who have taken their religion for granted. They have not been taught the principles of the gospel. I did my best to console my friend. He is not going to answer her letter for a while. I would like to hold that woman up to the country as an example of the highest type of sabotage."

Repeatedly we have received letters from our servicemen overseas pleading with the girls at home to be true to the ideals for which our boys thought they were fighting to preserve. Likewise, every girl has a right to expect constancy from the young man whom she trusts. A betrayal of this trust on the part of either is certain to result in doubts and gloom and despondency that are effective tools of the adversary in destroying individual self-respect.

The Importance of Ourselves

We must beware of the dangers that confront those who may find themselves, when they return home, misfits in the society they left before they went into military service. Employers who dismiss men from industrial service without helping them to make an adjustment into more suitable situations should not do so without due consideration for the individual's self-confidence, loneliness, defeatism and bitterness. Many men now languishing in jails mark the beginning of their downfall to the day when they thought no one understood them and they lost self-respect for themselves and confidence in their ability to cope satisfactorily with social problems.

What of the Fallen?

But what of those who have fallen? What does life hold for them? It was MacDougall, the great psychologist, who declared that "the first thing to be done to help a man to moral regeneration is to restore, if possible, his self-respect." Perhaps many of us have had experience in attempting to aid in the rehabilitation of one who has fallen into serious error to regain his balance and to reestablish himself in the society from which he has been ostracized. After I had been instrumental in helping one such, I had expected in return for my efforts an expression of gratitude, that the one liberated from prison would leap out into the fresh air with joy at his newborn freedom and resolve in his heart never again to enter the life that had led him to this forbidding place. Much to my chagrin, within two weeks he had committed another error worse than the first and was back again in jail. As I began to analyze the possible feelings of this man, I remembered that in his youth he was a shy, backward boy. He had but little schooling; he had not in his later years had the privilege of the counsel and example of a kind father; he had made no church contacts; he had taken up the habit of smoking and frequently had taken liquor to flag his courage, and then had sought the only company where he felt he could be a recognized citizen and a leader, —among those who were likely living more nearly the primal, savage law of the survival of the fittest than any other. He was afraid of life and with a queer look on his face and a side-long glance, he was shuffling away from me, back into the life of an habitual criminal that had become easier than liberty.

Value of the Gospel

The transcendent value of the gospel in emphasizing the dignity of the individual human personality as a fortification against the forces that would tear down and undermine one's character must be recognized by all

teachers of youth. I am indebted to the late President
Stephen L Richards for the declaration of a great truth
respecting this matter:

"It is largely because we have such faith and confidence in the perpetuity of home and family that we
have built our most elaborate and expensive structures,
temples of God, wherein man and wife and children
have been bound in an everlasting union transcending
the limitations of mortal life. How inestimable is the
comfort this surpassing concept has brought to the
families of the Church. Every aspect of home and individual life has been influenced by it. It has vastly
increased love and respect for parents. It has induced
deeper affection and more mutual concern among the
inmates of the home. One of the greatest deterrents of
wrong-doing has been the fear of losing a place in the
eternal family circle." (Address of Stephen L Richards,
October Conference, 1944.)

What radiance of light in that lofty gospel teaching of our relationship to our Divine Parent whom we
call our Heavenly Father. *Male and female created
He them—In the image and likeness of God!* And
again, "Furthermore we have had fathers of our flesh
who corrected us and we gave them reverence: shall
we not much rather be in subjection to the Father of
spirits, and live?" (Hebrews 12:9), speaking of "the
Lord, the God of the spirits of all flesh." (Numbers
27:16.) *We are the sons and daughters of God! Every
man is our brother!*

Scriptures Quoted

The scriptures tell us, "Ye were also in the beginning with the Father, that which is spirit" (and that)
"man was also in the beginning with God"; (D. & C.
93:23,29) that we are here in mortality to see if we will
do all things whatsoever the Lord our God shall command. (Abraham 3:25.) "Know ye not that ye are
the temple of God, and that the Spirit of God dwelleth

in you?" and that "if any man defile the temple of God, him shall God destroy; for the temple of God is holy, which temple ye are." (I Cor. 3:16-17.) And finally, they who "keep" their second estate upon this earth by living as the gospel teaches shall have glory added upon their heads forever and forever. (Abraham 3:26.)

These precious gospel truths properly taught and understood by youth will be an effective block against the flood of emotions that results from their lack of due respect for that most important of all entities to every human being in the world, "Ourselves."

Learning is the beginning of action; nothing is really learned until it is applied. May you learn to know the truth by living it and "the truth shall make you free." (John 8:32.)

> "Thou must be true to thyself if thou
>   the truth would teach
> Thy soul must overflow, if thou
>   another's soul would reach.
> It needs the overflow of heart to
> give the lips full speech."
>
> Boner.

Years ago through the kindness of a friend I was permitted to read an interesting book by an American scholar and thinker entitled, "Ten Ways to Test the Fineness of a Man." I have forgotten the ten points discussed but I have remembered the general premise of his discussion. Superiority, he said, is not to be measured by what a person has in worldly possessions because often the man of wealth becomes independent of things that are good, and riches are not always the result of honest toil. One's abilities or talents likewise are not a true measure, for singers of renown in their private lives might be lewd, cheap and even immoral. The only true measure of superiority, he reasoned is one's answer to the question, What do you like? When you seek pleasure during your leisure hours, when you choose your associates, when you read books, when you satisfy your appetite, what do you choose? Your choices in all these and other like situations will indicate either your superiority or your inferiority.

A Mother's Teachings

I knew a superior mother judged by those standards who lived in near poverty with a large family. She has since passed away but the training she gave her children left its mark upon their lives. She taught them a true appreciation for the beautiful, an optimism that made bitterness impossible, that life had deeper values than the mere satisfaction of temporary desires. Guided by those lessons, one son in military service testified in a letter to his father which I read that he had been kept from sin; a daughter was inspired to put her thoughts in beautiful poetry; another daughter just two months ago was led to a holy temple where at the altar she entered into a sacred marriage partnership. Thus by selecting the beautiful, the good, the worthwhile, according to the writer I have referred to, they proved themselves far above the average of their associates despite their lowly economic station in life.

Choosing Ideals

The conclusions of this scholar suggests the need for setting up objectives and standards to guide one's life, and from the volumes that have been written on the subject, I would suppose that there is hardly any other thing more important than the choosing of ideals. The dictionary defines an ideal as "existing in idea or as a perfect pattern; a standard of perfection, beauty or excellence; a perfect type." It was Carl Schurtz who said, "Ideals are like the stars. You cannot succeed in touching them with your hands but like the seafaring man on the desert of waters, you choose them for your guides and by following them reach your destiny."

Children are great mimics. They learn to talk, to walk and form habits of conduct largely because of what they see others do. Every teacher knows that bad language habits in the home are most difficult to correct in school, and that little children from refined and cultured homes bring with them that refinement which is lacking in a child whose home is not so privileged. Good teachers are as careful of their dress and their personal habits as they are of their speech, knowing that untidiness in the care of the hair, fingernails or the dress of children might be induced by the poor example and slovenliness of the teacher. If one wants to see what a girl will look like and be like when she matures, it would be well to see the mother. A father lives again in his son. The ideal man or woman of your dreams that you plan one day to select as your life's companion very likely really doesn't exist, although you may think so when you fall in love, for your ideal is probably a composite of the best qualities you have observed in any number of your choice associates.

Importance of Example

The Apostle Paul impressed the importance of example upon members of the church who "sat at meat in the idol's temple," thus encouraging those who are weak "to eat those things which are offered to idols. But take heed," said he, "lest by any means this liberty of yours become a stumbling block to them that are weak. For if any man see thee which hast knowledge sit at meat in the idol's temple, shall not the conscience of him which is weak be emboldened to eat those things which are offered to idols; and through thy knowledge shall the weak brother perish, for whom Christ died? But when ye sin so against the brethren, and wound their weak conscience, ye sin against Christ." (I Cor. 8:8-12.)

Not only must we avoid sin but we must avoid the very appearance of evil. No person of high station ever fell in sin or into disrepute without shattering the ideals or dream castles of some youth who had faith in him. It was Phillips Brooks who said, "No man or woman of the humblest sort can really be strong, gentle, pure and good without the world being better for it, without someone being helped and comforted by the very existence of that goodness."

Some years ago I spent an afternoon with a feature writer of a nationally published magazine who had just come from an interview with a member of the First Presidency of the Church. This writer, after commenting about the courtesy that had been extended to him in this interview said, "You know I was never so greatly impressed with any of the hundreds of men I have interviewed throughout the world in my work as I was with your leader. He made me feel as if I wanted to quit smoking." So in a measure is the influence of every good man or woman.

The Power of Example

Realizing the power of example, manufacturers of liquor and tobacco, cosmetics or cereals endeavor to get great athletes or movie stars who have become heroes and ideals in the eyes of youth to indorse their products in order to promote their sales to youth. Some time ago one of our L.D.S. navy chaplains stationed at San Diego wrote about a conversation he had with Glenn Cunningham, the famous miler, who was then a naval officer there. Cunningham told the chaplain this story and has consented to my repeating it here: "One day I was sitting in my hotel room in New York City after a track meet. The phone rang and a person asked if he could come up and talk with me a few minutes. I consented. When the man came in he said, 'Glenn, I don't want to take up much of your time so I have this contract made out for your endorsement of our tobacco. You sign here and you can name your own price.' I looked the man straight in the eye and said, 'I don't know how much money your company has, but it hasn't enough to get me to put my name on that contract.' " The next time you see such an indorsement of things the Lord has condemned as harmful, just remember Glenn Cunningham's story and be assured that some athletes unlike him can be bought for a price. Sellers of worthless stocks and promoters of questionable undertakings always seek to get leading citizens of the community as well as church leaders to accept gifts or gratuities so that their names might be publicized as stockholders or directors in their schemes in order that those who have confidence in them will buy. I wish that all such men of influence, and youth who will face these decisions tomorrow, would read again the warning of the

Apostle Paul to those who fail to live as they profess and teach.

"Unfailing Ideals"

But all mortal men have their limitations and youth would do well to anchor their faith in ideals that do not fail. There will never be great happiness in the world any more, *until men have faith in one higher than themselves.* Without faith in God, men cannot have utter faith in themselves or in their work. Until a youth learns to "hitch his wagon to the stars," he will surely fail of his eternal goal.

If you will listen well you may find in the teachings of the Master Teacher, Jesus, the object of your search for an unfailing ideal for you to follow when you may have become wearied of finding that ideal among your fellows. Here it is from the lips of the Master Himself: "Be ye therefore perfect, even as your Father which is in heaven is perfect." Perhaps on first thought you may think that goal so lofty and so well-nigh impossible of attainment as to make you almost despair in the attempt. But let us think about it for a few moments.

A Profound Truth

As Jesus lifted up his eyes in prayer as "his hour was come." he gave expression to a profound truth that should be full of meaning to every soul: "And this is life eternal, that they might know thee the only true God, and Jesus Christ, whom thou hast sent." (John 17:3.) While this expression has deeper significance than I shall discuss here, I should like to take one thought from it. How can you know the Father and the Son? Well, how can you come to know Abraham Lincoln? How will one become acquainted with the poet Longfellow, or the great composer Mozart or with Hofmann, the artist? You can come to know them by

their works they have left with us, by a review of their
lives, by an understanding of environment and circumstances that prompted their acts, and finally, by ac-
quiring through practice the ability to produce similar
works by a study of the techniques they employed.
Just so, we can come to know God and his Son, our
Savior. We begin to acquire that knowledge by study.
The Savior counseled us to "Search the Scriptures, for
in them ye think ye have eternal life: and they are they
which testify of me." (John 5:39.) Therein will be
found a history of God's dealings with mankind in
every dispensation and the works and words of the
prophets and those of the Savior himself as given "by
the inspiration of God," as the Apostle Paul said, "and
is profitable for doctrine, for reproof, for correction,
for instruction in righteousness; that the man of God
may be perfect, thoroughly finished unto all good
works." (II Timothy 3:15-17.) Youth should let no day
pass without reading from these sacred books. But it
is not enough merely to learn of his life and works by
study. It was the Master who replied in answer to the
question as to how one might know of him and his
doctrine: "If any man will do his will, he shall know."
(John 7:17.) Would you think an authority on science
to be one who had never experimented in a laboratory?
Would you give much heed to the comments of a music
critic who did not know music or an art critic who
didn't paint? Just so, one like yourself who would
"know God" must be one who does his will and keeps
his commandments and practices the virtues Jesus
lived?

Foundation for Eternity

I am convinced that the Master was not merely
thinking relatively when he said, "Be ye therefore perfect, even as your Father which is in Heaven is perfect"; or that he merely meant that we should be
perfect in this life as he is perfect in his life. Would

you suppose the Savior was suggesting a goal that was
not possible of attainment and thus mock us in our efforts to live to attain that perfectness? It is impossible
for us here in mortality to come to that state of perfection of which the Master spoke, but in this life we lay
the foundation on which we will build in eternity;
therefore, we must make sure that our foundation is
laid on truth, righteousness and faith. In order for us
to reach that goal we must keep God's commandments
and be true to the end of our lives here, and then beyond the grave continue in righteousness and knowledge
until we become as our Father in Heaven. In wonderful
revelations the Lord has told us that those "who
overcome by faith and are sealed by the Holy Spirit
of Promise which the Father sheds forth upon all those
who are just and true. They are they who are the Church
of the Firstborn . . . into whose hands the Father has given
all things. They are they who are priests and kings, who
have received of his fulness and of his glory." (D. & C.
76:53-56.) "Every person who has this hope in him,
purifieth himself even as God is pure." (I John 3:3.)

Apparently the Apostle Paul thought this was a
true doctrine for we find him declaring to members of
the Church in his day: "Let this mind be in you, which
was also in Christ Jesus: Who, being in the form of
God, thought it not robbery to be equal with God."
(Philippians 2:5-6.) He furthermore pointed to the
course by which perfection comes. Speaking of Jesus,
he said, "Though he were a Son, yet learned he obedi-
ency by the things which he suffered; and being made
perfect, he became the author of eternal salvation unto
all them that obey him." (Hebrews 5:8-9.)

Ways to Perfection

Who has not seen the purifying that comes from
the suffering of one who has become a prey to an incurable malady; who is humbled by the mental anguish
of betrayal, or who is suffering grief and the godly sor-

row that worketh repentance from the appalling effects
of sin; or who has sacrificed all for a loved one or the
cause of truth? Then if you too have seen, you may
know your way to perfection.

I am always uplifted by the words of the Savior
just before his crucifixion, "Be of good cheer; I have
overcome the world," and by the Apostle Paul who
declared that in Jesus we did not have an example of
one who did not understand our problems and could
not "be touched with the feeling of our infirmities; but
was in all points tempted like as we are, yet was without sin." (Hebrews 4:15.)

As we read the story of the life of the Savior we
are impressed by the fact that he was stirred by human
emotions, just as we are. I wonder if he was not
angered when he saw the money-changers making his
Father's house a den of thieves. When the hypocritical
Pharisees challenged him because he healed a man
with a withered hand on the Sabbath day, the gospel
writer records that he looked on them "with anger
being grieved because of their hardness of heart." The
wise preacher of the Old Testament declared that there
"is a time to love and a time to hate." I can fancy the
Master hating sin, hating social conditions that op-
pressed the poor and yet loving those who "despite-
fully" used him. When the Ten Commandments were
thundered from Mt. Sinai, the Lord declared, "I the
Lord am a jealous God, and will have no other gods
before me." The Apostle Paul counseled the saints to
"be ye angry, and sin not," and spoke of being "jealous" over them with a "godly jealousy." Yes, Jesus
was "tempted as we are in all things" yet he was without sin. Although he was moved by human emotions
throughtout his life, there was an essential difference
between his expression of them and ours. His emotions were always under control. Frequently ours are
uncontrolled and end in bitterness that endangers our
own souls. He could hate sin yet have compassion on

the sinner. He was angered at the narrowness and bigotry that closed men's minds to truth, yet he was patient
in his teachings. He loved all mankind and jealously
shepherded them against the evils of the day.

Strength to Overcome

To have strength to overcome temptation is God-
like. The strong, the virtuous and the true of every
generation have lived pure, clean lives, not because
their emotions were less impelling nor because their
temptations were fewer but because their will to do was
greater and their faith in divine guidance won them
strength through prayer that proved their kinship with
the great Exemplar who gave us the pattern for the perfect life. The pervert that whimpers in his degradation
that his lot is hard because of his overpowering passion
but presents a dismal picture of one who is victimized
by his own unholy thinking. Because of his repeated
sinning he has divorced himself from the companionship
of the Spirit of the Lord wherein he would have found
the "strength of ten, because his heart was pure." Such
a one must climb the road of repentance through self-
denial, restitution and confession. In temptation he
must learn to do as Jesus said during the time of his
great temptation, "Get thee behind me, Satan."

To him who would learn the perfect law of charity
towards the sinner, let him hear the words of Jesus to
the accusers of the woman in sin, "He who is without sin,
let him cast the first stone," or understand the deep
significance of his words to the repentant thief on the
cross, "This day shalt thou be with me in paradise."

To you who have imbibed the so-called war spirit
of hate for all those of nationalities representing the
countries against whom we have waged battle, will see
again the picture of the cross and hear the Master's
words, "Father, forgive them, for they know not what
they do."

In contemplation of the great ideals left us by

Jesus, Lecky, the historian, has given us this summary: "The simple record of three short years of Christ's active life has done more to regenerate and soften mankind than all the disquisitions of philosophy and all the exploitations of moralists." Let then no day pass but that we learn from the great lesson book of his life his way to a perfect life and walk therein to our eternal goal.

"Lord, What Wilt Thou Have Me Do?"

7

Sometime ago I heard a leader in a high Church position explain his method of endeavoring to arrive at just and equitable decisions in his council meetings. He explained that as problems would be presented he would frequently ask himself the question, "As measured by the record of the Master's teaching, just what would he do in this given situation, or just how would he answer this question or solve this problem?" That remark reminded me of the story of a young prince of the nobility in India who was found by his friend teaching little outcast children on his veranda, although it involved the risk of breaking his caste rules, and he was asked by his friend why he did it. His reply was simple: "I thought it was the kind of thing Jesus Christ would do."

Perhaps even more important than trying to speculate as to what Jesus would do in a given situation is to endeavor to determine what Jesus would have you do. Of course in order to give intelligent answers to such questions, one must have intimate acquaintance with the life of the Master and the account of his ministry and an understanding of the applications he made to the lessons he taught. History, either religious or secular, is valuable to us; for by learning how others adjusted in the past to given situations, we ourselves form patterns of conduct that will guide us to act similarly under similar circumstances.

We may read of pioneer persecutions with measurable interest, but when we learn that our own ancestors were among the persecuted, we then view the monument to their memory, depicting a pioneer father and mother at the grave of the infant child who had just died, as a monument to our own, and the father and mother in the sculptured model as our grandparents who lost their own loved child. The sculptured figures of the monument might well have been our own loved ones, and we are therefore drawn more closely to the sculptured model in our understanding of those represented.

Before we can feel our kinship to our Savior and be influenced by his teachings in all our thoughts and deeds, we must be impressed by the reality of his existence and the divinity of his mission.

To have due reverence for God, our Heavenly Father, in our devotions requires an understanding of his personality and his existence. Indeed the expressed purpose of some of the most important revelations of the Lord through the prophets is "that you may understand and know how to worship, and know what you worship, that you may come unto the Father in my name, and in due time receive of his fulness." (Doc. and Cov. 93:19.)

A prophet of this dispensation taught us that "If any of us could see the God we are striving to serve, if we could see our Father who dwells in the heavens, we should learn that we are as well acquainted with him as we are with our earthly father; and he would be as familiar to us in the expression of his countenance and we should be ready to embrace him, if we had the privilege. We know much about God, if we but realized it, and there is no other item that will so much astound you, when your eyes are opened in eternity, as to think that you were so stupid in the body." (Brigham Young's Teachings.)

Yes, we all are well acquainted with him for we

lived in his house in the spirit world year after year. We are seeking to become acquainted with him when the fact is that we have merely forgotten what we previously knew.

The Prophet Joseph Smith confirms this teaching of the reality of God our Father as a person. He says: "God himself was once as we are now, and is an exalted man and sits enthroned in yonder heavens! . . . If you were to see him today, you would see him like a man in form—like yourselves in all the person, image and very form as a man; for Adam was created in the very fashion, image and likeness of God and received instruction from, and walked, talked and conversed with him, as one man talks and communes with another." (Joseph Smith's Teachings, p. 345.)

And finally this: "When the Savior shall appear we shall see him as he is. We shall see that he is a man like ourselves. . . . The idea that the Father and the Son dwell in a man's heart is an old sectarian notion and is false." (Doc. and Cov. 130:1, 3.) "The Holy Ghost has not a body of flesh and bones, but is a personage of Spirit." (Verse 22.)

One of the most beautiful pictures of the Master has come down to us in the writings of John the Beloved who was speaking both from his memories of Jesus and from a vision given him wherein the Lord appeared:

"His head and his hairs were white like wool, as white as snow. His eyes were as a flame of fire, and his feet like unto fine brass, as if they burned in a furnace; and his voice was as the sound of many waters; . . . and his countenance was as the sun shineth in its strength. And when I saw him, I fell at his feet as dead. And he laid his right hand upon me, saying, Fear not; . . . I am he that liveth and was dead." (Revelation 1:14-18.)

Suppose you try to put yourself in the place of one

who had received such a visitation from a holy personage. Hardly had the sting of mourning been soothed
after the death of Jesus when Mary, fearing that someone had stolen the Master's body from the tomb, was
searching for him in the garden. She heard him speak
her name and heard him say, "I ascend to my Father
and to your Father, to my God and your God." Then
she went and told Peter and the disciples as they
mourned and wept, "And they, when they had heard
that he was alive and had been seen of her believed it
not." After that he appeared to two of them near Emmaus in a form that they failed to recognize at first, as
they walked and went into the country. (Mark 16:10-
12.) He accepted their invitation to "abide with them"
when it was eventide and the day was far spent. He sat
at meat and gave a blessing on the bread that they ate,
and their eyes opened so that they knew him.
(Luke 24:29-31.) When they told their experience to
the disciples their story was treated as had been the
story of Mary Magdalene. He thereafter appeared to
the disciples without Thomas being present and again
when he was present and quieted their fears with his
blessing, "Peace be unto you." Here it was that he
"upbraided them with their unbelief and hardness of
heart, because they believed not them which had seen
him after he was risen." (Mark 16:14.) He invited
them to see the prints of the nails in his hands and feet
and the wound in his side and to handle him to make
them sure of his reality as a tangible resurrected being.
(Luke 24:37-41.) He dined on broiled fish and honeycomb
with seven of his disciples on the shores of the Sea of
Tiberias. After forty days he gathered them together on
Mt. Olivet near Jerusalem to witness his ascension and
they saw him "taken up, and a cloud received him out of
their sight." (Acts 1:9.) But there remained with them the
abiding memory of his last words to them, "Lo, I am with
you alway, even to the end of the world?" (Matt. 28:20.)
They knew that he meant what he said.

"Lord, What Wilt Thou Have Me Do?"

Perhaps if you, too, were to have such a visitation you would ask as did Saul of Tarsus when the Lord appeared to him on the way to Damascus, "Lord, what wilt thou have me do?" His appearances to his disciples after his resurrection convinced them of his continued existence. Though they could not have him continually in sight after his ascension, there certainly was no confusion in their minds as to the reality of his existence. Never again would they leave their ministry to go fishing without hearing his accusing question, "Lovest thou me more than these?" Peter who shrank from the consequences of revealing his identity at the time of the crucifixion now went unafraid to his ordained responsibilities of leadership and later to a martyr's death without fear because he had seen in the Master the rewards of a just life through a glorious resurrection. Would not the partaking of the sacrament in remembrance of him take on new significance now? How could the two at Emmaus thereafter ask a blessing upon their food and give thanks to God for it without remembering that the resurrected Lord had sat across the table from them and who now though invisible might be very near! No longer could Peter walk alone on the shores of Galilee without a feeling that he was not alone, nor when imprisoned at Antioch by Herod was he greatly surprised when he heard the voice of the angel commanding him to arise quickly, although he was securely bound to two sleeping guards. He never doubted because he knew the power of the risen Lord.

Paul Tells of Conversion

As the Apostle Paul stood before King Agrippa he retold the story of his conversion and of the appearance of the Lord and declared with boldness that now in his ministry he could not be "disobedient unto the heavenly vision." With zeal unbounded and unmindful of personal safety, he labored unceasingly to carry the Gospel to the gentile nations.

And so it was with the Prophet Joseph Smith in our own day, as he declared in his own story to the world: "I had actually seen a light, and in the midst of that light I saw two Personages, and they did in reality speak to me; and though I was hated and persecuted for saying that I had seen a vision, yet it was true; and while they were persecuting me, reviling me, and speaking all manner of evil against me falsely for so saying, I was led to say in my heart: Why persecute me for telling the truth? I have actually seen a vision, and who am I that I can withstand God, or why does the world think to make me deny what I have actually seen? For I had seen a vision; I knew it, and I knew that God knew it, and I could not deny it, nether dared I do it, at least I knew that by so doing I would offend God, and come under condemnation."

A Sublime Knowledge

After the vision left him, do you think for one moment that although he no longer continued to see the Father and the Son that he was not constantly assured amidst his persecutions and imprisonment that his Heavenly Father was mindful of his every act? With that sublime knowledge, it was only natural that as new problems presented themselves to him in carrying out instructions in the translation of the gold plates and in the setting up of the Kingdom of God on the earth as he was commanded to do, that he turned to the Lord in mighty prayer, and like the brother of Jared spoken of in the Book of Mormon, "Having this perfect knowledge of God he could not be kept from within the veil; therefore he saw Jesus; and he did minister unto him." (Ether 3:20.) One who has such perfect knowledge would, as did the Prophet Joseph or Peter and Paul, walk daily in the company of angels and have conversation with them and receive from them such instructions and authority as are necessary to establish the great work he might be called to do.

Not Many Have Seen the Savior

Not many have seen the Savior face to face here in mortality, but there is no one of you who has been blessed to receive the gift of the Holy Ghost after baptism but that may have a perfect assurance of his existence as though you had seen. Indeed if you have faith in the reality of his existence even though you have not seen, as the Master implied in his statement to Thomas, that even greater is the blessing to you who "have not seen, and yet have believed"; (John 20:29.) for "we walk by faith not sight," (II Cor. 5:7.) although not seeing, yet believing we rejoice with joy unspeakable in receiving the end of our faith, even the salvation of our souls. (I Peter 1:8-9.) The testimony of Jesus is the spirit of prophecy, (Revelation 19:10.) and comes only by the power of the Holy Ghost, for "no man can say that Jesus is the Lord, but by the Holy Ghost." (I Cor. 12:3.) If you have lived worthy of such a testimony you may have "a more sure word of prophecy," (II Peter 1:19.) by asking God "nothing doubting," and "by the power of the Holy Ghost, ye may know the truth of all things." (Moroni 10:5.)

Youth Go Not Alone

With such a testimony, the youth of this day go not alone. You "shall abide under the shadow of the Almighty." (Pslams 91:1.) If you are beckoned into dens of vice where danger lurks, if you are faced with temptations where wrong decisions mean disaster, if you are confronted with great problems to solve or obstacles to surmount, you will always ask, as did Paul, in the depths of your humility, "Lord, what wilt thou have me do?" I fancy I can hear the Master's answer to your question: "Be thou humble; and the Lord thy God shall lead thee by the hand, and give thee answer to thy prayers." (Doc. and Cov. 112:10.) "If any of you lack wisdom, let him ask of God, that giveth to all men liberally, and upbraideth not; and it shall be given him. But let him ask in faith, nothing wavering. For he that wavereth is like a wave of the sea driven with the wind and tossed." (James 1:5-6.)

You who are engaged in deadly combat where all the forces of earth and hell seem to be combined to destroy life, if you have the assurance of the existence of things divine, you will be at peace even in the face of impending doom and though you walk through the valley of the shadow of death, you will fear no evil, but will feel the nearness of God's presence. "Surely goodness and mercy shall follow (you) all the days of (your) life and (you) shall dwell in the house of the Lord for ever." (Psalms 23:6.)

If you are called into a position of great responsibility, such a testimony would make you answerable to your Divine Maker for the acts of your high office and would humble you with the realization that "he who would be greatest among you must be the servant of all."

If you are shrouded in deep mourning for him who was and is no more, by faith you will hear again that glorious promise, "In my Father's house are many mansions: if it were not so, I would have told you. I go to prepare a place for you. And if I go and prepare a place for you, I will come again, and receive you unto myself; that where I am, there ye may be also. And whither I go ye know, and the way ye know." (John 14:2-4.)

Youth Must Strive for Testimony

Youth must strive with all their hearts, with all their souls, with all their minds to gain an abiding testimony that God lives and that he is the Father of the spirits of all that are born into mortality, and that Jesus Christ, his Only Begotten in the flesh, still lives and says

today to all who have ears to hear: "Behold, I stand at
the door, and knock; if any man hear my voice, and
open the door, I will come in to him and sup with him,
and he with me." (Revelation 3:20.)

Mothers, with your little ones at your knees, you
must realize that yours is the golden opportunity to
plant in their hearts the first seeds of a beautiful testimony that "heaven lies about us in our infancy" and
that

> "Our birth is but a sleep and a forgetting
> The Soul that rises with us, our life's Star,
> Hath had elsewhere its setting
> And cometh from afar;
> Not in entire forgetfulness,
> And not in utter nakedness,
> But trailing clouds of glory do we come
> From God, who is our home."

The Church must realize its responsibility to provide youth the opportunity to strengthen that testimony
by study and service in the Church that through the
perils of life they might be kept as if in the hollow of
God's hand. Because there are those today who have
"forsaken their sins and cometh unto the Lord, who
have called on his name, obeyed his voice and kept his
commandments," some have seen his face and all such
know that he is. They know that in hours of great ex-
tremity they may reach out with the yearnings of a faithful son or daughter to their Heavenly Father and find in
him the wisdom to answer every question and the
strength to meet every problem. As one of the least
among you, I humbly bear my testimony that I know
that God is the Father of our spirits and that through
his Son Jesus Christ he exercises his "power over his
saints and shall reign in their midst" while his judgments descend upon the world because of their wickedness.

May you our youth be blessed and guided always
by the power of an abiding testimony of the tangible
reality of our Heavenly Father and his Son, our Savior.

The Constitution for a Perfect Life

8

"Who is greatest in the kingdom of heaven?" The answer to that question had been the subject of controversy among the chosen Twelve as they sat in council in the home of Peter at Capernaum. Perhaps the question had so recently come from the experience on the Mount of Transfiguration, as to which of these three would be the first in the Church next to the Master himself. It is more likely that they were merely trying to determine those qualifications in a man that fitted him for the highest place in the kingdom. At any rate, as Jesus entered the council room, he discerned the question at issue as though it had been asked. He called a little child to him, probably one of Peter's children, and sat the child in the midst of them and then took it in his arms and said:

"Verily I say unto you, except ye be converted, and become as little children, ye shall not enter the kingdom of heaven. Whosoever therefore shall humble himself as this little child, the same is greatest in the kingdom of heaven." (Matt. 18:3-4.)

I think similar feelings to those of the Twelve on that occasion were in the minds of a group of young women who wrote this question just the other day: "What are the steps a young man or woman should take to really live a full life?" Perhaps the Master would suggest a similar reply to the answer he gave to the Twelve, for to really live a full life is to strive with one's full heart to be greatest in God's kingdom, for of such, as little children, "is the kingdom of heaven." To humble one's self as a little child, therefore, is to live to the highest of the Master's expectations concerning us.

Those who constitute the membership of the kingdom have been referred to as "saints." Moses called the children of Israel "saints." (Deuteronomy 33:2.) Daniel in a great vision saw that the "saints" would possess the kingdom. (Daniel 7:22.) Both the apostles John and Paul in their writings referred to members of the Church as "saints." In our own day that name has been incorporated into the name of the Church by revelation. (Doc. and Cov. 115:3.) What is its significance? A great prophet in the land of Zarahemla on the American continent in delivering the last sermon of his life has given us a statement that throws light upon its meaning, and also gives additional explanation of the statement of the Savior to the Twelve. King Benjamin declared that to become a saint one must "put off the natural man and become a saint through the atonement of Christ the Lord (which means for one to repent and be baptized for a remission of his sins) and become as a child, submissive, meek, humble, patient, full of love, willing to submit to all things which the Lord seeth fit to inflict upon him, even as a child doth submit to his father." (Mosiah 3:19.)

Steps in Becoming a "Saint"

But then, you want to know the "steps" by which one can have his life patterned to that fulness that makes him a worthy citizen or "saint" in God's kingdom. The best answer may be found by a study of the life of Jesus in the scriptures, for is has been said that "our gospels are not merely the record of oral teachings; they are the portraits of a living man." (Dean Inge) Christ came not only into the world to make an atonement for the sins of mankind but to set an example before the world of the standard of perfection of God's

law and of obedience to the Father. In his Sermon on
the Mount the Master has given us somewhat of a revelation of his own character, which was perfect, or what
might be said to be "an autobiography, every syllable
of which he had written down in deeds," and in so doing has given us a blueprint for our own lives. Any one
clearly understanding the true import of his words
comes to the realization that an unworthy member of the
Church, although he might be in the Kingdom of God,
yet would not be of the Kingdom because of his unworthiness.

You may know you are living a full, rich life when
you have the real joy of living for "Men are that they
might have joy." (II Nephi 2:25.) What is it then that
gives you that high emotional ecstasy called joy? Does
it come to one from the unusual or does it come from
common things? He who is moved thus only by the unusual is as one who must flag a failing appetite with
strong spices and flavorings which destroy the true
sense of taste. You are making a serious error if you
mistake an emotional "thrill' that passes with the moment for the upsurge of deep feelings that is the joy of
living. If one feels strong surges of happiness and desire from the quiet of a happy home, from the unfolding
of a beautiful life, from the revelation of divine wisdom,
or from a love for the beautiful, the true and good, he
is having a taste of the fulness of the joy and the living
of a rich, full life only can bring.

Eight Ways to Joy

In that matchless Sermon on the Mount, Jesus has
given us eight distinct ways by which we might receive
this kind of joy. Each of his declarations is begun by
the word "Blessed." Blessedness is defined as being
higher than happiness. "Happiness comes from without and is dependent on circumstances; blessedness is
an inward fountain of joy in the soul itself, which no
outward circumstances can seriously affect." (Dum-

melow's Commentary) These declarations of the Master are known in the literature of the Christian world as the Beatitudes and have been referred to by Bible commentators as the preparation necessary for entrance into the kingdom of heaven. For the purposes of this discussion may I speak of them as something more than that as they are applied to you and me. They embody in fact THE CONSTITUTION FOR A PERFECT LIFE.

The Constitution for a Perfect Life

Let us consider them for a few moments. Four of them have to do with our individual selves, the living of our own inner, personal lives, if we would be perfect and find the blessedness of that inward joy.

Blessed are the poor in spirit.

Blessed are they that mourn.

Blessed are they that hunger and thirst after righteousness.

Blessed are the pure in heart.

To be poor in spirit is to feel yourselves as the spiritually needy, ever dependent upon the Lord for your clothes, your food and the air you breathe, your health, your life; realizing that no day should pass without fervent prayer of thanksgiving, for guidance and forgiveness and strength sufficient for each day's need. If a youth realizes his spiritual need, when in dangerous places where his very life is at stake, he may be drawn close to the fountain of truth and be prompted by the Spirit of the Lord in his hour of greatest trial. It is indeed a sad thing for one, because of wealth or learning or worldly position, to think himself independent of this spiritual need. It is the opposite of pride or self-conceit. To the worldly rich it is that "he must possess his wealth as if he possessed it not," and be willing to say without regret, if he were suddenly to meet financial disaster, as did Job, "The Lord gave, and the Lord hath taken away; blessed be the name of the Lord." Thus, if

in your humility you sense your spiritual need, you are
made ready for adoption into the "Church of the First
Born, and to become the elect of God."

"To Mourn"

To mourn, as the Master's lesson here would teach,
one must show that "godly sorrow that worketh repentance" and wins for the penitent a forgiveness of sins and
forbids a return to the deeds of which he mourns. It is to
see, as did the Apostle Paul, "glory in tribulations
knowing that tribulation worketh patience; and patience, experience; and experience, hope." (Romans
5:3-4.) You must be willing "to bear one another's
burdens, that they may be light." You must be willing
to mourn with those that mourn, and comfort those that
stand in need of comfort. (Mosiah 18:8-9.) When a
mother mourns in her loneliness for the return of a wayward daughter, you with compassion must forbid the
casting of the first stone. It is the kind of mourning
portrayed in the deep feelings of the marine on Saipan
who wrote to us during the war when his buddy was
killed. "As I lay in my fox-hole that night I wept bitter-
ly." Your mourning with the aged, the widow and the
orphan should lead you to bring the succor they require.
In a word, you must be as the publican and not as the
Pharisee. "God be merciful to me a sinner." Your reward for doing is the blessedness of comfort for your
own soul through a forgiveness of your own sins.

"To Hunger and Thirst . . ."

Did you ever hunger for food or thirst for water
when just a crust of stale bread or a sip of tepid water to
ease the pangs that distressed you would seem to be the
most prized of all possessions? If you have so hungered
then you may begin to understand how the Master
meant we should hunger and thirst after righteousness.
It's that hungering and thirsting that leads those away from
home to seek fellowship with saints in sacrament services

and that induces worship on the Lord's Day wherever we are. It is that which prompts fervent prayer and leads our feet to holy temples and bids us be reverent therein. One who keeps the Sabbath Day holy will be filled with a lasting joy far more to be desired than the fleeting pleasures derived from activities indulged in contrary to God's commandment. If you ask with "a sincere heart, with real intent, having faith in Christ, he will manifest . . . truth . . . unto you, by the power of the Holy Ghost," and by its power you "may know the truth of all things." (Moroni 10: 4-5.) Build "each new temple nobler than the last . . . till thou at length art free"; then "your whole bodies shall be filled with light and there shall be no darkness in you." (Doc. and Cov. 88:67.)

"The Pure in Heart"

If you would see God, you must be pure. There is in Jewish writings the story of a man who saw an object in the distance, an object that he thought was a beast. As it drew nearer he could perceive it was a man and as it came still closer he saw it was his friend. You can see only that which you have eyes to see. Some of the associates of Jesus saw him only as a son of Joseph the carpenter. Others thought him to be a winebibber or a drunkard because of his words. Still others thought he was possessed of devils. Only the righteous saw him as the Son of God. Only if you are the pure in heart will you see God, and also in a lesser degree will you be able to see the "God" or good in man and love him because of the goodness you see in him. Mark well that person who criticizes and maligns the man of God or the Lord's anointed leaders in his Church. Such a one speaks from an impure heart.

Entrance Into the Kingdom

But in order to gain entrance into the Kingdom of Heaven we must not only be good but we are required

to do good and be good for something. So if you would
walk daily toward that goal of perfection and fulness
of life, you must be schooled by the remaining four "articles" in the Master's Constitution for a perfect life.
These beatitudes have to do with man's social relations
with others:

> *Blessed are the meek.*
> *Blessed are the merciful.*
> *Blessed are the peacemakers.*
> *Blessed are they which are persecuted.*

A meek man is defined as one who is not easily provoked or irritated and forbearing under injury or an-
noyance. Meekness is not synonymous with weak-
ness. The meek man is the strong, the mighty, the man
of complete self-mastery. He is the one who has the
courage of his moral convictions, despite the pressure
of the gang or the club. In controversy his judgment is
the court of last-resort and his sobered counsel quells
the rashness of the mob. He is humble-minded; he
does not bluster. "He that is slow to anger is better than
the mighty." (Proverbs 16:32.) He is a natural leader and is the chosen of army and navy, business and
church to lead where other men follow. He is the
"salt" of the earth and shall inherit it.

"To Be Merciful"

Our salvation rests upon the mercy we show to
others. Unkind and cruel words, or wanton acts of
cruelty toward man or beast, even though in seeming
retaliation, disqualify the perpetrator in his claims for
mercy when he has need of mercy in the day of judgment before earthly or heavenly tribunals. Is there one
who has never been wounded by the slander of another
whom he thought to be his friend? Do you remember
the struggle you had to refrain from retribution? Blessed
are all you who are merciful for you shall obtain mercy!

Peacemakers—The Children of God

Peacemakers shall be called the children of God. The trouble-maker, the striker against law and order, the leader of the mob, the law-breaker are prompted by motives of evil and unless they desist will be known as the children of Satan rather than God. Withhold yourselves from him who would cause disquieting doubts by making light of sacred things for he seeks not for peace but to spread confusion. That one who is quarrelsome or contentious, and whose arguments are for other purposes than to resolve the truth, is violating a fundamental principle laid down by the Master as an essential in the building of a full rich life. "Peace and goodwill to men on earth" was the angel song that heralded the birth of the Prince of Peace.

"The Persecuted"

"Truth forever on the scaffold,
Wrong forever on the throne,
Yet the scaffold sways the future,
And behind the dim unknown,
Standeth God within the shadow
Keeping watch above his own."

To be persecuted for righteousness sake in a great cause where truth and virtue and honor are at stake is god-like. Always there have been martyrs to every great cause. The great harm that may come from persecution is not from the persecution itself but from the possible effect it may have upon the persecuted who may thereby be deterred in their zeal' for the righteousness of their cause. Much of that persecution comes from lack of understanding, for men are prone to oppose that which they do not comprehend. Some of it comes from men intent upon evil. But from whatever cause, persecution seems to be so universal against those engaged in a righteous cause that the Master warns us, "Woe unto you when all men shall speak well of you!

for so did their fathers to the false prophets." (Luke 6:26.)

May youth everywhere remember that warning when you are hissed and scoffed because you refuse to compromise your standards of abstinence, honesty and morality in order to win the applause of the crowd. If you stand firmly for the right despite the jeers of the crowd or even physical violence, you shall be crowned with the blessedness of eternal joy. Who knows but that again in our day some of the saints or even apostles, as in former days, may be required to give their lives in defense of the truth? If that time should come, God grant they would not fail!

Gradually as we ponder prayerfully all these teachings, we will make what may be to some the startling discovery that after all God's measure of our worth in his kingdom will not be the high positions we have held here among men nor in his Church, nor the honors we have won, but rather the lives we have led and the good we have done, according to that "Constitution for a Perfect Life" revealed in the life of the Son of God.

May you make the Beatitudes the Constitution for your own lives and thus receive the blessedness promised therein.

Why the Church?

9

No doubt you have all been impressed when you have read in current publications bitter denunciations of the churches from the young person's point of view because of their apparent failure and ineffectiveness in successfully coping with the problems that are at root in the present evils with which the world is afflicted. These writers have particularly asked the question, "What does the returned serviceman think of the church?" They say that the answer to that question is, "He doesn't." They claim that the serviceman has "complete and colossal indifference" toward the church and point out that as a returned serviceman he is merely a reflection of the mind of any average man on the street, for after all he is simply a civilian in uniform and his mental outlook has not been radically altered by the entirely different environment in which he finds himself. He sees little vitality in a church "which has so signally failed to impress itself on the consciousness to say nothing of the conscience of a generation." Attention is called to the fact that the boys when they came home needed the church and the church needs them. They and all men are seeking leadership in the rebuilding of a wrecked society. "That leadership must come from a church which has given evidence . . . that it is worthy to direct the reformation of mankind."

When I noted by the signature of the writer of one of these articles that he was a licensed minister of his church, I assumed that probably he was in reality confessing the sins of his own ineffectiveness as a leader of his church. Possibly by inference he was condemning the teachings of the sect with which he is affiliated as lacking in force and authority to impress its members with the vitality of the gospel it teaches.

As I have read such opinions I am reminded of one of the dreariest quotations I know of in English literature commenting on the effect of a religion without spiritual power. This is the quotation: "Spiritual teaching, spiritual guidance,—these poor peasants had none, and when the Monday came they went to their work in the marshes and elsewhere, and lived their blind lives under gray skies, with nothing in them of the Sunday save the recollection of a certain routine performed which one day might save them from some disaster with which flames and brimstone had something to do. It was not, however, a reality to them. The wheelwright and his wife, the six laborers and their wives, listened as oxen might listen, wandered home along the lanes heavy-footed like oxen, with heads toward the ground, and heavily went to bed." (The Revolution in Tanner's Lane by Rutherford)

Two Different Meanings

The term "church," as it is frequently but loosely used with reference to professors of various beliefs, has two different meanings. It may mean the whole body of Christian worshipers everywhere, or it may refer to any specific religious society or body. "The Church" as spoken of in the scriptures had a much more significant meaning. The Church that the Master spoke of required the conferring upon the earthly head thereof, certain rights known as "the keys to the Kingdom of heaven" and to whom would be given the authority "to bind on earth and to loose on earth." with the assurance that such acts so performed would be bound or loosed in the heavens. Furthermore he declared to the Apos-

tle Peter that the testimony he, Peter, had received of
the divinity of the Savior was a revelation from his father in Heaven and that upon "this rock," confession of
faith or principle of divine revelation, he would build his
Church and the gates of hell would not prevail against it.
(Matt. 16:15-18.) If there be those who believe falsely
that his Church was to be built upon the Apostle Peter
to whom he spoke, remind all such that the Master said
on another occasion that he, himself, was the "stone"
which men had rejected that was now to become
"the head of the corner." (Matt. 21:42; Eph. 2:20;
Col. 1:18) or the head of the Church. A church founded
upon Peter or upon any other man would not be the
Church of Jesus Christ but the church of Peter or that
of any other man upon whom it was founded. This
Church of Jesus Christ was to be "the power of God
unto salvation." (Romans 1:16.) It was to have the
only door to the sheepfold of his flock and any person
whosoever would climb up any other way the same
would be "a thief and a robber." (John 10:1-7.) Any or-
dinations performed without authority from the Lord's
anointed were required to be repeated by proper authority. (Acts 19:1-6.) The Church that Jesus established
was to have a definite organization with apostles and
prophets presiding over it, and including pastors, teachers, evangelists, bishops, elders, priests, teachers and
deacons, with Jesus Christ himself as the chief Cornerstone. (Ephesians 2:19-20.) Such an organization was
to be devoted to the work of aiding every member thereof to become perfect and to preach the Gospel unceasingly to every people that all might receive the blessings
of salvation administered therein; that through its educational system all might come to a unity of the faith
and to a knowledge of the Son of God as a perfected
Man. It was expected that such appointed officers and
teachers should be as shepherds tending their flocks to
keep out the "wolves" of false doctrine that might break
in and destroy the faith of the "flock." (Acts 20:28-29.)

Eternal Counterfeits

Without doubt the Master realized that every genuine article has its eternal counterfeit, and just so, there would come a time when false Christs and false prophets, claiming authority the Lord had not given them, would arise and would deceive many, even members of the Church, by signs and wonders performed by occult powers derived from sources of evil. (Matthew 24:4-24.) Such deceivers, he foretold, were to bring in damnable heresies or doctrines of devils, such as lies spoken in hypocrisy, forbidding to marry or commanding to abstain from meat; (I Timothy 4:1-3.) and churches would be built up to say, "Come unto me and for your money you shall be forgiven of your sins." (Mormon 8:32.) These misguided, uninspired, man-appointed leaders, he said, would blaspheme God's name and his tabernacle and would make war on the saints and even kill them, all the while thinking they were doing God a service. (John 16:2.) He made it clear, however, that any such institution so established, if it were not built upon his gospel, would have success and joy in their works for a season but by and by the end would come and they would be hewn down and cast into the fire from whence there is no return. (III Nephi 27:11.)

It was not surprising in view of all this opposition that the Church would be driven into the "wilderness" of apostasy for a season and that there would come a time of famine in the land, "not a famine of bread nor a thirst for water but of hearing the words of the Lord," as had been predicted. (Amos 8:11-12.) But a kind and loving Father, ever mindful of the need of his children in this school of mortality in that most forlorn day when darkness and unbelief covered the earth, cheered the remaining faithful and the honest seekers after truth with this thrilling promise through John, his apostle:

"And I saw another angel fly in the midst of heaven, having the everlasting gospel to preach unto them that dwell on the earth, and to every nation, and kindred, and tongue, and people, Saying with a loud voice, Fear God, and give glory to him; for the hour of his judgment is come: and worship him that made heaven, and earth, and the sea, and the fountains of waters." (Revelation 14:6-7.)

Thus not only was the fulness of the truths of the gospel to be restored by an angel but from similar divine sources, power to preach that gospel and to administer the ordinances thereof was to be given by which the world would be judged either to their salvation or to their damnation.

When we hear a professing representative of a so-called church, such as our soldier friend, declaring that the church of his acquaintance "has (to use his own quotation) signally failed to impress itself on the consciousness, to say nothing of the conscience, of a generation," we are certain he is bearing solemn testimony to the fact that the body of professing Christians of which he speaks is as a body without the spirit and "having a form of godliness but denying the power thereof." Have such congregations of worshipers come to a time when "they will not endure sound doctrine, and after their own lusts . . . heap to themselves teachers having itching ears and thus be turned from truth unto fables"? (II Timothy 4:3-4.) How many of such teachers have been thinking not of truth but merely of convention?

Surely of such is not the Church which Jesus established. As one listens down the ages, he does not hear the blatant commands of assumed authority demanding confession on pain of death issuing from the Church of the lowly Nazarene. It was not the doctrine of an eye for an eye or a tooth for a tooth given to a people who had been divorced from the fulness of his gospel. His was the voice of a little baby, given as a sign, crying in the manger, and at the end, the whispered prayer from tortured lips at Gethsemane, "Father, forgive them, for they know not what they do."

Doctrine of Love

It was the doctrine of love. "For God so loved the world, that he gave his only begotten Son, that whosoever believeth in him should not perish, but have everlasting life." (John 3:16.) It was a doctrine that changed men's lives: that built for them who accepted and did his will a house upon a rock, that when "the rains descended, and the floods came, and the winds blew, and beat upon the house; it fell not for it was founded upon a rock." (Matthew 7:25.) It was a power that has wielded more influence for good than any worldly powers ever known to man.

In contrast with the lament of one who knows not the truth, may I have you listen to a testimony I once heard in the city of Toluca, about forty miles west of the City of Mexico. A young married man of culture and refinement and of Mexican birth was asked to speak at a meeting being held by The Church of Jesus Christ of Latter-day Saints of which he was not a member. This was his story: Until he was married and became the father of two little children he had never thought seriously of the social dangers in the midst of which he had to raise his children. For two years he had given serious thought to the finding of a refuge in which to bring up his children and have them taught correct principles to prepare them against the moral dangers brought on by war conditions. He was crossing a small park one night on his way to town and heard the voices of singers coming from a small building at the corner. Peering through a small hole in a broken window he heard a prayer being offered and went on his way supposing this to be but another Protestant organization. Later he was invited to a social at the home of a prominent attorney of that city and there recognized among the guests the two young men he had seen at the Church meeting through the broken window a few days before.

He became acquainted with them and learned that they were missionaries of The Church of Jesus Christ of Latter-day Saints. Five days later he had a visit from the missionaries who explained the necessity of the authority of the Priesthood in performing the ordinances of the Gospel, as taught in the fifth and seveneth chapters of the book of Hebrews wherein it is stated that "no man taketh this honor unto himself, but he that is called of God, as was Aaron," (Hebrews 5:4.), which authority these young men testified they had received and was being exercised by them in accordance with that instruction. He began attending services at their little meetinghouse and found the members friendly and sincere and at their invitation had taken delight in assisting them with the music and singing. He had just been presented with a copy of the Book of Mormon and had been greatly impressed by his reading of I Nephi the 13th chapter, and prayed that he too might one day be a "messenger upon the mountains." He closed by announcing that he and his wife were soon to become members of the Church, for at last they had found the refuge they had sought by the teachings of which their children could be prepared to meet the problems of their generation.

Church An Integral Part of Lives

One of our army chaplains who wrote us during the war from the Philippines made the following comment:

"A recent article in a magazine, making an attack upon the decadent Protestant world for its failure to influence the lives of its communicants, can certainly have no application to L.D.S. men, for the Church is an integral part of their lives, one of the values of a practical religion. The influence of the gathering spirit is as predominant in the Philippines today as it ever was when the saints began to gather to Zion. As a chaplain I have experience with many groups, many denominations, and I have yet to find another organization which evidences this same characteristic with all its desirable results."

If the observation of the chaplain is true, and I am convinced it is, why does the Church mean more to these soldiers than this other writer claims for members of other sects for which he speaks? From the many testimonies that have come to us, perhaps we could answer by summarizing some of their statements in these words: Because the Latter-day Saints realize that the spiritual, mental and physical factors of life must be balanced in order to have a fulness of life, they have been prepared to meet the emergencies of life and do not falter under the strain, no matter how great it may be. Most all of those who are members of the Church will come back with sterling characters and be a credit to their parents, teachers and their God. If they and their parents have kept the commandments of God before this war, you can feel assured that most of them will come home clean and pure. If they have heeded its teachings, while in the service, the gospel will have been as an armor of righteousness.

Source of Power

From what source have come such power and influence, wielded with an authority always characteristic of the Church of Jesus Christ? Listen to the testimony of a youth just as earnest as youth today in seeking for truth amidst a world of confusion; seeking to find the true Church of Jesus Christ as distinguished from those of worldly origin. He "asked of God," the only One to whom he could appeal for guidance with this most startling result, as related by that youth, Joseph Smith: "I saw a pillar of light exactly over my head, above the brightness of the sun, which descended gradually until it fell upon me. . . . When the light rested upon me I saw two Personages, whose brightness and glory defy all description, standing above me in the air. One of them spake unto me, calling me by name, and said, pointing to the other—This is My Beloved Son. Hear him!

"My object in going to inquire of the Lord was to know which of all the sects was right, that I might know which to join. No sooner, therefore, did I get possession of myself, so as to be able to speak, than I asked the Personages who stood above me in the light, which of all the sects was right—and which I should join.

"I was answered that I must join none of them, for they were all wrong; and the Personage who addressed me said that all their creeds were an abomination in his sight; that those professors were all corrupt; that: 'they draw near to me with their lips, but their hearts are far from me; they teach for doctrines the commandments of men, having a form of godliness, but they deny the power thereof.' " (History of the Church, Vol 1, pp. 5-6.)

Before you of hasty judgment criticize that simple, straight-forward declaration concerning the so-called Christian world, I bid you remember that the words quoted by Joseph Smith were not the words of a man but were spoken by our Lord and Savior. He is the same Personage who said that "Strait is the gate, and narrow is the way, which leadeth unto life, and few there be that find it," (Matthew 7:14), and who inspired another prophet to declare that there is but "One Lord, one faith and one baptism." (Ephesians 4:5.) If you will "ask of God," you too may know the truth of these things.

The subsequent restoration of the Gospel, as foretold by John the Revelator, and the organization of the Church with the authority to teach it to the world in preparation for just such conditions as we are now experiencing, I bear solemn witness has taken place "as a stone cut out of the mountain . . . never to be destroyed or left to other people, and shall stand forever." (Daniel 2.)

May the world always be blessed and guided by its influence.

Imagine yourself on the oceanside watching a crew of men engaged in trying to slide or pull a huge boat off into deeper waters from a sandbar on which it is stranded. As the tide goes out, the prow of the huge vessel will be left exposed high above the water. With the returning tide the water will surge up around the boat but not in sufficient depth to give it the buoyancy necessary to make it float off the sandy bottom. It is too heavy to lift and too much to pull. Suppose you offer a suggestion to the foreman of the crew that he have his men construct broad platforms that might be fitted under the shoulders of the great vessel while the tide is out so that when the surging ocean returns, its added lifting power underneath the platforms will accomplish that which man with his man-made tools had failed to do. What was the secret of your success? You had merely harnessed the powers of the universe and had made them serve you in the solution of a problem too great for human strength.

The Touch of Divinity

You young folks have but to look around you to see evidences of the continual workings of some great Intelligence or power beyond your own. Contemplate man's own body for a moment and consider the stupendous miracle of his existence, his birth, his development, the functioning of life processes and the touch of divinity that seems inherent in him, and with awe you will exclaim at the wonder of it all. "What is man that thou art mindful of him?" (Psalms 8:4.) Go out into the stillness of the night and observe the myriads of stars that are inlaid in a background of ebony and watch them night after night moving in exact patterns and regularity. The morning breaks and the shadows flee, and at night the earth is enveloped in darkness except for heavenly light issuing from a lesser light seemingly placed there by someone who was concerned about the welfare of beings upon the earth who needed that light. Winter comes with its chilling blasts and all nature seems shrouded in a white mantle of death, but with the touch of gentle spring and the succeeding march of summer and autumn, earth yields her abundant harvest as a gift from unseen forces that thus minister to human needs. All these and more are perpetual evidences of power with purpose. That power, the testimony of tradition, history and revelation calls God, and that purpose is "to bring to pass the immortality and eternal life of man." (Moses 1:39.) Indeed, "The heavens declare the glory of God and the firmament showeth his handiwork," (Psalms 19:1.) for "the earth rolls upon her wings, and the sun giveth his light by day, and the moon giveth her light by night, and the stars also giveth their light, as they roll upon their wings in their glory in the midst of the power of God. . . . Behold all these are kingdoms and any man who hath seen any or the least of these, hath seen God moving in his majesty and power." (Doc. & Cov. 88:45, 47.)

Quality of Assurance

That quality of assurance or abiding conviction in an individual of the existence of things unseen, "which to him may not be demonstrated or for that matter may not be demonstrable," is called faith. That quality inherent in an individual applies to other things than the supernatural. One may "know" that there is an England, that there is such a person as Richard Nixon, or that there is a Middle-East conflict, only because of his faith in the correctness of the evidences that these things are a reality. So certain in fact is he, although he has not seen, one may say that he has a perfect faith or assurance that approaches absolute knowledge. So we might, if time would permit, carry our illustrations into the findings of science, art or mechanics and show the application of the principle of faith there also.

But all do not possess it in like degree. Some seem to have intuitive qualities of mind to impress each truth with the stamp of the genuine, while others are perennial doubters by nature. The Apostle Paul declared that faith is "not of yourselves: it is a gift of God." (Ephesians 2:8.) I am convinced that everyone, if he is honest in his desires, has sufficient of this gift to lead him eventually to eternal salvation through a faith in and understanding of God, our Creator, and his plan and purposes concerning us. Faith is based on the testimony of witnesses and in order to avoid the building of a false faith, the individual is required to examine carefully all such witnesses and in the language of the scriptures, "Prove all things and hold fast to that which is good."

Faith Applied to Religion

Faith applied to religion is its foundation principle and indeed the source of all righteousness that directs man in his efforts to gain eternal life in the world to come. It centers in God who by faith is recognized as the source of all power and all wisdom in the universe and who is the directing Intelligence of "all things visible or invisible that demonstrate his wisdom." By faith in God then, you too as youth can become attuned to the Infinite and by power and wisdom obtained from your Heavenly Father harness the powers of the universe

and have them serve you in your hour of need in the
solution of problems too great for your human strength
or intelligence.

How may youth develop this faith? The answer
is by study, by work and by prayer. Paul the Apostle
asked the question, "How shall they believe in him of
whom they have not heard? and how shall they hear
without a preacher?" (Romans 10:14.) We must answer, they cannot. So then faith can only come by
hearing the word of God from preachers of truth. The
preaching of the truth concerning God and his purposes has been compared to the sowing of a seed,
which if a good seed will begin to sprout and grow in
your hearts on these conditions: First, that it is planted
in the rich, fertile soil of sincerity and real desire; second, that it is cultivated with diligent study and searching; and third, that it is watered by genial spiritual
"dews" and warmed by rays of inspiration that come
from humble prayer. The harvest from such planting
comes only to that individual who acts upon the truths
he has learned and reforms his life of sin and fills his
days with purposeful conduct in keeping the commandments of God in whom he has faith, and in service toward his fellowmen.

Power Derived from Faith

From the experiences of great leaders of the past
and from sermons that have been written concerning
the power derived from faith, I should like to take some
lessons that you may apply as your faith increases and
grows by the light of the Gospel. The Apostle Paul
commences his sermon on faith with a statement of the
prime requisite in order to gain the right to God's infinite power; "Without faith it is impossible to please
him, for he that cometh to God must believe that he is
and that he is a rewarder of them that diligently seek
him." (Hebrews 11:6.)

In the reign of King Nebuchadnezzar of Babylon,

the house of Judah had been captured, and the king had requested several of the young men of the captured Israelites to teach their language and learning to the king's agents. He specified that these young men should be "without blemish and be well favored, skillful in all wisdom, and cunning in knowledge and understanding, and such as had ability to stand in the king's place." The king further stipulated that these choice young men should be nourished for three years on a diet that consisted of a daily provision of the king's meat and the wine which he drank, which according to a word of wisdom given to ancient Israel was not good for their bodies. Daniel, one of these young men, "purposed in his heart that he would not defile himself with the portion of the king's meat nor with the wine which he drank," and so advised the king's servant who came to serve them, but requested that instead they be served a vegetable food called pulse and pure unadulterated water. After ten days of this simple fare, "their countenances appeared fairer and fatter in flesh . . . and in all matters of wisdom and understanding ten times better than all the astrologers and magicians in the realm" and all the others which ate the food prescribed in the king's diet, thus proving the wisdom of the Lord's word of wisdom that superseded the wisdom of a mere king. (Daniel 1:3-21.)

Times have not changed for the choice of youth without blemish today. The Lord's word of wisdom commanding abstinence from a worldly "king's portion" of tobacco, tea and coffee and alcoholic beverages that are habit-forming, and which counsels the simple diet of fruits, grains and vegetables in season, with meats used sparingly, has been given you as a revelation of God's great law of health. It stands today as a challenge to a world surfeited with things condemned as unclean and unfit for the human body. If you have faith as the youthful Daniel and his brethren and purpose in your hearts that you will not defile yourselves with "king's meat and wine," even though you may be two thousand miles east of the Suez Canal, your faith will have the reward of hidden treasures of knowledge, of strong bodies that can "run and not be weary and walk and not faint." If by faith in this great law, you refrain from the use of food and drink harmful to your bodies, you will not become a ready prey to scourges that shall sweep the land, as in the days of the people of Moses in Egypt, bringing death to every household that has not heeded the commandments of God.

Joseph, the son of Jacob, as just a youth of tender years, was sold to the Egyptians by his jealous brothers. When Potiphar in Egypt saw him he recognized in him superior qualities, because of his heritage and the training of his youth, and made him overseer in his house. Joseph was described as a handsome, good-looking lad and "well-favored," and just the age when temptations are strongest, he was far removed from the restraining influences of home and family. When the young, beautiful but apparently unloved and evil-minded wife of Potiphar invited him to join with her in the commission of a sin which God had declared in every generation as second only to murder, he shamed her with his simple words that gave evidence of a great faith: Behold my master trusts me and "thou art his wife: how then can I do this great wickedness and sin against God?" (Genesis 39:6-16.)

Potiphar's wife then did that which is universally the accompaniment of immorality, she lied to her husband, and had Joseph thrown into prison, but this was his reward. "The Lord showed him mercy and gave him favor in the sight of the keeper of the prison." (Genesis 39:21.)

You with the hot blood of passionate youth in your veins, when faced with the lewd invitations of immoral princesses or slick-tongued princes of the earth under the spell of the influence of Satan whose servants they are, have you the faith of a Joseph to make the consciousness of God's presence and intervention in your affairs a vital principle of your actions and law of your life? Remember that in the wake of your submission to any such invitations there follow remorse of conscience and a sense of guilt and unworthiness that drive you from the presence of God, from whom you might otherwise have found mercy as did Joseph, and will make you an inmate of a lonely prison in the sight of whose keeper "you will not find favor," and who will require you to pay the uttermost penalty in recompense for your sins.

Now for a moment let us become fellow-travelers with Paul the Apostle, a young man on a voyage across the Mediterranean to Rome, where he was in the custody of Roman officers because of his "offense" to the guilty sinners of his day in preaching the truths of the Gospel. He had just given an exhibition of a wonderful faith in the recital before King Agrippa of his vision wherein the Lord spoke to him. With such power did Paul speak that the king was almost persuaded to become a Christian. As we voyage together toward Rome a furious storm breaks and after five days most all on board have despaired of living out the storm. Not so with this young man whose faith had brought him the peace of heavenly vision. He stood before his cowering mates and said: "And now I exhort you to be of good cheer: for there shall be no loss of any man's life among you, but of the ship. For there stood by me this night the angel of God, whose I am, and whom I serve, saying, Fear not, Paul . . . Wherefore, sirs, be of good cheer: for I believe God, that it shall be even as it was told me." (Acts 27:22-25.)

Again, you youth of today, we voyage together. It may as well be out from Golden Gate Harbor or from any international airport to an overseas destination. It may be a storm where nature's fury is unleashed or it may be a mental or an emotional storm that threatens shipwreck.

Whatever the occasion or the cause, you may by faith, intensified by fasting or "after long abstinence" like Paul, have standing by your side during "that night" of turmoil a guardian angel of God "whose you are and whom you serve."

If by "faith we understand the worlds were framed by the word of God" (Hebrews 11:3), what think you of the possibility of your business problems, your farm difficulties or your personal anxieties being righted by that same power. If you have faith, and it is God's will, it will be so.

I can imagine the ridicule and scorn that Noah suffered during the months he was building a great ship out in the middle of a comparative desert to house himself and his family and the selected of earth's bounties in preparation for the flood that through his faith in God's prophetic revelation he knew was coming to destroy the earth. Don't you be as the foolish virgins with no oil in your lamps because of your unbelief in God's warning of things to come. Dare to listen to the leaders of the Church, the prophets of God, without a revelation to whom, God said he would do nothing (Amos 3:7.) despite the jeers of the worldly and unrighteous who have no faith and who dare not because of their own sinning believe that these threatened judgments might be so. Through your faith in the inspired revelations, you will always be given time to build an ark of safety that will eventually land you on a Mount Ararat. Beware you of little faith who place your trust in the arm of flesh rather than in the power of God as declared by his prophets.

If you haven't faith to sacrifice for the work of the Lord, if you have doubts about the possibility of one being raised from the dead, will you stand aside and witness the workings of the faith of Father Abraham. His faith was so great that even though he was commanded to sacrifice the life of his son Isaac, through whom only he could realize the promise of great posterity, he confidently prepared for the sacrifice with full faith that Isaac could even be raised from the dead, if necessary, to fulfill the promise of posterity.

Has enough been said to my youthful friends to indicate the way to power by the demonstration of your faith by prayer and by living lives of purity and sacrifice? By obedience to God's laws you might, by thus keeping in tune with the Infinite, subdue all things including Satan's power, and save yourselves in this world and in the world to come.

God grant that such faith might abound in youth today.

The late President Calvin Coolidge was known as a master of brevity in his speech. Upon returning home from church on one occasion, as the story goes, he was asked by his wife what the minister had talked about in his sermon. "Sin," was the president's terse reply. "What did the minister say about sin?" his wife again inquired. "He was against it," was the president's answer.

Sin is something so universal that all of you know about it, and all preachers of righteousness and indeed all honest souls are opposed to it. Sin may be defined as any want of conformity to or transgression of a rule or law of right or duty, as made known by your conscience or the revealed word of God. Such non-conformity or transgression of divine law might be either by omission or commission, or in other words sin may be either the willful breaking of divine law or you may sin by your failure and neglect in thought, word or deed to keep the commandments of the Lord. One may sin by being hasty in judgment on vital issues or where the welfare of a human soul is at stake, and "he that forgiveth not his brother his trespasses standeth condemned before the Lord; for there remaineth in him the greater sin." (Doc. & Cov. 64:9.)

Free Agency by Divine Right

All blessings that we receive from our Heavenly Father are predicated upon obedience to law, "and when we obtain any blessing from God, it is by obedience to that law upon which it is predicated." (Doc. and Cov. 130:21.) Free agency, or the privilege of choosing your course in life, has been given to every one of you as a divine right. You are "free to choose liberty and eternal life (by putting into practice in your lives the teachings of the Gospel) or to choose captivity and death according to the captivity and power of the devil" by your disregard of the laws of the Gospel and your failure to live according to Gospel standards.

The laws of God given to mankind are embodied in the Gospel plan and the Church of Jesus Christ is made responsible for teaching these laws to the world. They are given by our Heavenly Father for only one purpose, that you who are governed by law might also be preserved by law and perfected and sanctified, or made holy by the same. (Doc. and Cov. 88:34.) The greatest of all gifts of God to us is the gift of salvation in his Kingdom. But in the Lord's revelation he asks this pertinent question regarding this priceless privilege:

"For what doth it profit a man if a gift is bestowed upon him, and he receive not the gift? Behold, he rejoices not in that which is given unto him, neither rejoices in him who is the giver of the gift." (Verse 33.)

Perhaps a simple illustration will help you to see the necessity of your compliance with the "rules" of this "game" of life if you are to be saved in our Father's Kingdom after you live these few years here in mortality.

An Illustration

Suppose you have a great-hearted friend who calls you in for a consultation and makes the proposition that he has decided to give you the opportunity of going to college to get an education, at his expense, which will give you training to become a competent and well-trained artisan, executive or mechanic. Beyond this

you may continue to take post-graduate work and receive higher education after you graduate from the university. If you successfully complete this university
course offered you, your generous friend agrees to take
you into his business where you will have the opportunity of becoming a partner and joint owner, thus giving you security to the end of your days. But this wonderful opportunity is yours only on certain conditions.
You must complete your university education in a limited number of years. You must make passing grades
in each course you take, or if you should fail to get a
passing grade you must spend extra hours to make up
your losses. The courses are so exacting that your
mind must be clear and your body strong. If you cloud
your mind and weaken your body through the use of
substances that are harmful or by practices that sap
your vitality, you will fail in your final examinations and
will be "washed out," as they say in the army. You
will find plenty of play-boys along the way who will
try to persuade you to "sow some wild oats" in disregard of the possible consequences. All your tests will
be private. There is no chance to cheat. You can't
make amends for your failures by merely saying, "I'm
sorry." The one who gives the tests will base his judgment not alone on the actual results as written on your
examination papers, but will take into account the vital
factor as to whether or not you have done all you could
have done according to your native ability. Thus even
if you are physically or mentally handicapped, you have
an equal opportunity with him who seems to have greater physical strength or mental vigor.

What would you think of such a proposition? Is
it fair? If you failed to meet the requirements, would you
have anyone to blame but yourself as the cause of your
failure? If you lose the business partnership promised
you and are limited to the position of merely a hired man
or servant in the house of the man who offered you a
place of ownership in his business, could you blame

your friend for your failure? Should you fail he would probably feel as badly as you because he needed you and wanted you in his business and was always ready to give you counsel and advice any time you wanted to go to him and were prepared to listen to his voice.

An Application

Let me see if I can apply some of the principles of that illustration: God our Heavenly Father is the great-hearted Friend of my analogy. Mortality is the name of the university where you are to receive your education. The reward for successful completion of your lives is the privilege of becoming "heirs of God and joint-heirs with Christ" (Romans 8:17) in our Father's Kingdom. To these faithful the Lord has promised that "he shall reveal all things—things which have passed, and hidden things which no man knew, things of the earth by which it was made, and the purpose and the end thereof." (Doc and Cov. 101:32-33) All this and more the faithful may receive "until he is glorified in truth and knoweth all things." (Doc. and Cov. 93:28.)

The rules of conduct in his gospel plan of salvation are for the sole purpose of helping you complete this schooling with as few failures as possible, so that at the end you will not fail of the priceless opportunity that is afforded. If you fail in any given test, there is provided through repentance a way by which you can make good your losses and gain a forgiveness for your mistakes. Your failure to observe these laws or rules that have been laid down in the Gospel plan is to make mockery of the rules imposed, or in other words, to sin against God in that you unfit yourselves for service in his kingdom and also sin against yourselves because you thus fail of the great opportunities that otherwise could have been yours. They "which breaketh a law, and abideth not by law, but seeketh to become a law unto (themselves), and willeth to abide in sin, and altogether abideth in sin, cannot be sanctified by law, neither by mercy, justice, nor judgment. Therefore, they must remain filthy still." (Doc. and Cov. 88:35.)

Just as a university course is limited as to time, as suggested in my illustration, so our days here in mortal life are limited to an average normal span of years. "The day of this life is the day for men to perform their labors. . . . If we do not improve our time in this life, then cometh the night of darkness wherein there can be no labor performed. Ye cannot say, when ye are brought to that awful crisis, that I will repent, that I will return to my God. Nay, ye cannot say this; for that same spirit which doth possess your bodies at the time that ye go out of this life . . . will have power to possess your body in that eternal world." (Alma 34:32-34.) You are building today the castles you will live in throughout eternity and deciding the place you will occupy in your Father's business hereafter. There is joy in heaven when you who are failing reform your ways and return to a standard of activity that assures your success. There will be mourning in heaven if you fail in life's education, but there is nothing your Heavenly Father can do about it unless you open the door by prayer and the living of a good life and invite him to counsel with you.

Acceptance of the Plan

The fact that you are here in this mortal existence is an evidence that you accepted our Heavenly Father's plan and entered into covenant with him to keep his commandments in return for which you were to be given a glorified place in his Kingdom. One-third of all those in the spirit world before you came to this earth were cast out because they refused the gift of this education in the "University of Mortality" on the terms provided. They are the tempters who, like yourselves, have their free agency and are endeavoring to persuade you to "eat, drink, and be merry, for tomorrow we die" (2 Nephi 28:7) and thus be miserable like themselves. Whatever may be the ratio of evil spirits to every human soul one thing is certain, that the power of temptation is great. Someone has said that "man is as prone to do evil as sparks are to fly upward." The Apostle Paul puts it this way: "For the good that I would I do not; but the evil which I would not, that I do. . . . The law in my members always warring against the law of my mind." (Romans 7:19, 23.)

Unless the good and the truth are taught just as effectively and as militantly from home and pulpit, by the radio and television, the billboards and the moving pictures as are things that tempt us to do evil, we are giving Satan and his hosts great odds in this contest for eternal life.

Fatal Mistakes

Build a bonfire sometime and watch the beautiful moths and insects come wheeling in because of the enticement of the bright lights. Round and round, closer and closer they whirl until their daring prompts a fatal mistake and they fall with singed wings to their doom in the burning furnace of tempting fascination. I've seen beautiful young human butterflies playing with the tempting fires of sin. They want to see the bright spots of a big, sinful city while they are away from home. If married and forced to be separated from their companions through the demands of employment or training, they accept dates to parties and entertainments in disregard of their marriage vows. They seek promiscuous associations with strangers at dances. By improper dress and look and cheap conversation, they issue invitations for the advances of the unholy. They listen to and repeat the filthy and obscene story. They tell themselves that experience with vice and sin is necessary preparation for protection against it. They draw a distinction between the "kill, rob and cheat" kinds of sin and the "pleasant sort of sinning," which they consider less serious. They forget the warning of the wise man who said that "The knowledge of sin tempteth to its commission," and that you can't come in contact with sin in any form without losing a certain pure-mindedness. They little realize that:

> Vice is a monster of so frightful mien,
> As to be hated needs but to be seen;
> Yet seen too oft, familiar with her face,
> We first endure, then pity, then embrace.

Many of these beautiful human butterflies winged for heavenly flight have fallen with wings singed and badly seared because of their curiosity about the forbidden. The more I see of life, the more I am convinced that we must impress you young people with the awfulness of sin rather than to content ourselves with merely teaching the way of repentance. I wish that someone could warn you of the night of hell that follows the committing of a moral sin or of a beastly act, as one who has sinned has described it in these words: "No one knew anything about it. You told no one, and no one found out, no one condemned. But your face flushed, your heart beat against your ribs. Perspiration broke out upon your brow. You went to bed that night, you tied a bandage around the eyes of your soul, you built a little shelter in which to hide, you tried to sleep, but no sleep came. You said to yourself, 'Other people do it,' or 'I had to do it,' or 'No one else can ever find it out.' But there were hands from the unseen world that came through the darkness and tore the bandage from the eyes of the soul, and smashed down the little shelter you had made for your cowering spirit." (Weatherhead)

I saw at one time the effect of that accusing conscience in one who had stolen money from an employer for twenty years without being suspected, who is now so haunted by the knowledge of his guilt and a sense of unworthiness that he is making a complete confession and risking the penalty of his crime in an attempt to gain back the right to an answer to his prayers. It was so with a confessed murderer I met in Mexico some years ago who after twelve years had found life so intolerable, although his crime was not known to law enforcement officers, that he was ready to give up his life as an atonement for his great sin rather than to continue to live in the torture chamber of his own accusing thoughts. Have you ever known of the agony of the mother of beautiful children because of the burning feelings of unworthiness that result from an unconfessed immoral stain?

Sinner Loses Light of Spirit

I interviewed a man recently who had been excommunicated from the Church for a grievous sin. He bore testimony to this significant truth that when he was cast out of the Church he lost not only his membership in the Church but also the light of the spirit of the Holy Ghost which he had been promised at his baptism would be a lamp to his feet and a guide to his way, and that he had wandered as a traveler in a fog without sense of direction or the Spirit of the Lord to guide him. How true are the words of the prophet, "The wicked are like the troubled sea when it cannot rest, whose waters cast up mire and dirt. There is no peace, saith my God, to the wicked." (Isaiah 57:20-21.)

Years ago I read the life story of Jack Black, who for thirty years was a professional criminal who plied his nefarious trade in and around Salt Lake City and the Intermountain country. His book was entitled, "You Can't Win." In his conclusion he answers his own question, "What price larceny, burglary, and robbery?" Half of this thirty years of underworld life was spent in prison. He had stolen a total of $50,000, or about $5.00 a day on an average, but here he was at fifty years of age, penniless; his nerve was gone; he had no home, no wife, no friends and not even a dog. What might have been a flower garden of memories of good deeds and pleasant associations was a weed patch of bitter, rueful reflections of a wasted life and even the future held no promise. If he ever repented of his sins, perhaps today, wherever he may be, he could say as did the prophet, "And I will tell you of the wrestle which I had before God, before I received a remission of my sins." (Enos 2)

Subjected to Devil

Those who sin and procrastinate the day of their repentance, "even until death . . . have become subjected to the spirit of the devil, and he doth seal you his; therefore, the Spirit of the Lord hath withdrawn from you." (Alma 34:35) The hell to which we will be consigned if we sin and repent not will be a "bright recollection of all our guilt" (Alma 11:43) for in the day of judgment "our words will condemn us . . . and our thoughts will also condemn us . . . and we would fain be glad if we could command the rocks and the mountains to fall upon us to hide us from his presence." (Alma 12:14.)

Youth of today, by your conduct you become the servants of that power whom you thus serve. Your reward for a good life is to live in the sunburst of heavenly light and intelligence that will guide you into all truth. "The wages of sin is (spiritual) death," (Romans 6:23) which separates you from the influence of the Spirit of the Lord wherein you would have found peace and leaves you in the dungeon of darkness and subject to the torment of evil spirits until you free yourselves from the bondage of sin by a sincere repentance.

And so the anxious Shepherd of his flock, of which you are a part, pleads with us, his "sheep": "Therefore, what I say unto one I say unto all: Watch for the adversary spreadeth his dominions, and darkness reigneth. . . . Go your ways and sin no more; but unto that soul who sinneth shall the former sins return, saith the Lord your God. . . . I give unto you directions how you may act before me, that it may turn to you for your salvation. I, the Lord, am bound when ye do what I say; but when ye do not what I say, ye have no promise." (Doc. and Cov. 82:5-10.)

But is there no hope for him who sins? In another discussion we will concern ourselves about the eternal plan of restitution by which the human soul may return from his evil ways and find a forgiveness for his sins by true repentance and the turning away therefrom.

I plead with youth everywhere to heed the call of the master to forsake their sins and come unto him, and to "shun the devil that he will flee from you." I pray that you might have strength so to do.

The "Successful" Sinners

Are there actually any successful sinners? Well, perhaps what you are thinking about is the man of independence who, despite the fact that his money may not always have come to him from honest toil or from legitimate enterprise, apparently lives a life of luxury and ease. He spends his Sundays playing golf, at a baseball game or at the races instead of struggling or worrying with difficult church problems as a responsible church officer or otherwise keeping the Sabbath Day holy; he takes long excursions into interesting places by spending money, a part of which at least as a faithful church member he would have paid in tithing contributions or in donations for the building up of the church or for the care of the needy; he hasn't time to fill a mission at his own expense for the church. Because of the worldly company he keeps, he has no scruples about drinking or gambling at the club and even immorality is winked at by his crowd who absent themselves from church contacts, where such conduct as measured by gospel standards would be seriously frowned upon and vigorously condemned. At the same time you may have observed that woman who lives at his house whom he calls his wife who has completely ignored the first great commandment "to multiply and replenish the earth." She can't be bothered with children; they might interfere with her career or her social activities. She thinks herself beyond the pale of the church and quiets her conscience with the constant expression that after all religion and the church are only for the poor and the unsophisticated. The expenditure of her husband's wealth has freed her from home responsibilities so that her days must be kept from monotony by bridge parties, with small bets and substantial prizes that act as condiments to her interest, and where smoking and drinking are indulged in with little or no regard for church injunctions to the contrary. She is able to dress in the latest and most expensive fashions; she avoids the tell-tale marks of a mother's home cares and worries about the children, and her face and figure are proper for all occasions.

A Higher Vantage Point

Perhaps as you, our youth of today, look at such pictures of seemingly successful sinners against the Lord's commandments, you may from your lack of perspective of the entire span of life and its purposes conclude that such have chosen the better way. You may think by comparison that the life of one active in the church is not easy with its constant inhibitions and restraints, with the service and the sacrifices entailed that require his time and talents and money, and the disquieting shocks that come to his conscience when he acts below the standards he professes. You may think that your energies expended in other endeavors might pay you greater dividends and that religion should be left to those who can't afford anything better. But before you make your final decision as to the course you will take, let me help you lift your vision to a higher vantage point so that you can see these things as they really are.

Beautiful, luscious fruit does not grow unless the roots of the parent tree have been planted in rich, fertile soil and except where due care is given to proper pruning, cultivation and irrigation. So likewise the luscious fruits of virtue and chastity, honesty, temperance, integrity and fidelity are not to be found growing in that

individual whose life is not founded on a firm testimony
of the truths of the gospel and of the life and mission of
the Lord Jesus Christ. It was the Apostle John who
said, "By this we know that . . . we love God, (we) keep
his commandments." (I John 5:2.) In order for good
to blossom it must be cultivated and exercised by constant practice, and to be truly righteous there is required
a daily pruning of the evil growth of our characters by
a daily repentance from sin.

This daily repentance is necessary because there
is "opposition in all things, the forbidden fruit in opposition to the fruit of the tree of life," the evil ofttimes
seeming to be the sweeter and the good the more bitter
to our first taste. I have heard youth state it this way:
"It seems that the most desirable and tempting things
in the world are either illegal, immoral or fattening."

Lucifer, Author of Program

Who is the author of this program that thus dresses
up the evil and the wrong to become so desirable to our
appetites? There was war in heaven. Lucifer, a son
of God in the spirit world before the earth was formed,
proposed a plan under which mortals would be saved
without their effort or choice, and for which service he
demanded the glory and honor of God. The plan of
our Savior, Jehovah, was to give to each the right to
choose for himself the course he would travel in earth
life, and all was to be done to the honor and glory of
God our Heavenly Father. A Savior was to be named
to redeem us from the spiritual death or temporary separation from the presence of the Lord that all in mortality must experience. Jehovah's plan was accepted.
Satan's plan was rejected. There was sharp disagree-
ment and finally war in heaven over this issue, and Lucifer succeeded in persuading one-third of all the spirits
to rebel. He and they were cast out upon the earth
without mortal bodies and he became Satan. Some have
seen his satanic majesty in his spiritual form, in bodily

shape like a man. Some have seen individuals who have been possessed of evil spirits. Others there are who have felt the awful influence of his "hellish" suggestions. All of you have known individuals who because of their own sins are in his power and subject to his will. Make no mistake about his reality as a personality although he is not possessed of a physical body. Since the beginning of time he with his hosts, who are likewise beings in spiritual form, have waged relentless war to destroy "the free agency of man and to lead captive as many as would not hearken unto the voice of the Lord," (Moses 4:4) as revealed in the teachings of the gospel.

Right to Choose

But, you ask, Why does God, if he truly loves his children, permit Satan to tempt us and thereby jeopardize our chances to gain the experiences of mortality and return back to enjoy eternal life in his presence? The answer is given by a great prophet-teacher: "Wherefore, the Lord God gave unto man that he should act for himself. Wherefore, man could not act for himself save it should be that he was enticed by the one (which is evil) or the other (which is good)." (II Nephi 2:16.) You think about that for a moment. If there were no opposition to good, would there be any chance to exercise your agency or right to choose? To deny you that privilege would be to deny you the opportunity to grow in knowledge, experience and power. God has given laws with penalties affixed so that man might be made afraid of sin and guided into paths of truth and duty. (Alma 42:20.)

> Good timber does not grow in ease,
> The stronger the wind, the tougher the trees;
> The farther the sky, the greater the length;
> The more the storm, the more the strength
> By sun and cold, by rains and snows,
> In tree or man good timber grows.

When you see a person so overpowered by evil habits that his passion is the master, there you are beholding one over whom Satan has dominion, who thus seeks to destroy in him his individual agency. Satan's forces are most powerful. I fancy as I grow in experience that I can see his methods in his relentless warfare, with the damnation of the human soul as his stake. He has effective secret agents organized and always at work behind our defenses, putting doubts into our minds by the medium of false philosophies; bringing discouragement when we lose the perspective of faith; and sowing seeds of gloom and despondency that give vent in the dangerous expression of youth, "Oh, what's the use!"

Besides these saboteurs Satan has a spy system that has discovered the weakest places in our defenses and has ports marked for invasion carefully charted in each one of us. The D-Day of your invasion is that day when you lower your defenses. Those ports, through which you are most likely to be "invaded," are declared by inspired men to be your virtue, your conduct, your ideals or objectives in life, and your thinking. Let the defenses of those ports be weakened by carelessness or negligence and the enemy has taken you into his captivity.

How One Might Repent

Some time ago a young girl came to our home with her companion to discuss some problems which were troubling her. She wanted to know how one who had sinned could repent. We spent some time discussing that wonderful Gospel principle by which the man of sin might be buried and the man of righteousness raised to a newness of life. As we concluded our discussion, she sat for several moments with a far-away look in her eyes and then asked simply, "Why does not the Church teach youth to really understand the principle of repentance?" I fancied that behind that question was a knowledge of the evil acts of human souls that were committed because they listened to those foolish promptings of the tempter following their first mistake: "Be a good sport; you have the name, why not the game; don't be a prude or a dud; everybody's doing it; now that you've made a serious mistake you can't come back anyway, so you might as well make the best of it."

Before I attempt to explain this precious refining process of the human soul called repentance, may I state two simple but fundamental truths. First: Satan with all his cunning cannot overthrow you if you strive with all your might to keep the commandments of the Lord. And second: With the first breaking of one of these commandments, you have taken your first step into the devil's territory.

One of the most scenic drives in the State of Arizona is through Oak Creek Canyon that lies between Flagstaff and Jerome. To enter the canyon from Flagstaff the descent is very steep, requiring expert roadbuilders to construct the winding highway, with sharp hairpin turns to get the traveler to the floor of the canyon. Just as with all paths that lead downward, no effort at all is required to go all the way to the bottom; indeed all the going is so easy that unless you apply your brakes at the dangerous turns, you would meet early disaster. When you arrive at Jerome, however, the situation is just reversed. Before you is the sheer wall of the canyon that can only be surmounted by a series of ladder-like roads constructed on ascending levels. What energy or gasoline you think you saved in coming down, you now must expend and more to climb back up. Woe be to the motorist if his gasoline is poor or the spark plugs are fouled. If a tire should go flat or some mechanical defect should develop, Jerome would have an unwilling visitor added to its population.

"As Ye Sow . . ."

A reckless life is that trip through Oak Creek Canyon. In the early stages the road of temptation and sin

seems much the easier, but each of us must eventually
face the judgment of God's inexorable law: "As ye sow,
so shall ye reap." The shadows fall quickly in the
bottom of the canyon, and one so traveling has lost
the vantage point of the mountain peaks, where the sun
shines brighter and the power of vision is enlarged.
Always, but sometimes too late, the "Successful" sinner of yesterday realizes his loss of the quiet and peace
of a well-spent life. If his debauchery is great, he finds
too late that body and mind are not prepared for the
split-timing competition he meets in the world of action.
His money won't purchase lungs and brain and heart
and stomach destroyed by licentious and riotous living.
Yes, as the prophet said "the way of transgressors is
hard." (Proverbs 13:15.) When the need for spiritual
strength comes to meet a crisis in life, or perhaps to face
incurable sickness and death, all who have chosen the
downward road cry out today, as they have done since
the beginning of time to the prophets of the Lord and
the leaders of his Church, "What must we do to be
saved?" The answer is always the same: "Repent, and
by baptized every one of you in the name of Jesus Christ
for the remission of (your) sins, and ye shall receive
the gift of the Holy Ghost," (Acts 2:38) which shall be
lamp to your feet and a guide to your path. Like the
traveler with motor trouble in the deep canyon in Arizona
they must commence the "repair" of their machine, if
they would make the steep climb from the floor of their
"canyon" of sin.

Up the Road of Repentance

Now what are the steps to be taken on this climb
up the road of repentance in order to be worthy of God's
forgiveness through the redemption of the Master's
atoning sacrifice and the privileges of eternal life in the
world to come? An all-wise Father, foreseeing that
some would fall in sin and all would have need to repent,
has provided in the teachings of his gospel and through

his Church the plan of salvation that defines the clear-cut way to repentance.

First, those in sin must confess them. "By this ye may know if a man repenteth of his sins—behold, he will confess them and forsake them." (Doc. and Cov. 58:43.) That confession must be made first to him or her who has been most wronged by your acts. A sincere confession is not merely admitting guilt after the proof is already in evidence. If you have "offended many persons openly," your acknowledgment is to be made openly and before those whom you have offended that you might show your shame and humility and willingness to receive a merited rebuke. If your act is secret and has resulted in injury to no one but yourself, your confession should be in secret, that your Heavenly Father who hears in secret may reward you openly. Acts that may affect your standing in the Church, or your right to privileges or advancement in the Church, are to be promptly confessed to the bishop whom the Lord has appointed as a shepherd over every flock and commissioned to be a common judge in Israel. He may hear such confession in secret and deal justly and mercifully, as each case warrants. The unbaptized who is in sin may by following a similar course receive at the hands of an authorized elder of the Church, if otherwise prepared by an understanding of the gospel, baptism for the remission of his sins. Following confession, one in sin must show forth the fruits of his repentance by good deeds that are weighed against the bad. He must make proper restitution to the limit of his power to restore that which he has taken away or to repair the damage he has done. He that repents thus of his sins and altogether turns away therefrom, to return no more to a repetition thereof, is entitled to the promise of a forgiveness of his sins, if he has not committed the unpardonable sin, as it was declared by the Prophet Isaiah, "Though your sins be as scarlet, they shall be as white as snow; though they be red like crimson, they shall be as wool." (Isaiah 1:18.)

But now, please do not misunderstand the true meaning of the scriptures with respect to this matter. One may not wallow in the mire of filth and sin and conduct his life in a manner unlawful in the sight of God and then suppose that repentance will wipe out the effects of his sin and place him on the level he would have been on had he always lived a righteous and virtuous life. May I quote from the words of a prophet of the Lord on this subject: "He may and will be forgiven if he repents, the blood of Christ will make him free, and will wash him clean, though his sins be as scarlet; but all this will not return him any loss sustained. . . . Nor will it place him in a position where he would have been had he not committed wrong. He has lost something which can never be regained notwithstanding the . . . forgiveness of God." (President Joseph F. Smith, *Gospel Doctrine*, p. 468.) It was undoubtedly this Law of Recompense the Lord was speaking of concerning those to whom the blessings and powers of the priesthood in his kingdom were given if they were to break their "oath and covenant" after they had received it. Said he, "They shall not have forgiveness of sins in this world nor in the world to come." (Doc. and Cov. 84:41.) Throughout the eternal worlds, they could never make up for that which they lost while they "procrastinated the day of their repentance." The Lord extends loving mercy and kindness in forgiving you of the sins you commit against him or his work, but he can never remove the results of the sin you have committed against yourselves by thus retarding your advancement toward your eternal goal.

Now just a moment; you were about to judge someone of your acquaintance because of the downward course he had taken and the losses he had sustained by his sinning. Don't you think we spend too much time confessing the other person's sins? What about yourself? How long have you postponed the day of a repentance from your own misdeeds? The judgment we shall face will be before the Righteous Judge who will take into account our capacities and our limitations, our opportunities and our handicaps. One who sins and repents and thereafter fills his life with purposeful effort may not lose as much in that day of righteous judgment as one who, though not committing serious sin, falls down miserably by omitting to do that which he had capacity and opportunity to do but would not. Look to your own salvation, then, and leave with God the judgment. Remember what the Lord said, "I, the Lord, will forgive whom I will forgive, but of you it is required to forgive all men." (Doc. & Cov. 64:10.)

Perhaps you are now prepared to understand in part at least the meaning of the great teaching of the Master: "Come unto me, all ye that labour and are heavy laden, and I will give you rest. Take my yoke upon you, and learn of me; for I am meek and lowly in heart: and ye shall find rest unto your souls. For my yoke is easy, and my burden is light." (Matthew 11:28-30.)

There are no successful sinners. All must one day stand before God and be judged, each according to the deeds done in the flesh. What do you think now? Is the burden of the sinner lighter than that of a saint?

May you be blessed and guided always in your search for the best in life.

A few years ago we had a visit from a prominent
educator and engineer who became greatly inter-
ested in the work of the Church in looking after the welfare of the needy among its membership, its missionary
work, its social and educational activities, and its deep-
laid principles of spiritual truths. He was very compli-
mentary in his statements and expressed a feeling that
he would desire to become affiliated as a member of the
Church except for one thing. He did not have faith in
nor did he accept the teachings of the Church that God
"has revealed, does now reveal, and will yet reveal"
through the president of the Church, God's earthly representative, "many great and important things pertaining to the Kingdom of God." (9th Article of Faith.) He
would have the Church to be only a social institution
without power and authority to receive continued revelations from the Lord.

A Vital Principle

By his expression, he has touched upon a most
vital issue and a principle, which if clearly understood
by youth and indeed by the world, would save them
from the pitfalls of Satan's sophistry, wherein he constantly "lies in wait to deceive," and to lead astray those
who have not this rock-bottom principle of divine revelation upon which the Master told Peter he would build

his Church that "the gates of hell would not prevail against it." (Matt. 16:15-18.)

We have previously given consideration to the Church of Jesus Christ as the earthly Kingdom of God. If such a divine institution be established upon the earth, obviously such must have the leadership and be headed by that One whose name it bears. So we find an apostle with reference to Jesus, making this statement: "And he is the head of the body, the Church: who is the beginning, the firstborn from the dead; that in all things he might have the preeminence." (Colossians 1:18.) It is true, however, that in each dispensation when his gospel has been upon the earth and his Church has been established, the Lord has appointed and has vested authority in one man at a time in each such dispensation who has borne the title of president of the Church, or prophet, seer and revelator to the Church. Such titles, or the conferring of such authority, does not make of one "the Head of the Church," which title belongs to Jesus Christ. It does make of him, however, God's mouthpiece and the one who acts in God's stead and through whom he speaks to his people by way of instruction, to give or to withhold principles and ordinances, or to warn of judgments. To him is committed the "keys of knowledge, power and revelations (and) who should hold this testimony to the world." (Joseph Smith's Teachings, p. 364.) When the Lord authorized Moses to call and ordain Aaron, his brother, to be his spokesman he very clearly set forth the relationship Moses was to bear toward Aaron in these words: "And he (Aaron) shall be thy spokesman unto the people; and he shall be even . . . to thee instead of a mouth, and thou (Moses) shalt be to him instead of God." (Exodus 4:16.) While there could be other spokesmen to declare the revealed truths, there could only be one mouthpiece of God and that was his prophet. How do you think that any church without such an authorized representative could claim to be the Church of Jesus Christ?

Prophet Joseph Explains

The Prophet Joseph Smith explained in answer to a question that one so appointed was only a "prophet when acting as a prophet," or in other words, when the spirit of prophecy was directing him to say or do that which the Lord commanded. Such prophecy "came not in old time by the will of man; but holy men of God spake as they were moved by the Holy Ghost." (II Peter 1:21.)

A former president of the Church declared that "if any man in that position should become unfaithful, God would remove him out of his place; that God would not suffer him to transgress his laws and apostatize and that the moment he should take a course that would in time lead to it, God would take him away. Why? Because to suffer a wicked man to occupy that position would be to allow; as it were, the fountain to become corrupted, which is something he will never permit." (*Gospel Doctrine*, by President Joseph F. Smith, p. 44.)

Now again the Lord has said that "there is never but one on the earth at a time on whom this power and the keys of this priesthood (or authority to act as the Lord's representative) are conferred." (Doc. and Cov. 132:7.) If you will think for a moment you will see great wisdom in this provision in order to avoid the confusion that might otherwise result in the Kingdom which the Master referred to as "His Father's business."

"Keys of the Priesthood"

Let me see if I can make this principle of divine authority called "Keys of the Priesthood" a bit more understandable. Suppose I take a journey of several months' duration to Europe. Before I leave, I arrange with a caretaker to look after my house during my absence. In order that he may properly discharge his duties, I give him the keys to my front and rear doors, and give him permission to occupy the entire house and to use the

piano and to have freedom to invite in his friends to enjoy
the comforts thereof and the fruits of his responsibility.
I refrain, however, from giving him the keys to my
storeroom wherein my small stockpile of foodstuffs is
stored, or to my safe where my few, if any, jewels and
money are kept. But in my absence he takes license
from the authority I have given him and breaks the door
to my storeroom, to which I had not given him my key,
and with his friends proceeds to devour the foodstuffs
I had there for my family; or suppose he breaks the lock
to my safe and pawns my jewels. Has he acted within
his authority? Clearly his conduct has been such as to
warrant my refusing him the further privileges of my
house and my seeking due process of the law to punish
him for his infidelity in thus robbing me of my substance.

Principles Are Operative

In the Church of Jesus Christ principles are oper-
ative that show some parallel to those set forth in my
illustration. The president of the Church is the keeper of the Lord's House or Kingdom. Into his hands are
committed the keys to every part. At the Lord's direction
he gives keys of authority to other members of the Church
to baptize, to preach the gospel, to lay hands on the sick,
to preside or to teach in various offices. To a few only
he gives the authority to officiate in the ordinances of the
temples or to perform marriages therein "to bind on earth
and in heaven." Authority to perform some ordinances
he reserves to himself only. This authority, according
to the revealed pattern, is conferred by the laying on of
the hands. What would you think of a person in the Church,
to whom had been given certain limited rights or authority,
if he were to usurp prerogatives that had been reserved
to only a chosen few or to the president of the Church
himself? Let me give you the Lord's answer to that
question: "Behold, the heavens withdraw themselves;
the Spirit of the Lord is grieved; and when it is with-

drawn, Amen to the priesthood or the authority of that man." (Doc. and Cov. 121:37.)

There is an eternal principle that governs the relationship between God and his children and the obedience which his children are to yield to his commands. The Lord gave that principle in a revelation to Joseph Smith in June, 1831, at Kirtland, Ohio, wherein he said: "Wherefore I, the Lord, command and revoke, as it seemeth me good; and all this to be answered upon the heads of the rebellious, saith the Lord." (Doc. and Cov. 56:4.)

Now let us examine a few instances to show how this authority has been exercised in past generations. In the days of the apostles, after the crucifixion of the Savior, they still observed the law of the Jews that it was "an unlawful thing for a man that is a Jew to keep company or to come unto one of another nation." (Acts 10:28.) Peter was the Lord's earthly representative at that time in his Church. As Peter went upon the housetop to pray, he was given a vision that was repeated three times, in which he was shown that the law restricting the preaching of the gospel and the baptizing of others than the Jews was now to be revoked and the gospel was to be given to "him in every nation that feareth him, and worketh righteousness." (Acts 10:35.) At almost the same time the Lord appeared to Saul of Tarsus and in a vision told him that he, Saul, was to be "a chosen vessel . . . to bear the Lord's name before the gentiles, and kings, and the children of Israel." (Acts 9:15.) Here we have an instance where the Lord at first, for reasons best known to himself, restricted the taking of the gospel to the Gentiles and then later reversed the former restrictions in a vision to his mouthpiece, Peter. Before Saul could commence that mission to the Gentiles, however, he had to be baptized and confirmed a member of the Church by the humble Ananias, and later was taken by Barnabas to the apostles. For what purpose? It was for the purpose of receiving from Peter and the twelve apostles his commission or authority to fulfill the mission of which he had learned in heavenly vision.

The Mosaic Law

The Lord gave to Moses, because of the "hardness of heart" among the Israelites, a code of laws called the "carnal commandments" or the Mosaic Law, and certain of the rights of the higher priesthood were withdrawn from among the people. Does anyone question the rights of Moses as God's prophet to take away these rights if the Lord inspired him to do so? (Doc. and Cov. 84:24-26.) In the light of our experience today, I imagine that some in the day of Moses rebelled when their former rights were taken away. What happened to those who continued to attempt to exercise those rights without the authority of the Lord through Moses? The history is complete. They were cut off from among the people and were denied the blessings of the Lord.

This same principle has been applied to the doctrine of plural marriage. In the days of Abraham, Jacob and David, by divine commandment through the Lord's mouthpiece, certain leaders were permitted to have more than one wife. At another period on this continent through his prophet, Jacob, son of Lehi, the Lord prohibited the practice of the principle and commanded the Nephites, "For there shall not any man among you have save it be one wife and concubines he shall have none." (Jacob 2:27.) Still later in our own dispensation, the Lord through his prophet, Joseph Smith, in 1843 reestablished the practice of plurality of wives by a worthy few who were especially chosen. This practice was commanded as a principle of sacrifice which the Lord compared as similar to that he had commanded at the hands of Abraham, who was told to offer up his son Isaac. (Doc. and Cov. 132: 50.)

The Manifesto

Still later, in October, 1890, Wilford Woodruff, then the president of the Church, pursuant to a revelation from the Lord, announced the withdrawal again of the practice of that principle in a written document or proclamation to the Church which he called the Manifesto. This action was sustained by the unanimous vote of the Church members at the general conference in October, 1890. Of this proclamation President Woodruff made this significant statement: "The God of heaven commanded me to do what I did do . . . I went before the Lord, and I wrote what the Lord told me to write." (Sermon of Wilford Woodruff, Logan, Utah, November 1, 1891. *Deseret News*, November 7, 1891. See Woodruff sermon, fourth session of dedicatory services of Salt Lake Temple.)

This decision has been repeatedly reaffirmed by every president of the Church since that time down to the present.

That the president of the Church has the due and recognized authority in such matters was declared by Orson Pratt, one of the vigorous leaders of the Church during the days of the practice of plural marriage. These are his words:

"But then another question will arise: How are these things to be conducted? Are they to be left at random? No. We find they were restricted in ancient times. Do you not recollect the circumstance of the Prophet Nathan's coming to David? Nathan the prophet, in relation to David, was the man who held the keys concerning this matter in ancient days; and it was governed by the strictest laws. So in these days; let me announce to this congregation that there is but one man in all the world, at the same time, who can hold the keys of this matter; but one man has the power to turn the key to inquire of the Lord and to say whether I, or these my brethren, or any of the rest of this congregation or the Saints upon the face of the whole earth, may have

this blessing of Abraham conferred upon them; he holds
the keys of these matters now, the same as Nathan in
his day." (Journal of Discourses Vol. 1, pp. 63-64.)

The United Order

The Lord acted upon the same general principle
when he first established the United Order and then
after the people had shown that they were not righteous
enough to live the law, he withdrew it until after the
"redemption" of Zion. (Doc. and Cov. 105:34.) So the
Lord will do with principles and practices which he has
set up when the people are no longer able to abide them
because it is better we should lose the blessings of obedience than that we should incur the penalties of disobedience; but after any such withdrawal, the Lord himself through his appointed mouthpiece will declare the
restoration at the proper time.

What then becomes of the claims of charlatans
and misguided persons who rise up to claim authority
and revelations for the Church contrary to and without
the keys from him whom God has sent to preside as his
prophet, seer and revelator? Should not they likewise,
as the caretaker of my illustration, be cast out because
of their infidelity and be dealt with according to the law
that condemns their practice as unlawful? When the
judgment of the law descends upon those who are sinners before the law of God and the law of the land, as
with the transgressor who steals my goods, they shall
be cut off from among those whom they have betrayed.
Let no one persuade you that such lawful prosecution
should claim the blessedness of which the master spoke
when persecution should descend upon the righteous
"for his name's sake." Judgment in all justice under
these circumstances does not prove such a cause to be
true.

So you, the youth to whom I speak, be on guard
against the sophistry of him who comes to you claiming

to be "one mighty and strong," to set the Church in order; or to set up a so-called Order of Aaron in contradiction of divine authority, or to set up a system where they
have things in common, as in the days of the apostles
(Acts 4:34-37) and in the commencement of our own
generation. There are some among us who would have
us believe that they alone are the true blood of Israel
and that the time is now ripe for them to take over the
reigns of authority already held by an authorized representative of the Lord. If any such come to you as members
of the Church, claiming divine revelation for the Church
with respect to the law of marriage, or with any other
matters pertaining to the affairs of the Kingdom of God,
challenge all such claims until they show proof that they
have been properly authorized by the president of the
Church who presides at the present time and is the
only man on the earth who holds the keys of authority to
speak for the Church. Each prophet speaks for his own day
and time in harmony with God's will.

If they come to you not being members of the
Church, ask them where they get their authority. Remind
them of the words of the Apostle Paul that "No man
taketh this honor unto himself, but he that is called of
God, as was Aaron," (Hebrews 5:4) which means being
called of God "by prophecy and by the laying on of
hands by those who are in authority." (Fifth Article of
Faith.)

You are commanded by the Lord in all things, "to
ask of God . . . doing all things with prayer and thanksgiving, that ye may not be seduced by evil spirits, or
doctrines of devils, or the commandments of men; for
some are of men, and others of devils." (Doc. and Cov.
46:7.) The Prophet Joseph Smith gave us this as a rule
by which to detect these who would deceive. This is
what he said: "That man who rises up to condemn
others, finding fault with the Church, saying that they
are out of the way, while he himself is righteous, then
know assuredly that that man is on the high road to

apostasy, and if he does not repent he will apostatize, as God lives." (History of the Church, Vol. 3, p. 385.) Look about you. Do you know of any one soul who has apostatized from the truth that has prospered spiritually in your day? Contrary to that, they are "left unto themselves to kick against the pricks, to persecute the saints and to fight against God," The works of the apostates are but a solemn witness to the truthfulness of these words of the Lord: "No weapon that is formed against (the leaders) of the Church shall prosper and if any man lift his voice against (them), he shall be confounded in (the Lord's) due time." (Doc. and Cov. 71:9-10.)

Revelation of Warning

Early in our day the Lord gave a revelation of warning against these things: "Behold, verily I say unto you, that there are many spirits which are false spirits which have gone forth in the earth, deceiving the world. And also Satan hath sought to deceive you, that he might overthrow you. . . . Behold, verily I say unto you, there are hypocrites among you, who have deceived some, which has given the adversary power; but behold such shall be reclaimed; but the hypocrites shall be detected and shall be cut off, either in life or in death, even as I will; and wo unto them who are cut off from my Church, for the same are overcome of the world. Wherefore, let every man beware lest he do that which is not in truth and righteousness before me." (Doc. and Cov. 50:2-3, 7-9.)

May youth live such lives as to entitle them to the companionship of the Spirit of discernment by which they might be guided from the errors of Satan's sophistry.

The Worth of a Human Soul

14

A few years ago with a representative of an international news service, I stood on the west bank of the Willamette River near Portland, Oregon. It was near midnight. Across the river we witnessed the amazing spectacle of the huge shipyards where eleven ships were undergoing construction. These ships were being hastily constructed for the army and navy to meet the emergency problems of transportation and combat. The ultimate purpose of all this feverish activity was the destruction of human beings.

As we stood there that night gazing upon this stupendous activity, the news representative made the comment that formerly whenever there was an airplane crash where lives had been lost, he had been required to make his report in the most complete detail, but now such happenings were dismissed with the most meager report. "Seemingly," he said, "life has become so very cheap that with all that's going on we pay but scant attention to the loss of a mere human life."

Greatness of Men's Worth

How much is a human soul worth? The Psalmist exclaimed about the greatness of man's worth: "For thou hast made him a little lower than the angels, and hast crowned him with glory and honor. Thou madest him to have dominion over the works of thy hands; thou hast put all things under his feet." (Psalms 8:4-6.) The cynic describes a man as being 90 per cent water, containing considerable carbon, with enough iron for a ten-penny nail, lime sufficient to whitewash a chicken coop, with enough phosphorus to fire a toy cannon and the fat required to make two bars of soap. As though to evaluate inversely a man's worth, or at any rate to figure the cost of destroying him in terms of dollars and cents, there appeared recently a statement of someone who had figured out that "during Caesar's campaign of war, the killing of one soldier involved the expenditure of 75 cents. In Napoleon's time it required about $3000 in terms of American money. During the Civil War the cost advanced to about $5000, and in the first World War it reached $25,000." I leave with you the question as to whether these increasing costs indicate the tendency to place a greater or lesser value on a human life.

The feelings of the soldier at the battle-front about this matter are summed up in the statement of a chaplain, the late Marsden Durham, who had just gone through his first bloody experience. He wrote, "The sight of but one man, in the image of God, mutilated on the battlefield, causes one to ponder the worthwhileness of it all, and to ask 'Why?' But the question turns into one of pure rhetoric. The premium for free agency is high. One does well to remember that 'All things are done in the wisdom of him who knoweth all things' and that the essential justice of God is not to be impugned." Chaplain Durham no doubt had in mind the truth declared by a prophet-warrior of another day who said: "For the Lord suffereth the righteous to be slain that his justice and judgment may come upon the wicked." (Alma 60:13.)

A Mother's Evaluation

A mother has a different sense of values in considering man's worth. Whether it be a son lying dangerously ill in a hospital bed or a son or daughter caught in the merciless web of sin and crime, she counts the cost in tears of anguish and lonely vigils filled with pleadings and supplications. A mother's love prompts agonized suffering in her almost commensurate with that of her offspring. Since the days of mother Eve, a mother's sorrow has been greatly multiplied in her conception, and in sorrow has she brought forth children. (Genesis 3:16.) After months of travail she has gone to the gates of death that she might ascend the mountains of life, and to her the cry of her infant child, giving evidence that it is alive, is ample reward for her pain and sacrifice. In union with the father of her babe, she has linked hands with God in the creation of a human soul. She knows the cost of a human soul in terms of care and patience while her child climbs "Fool's Hill" in its youth, for parents see themselves in their children living again as youth through their own foolish years. She counts it all worth-while if the son grows to maturity to become a God-fearing man, a useful citizen and a kind husband and father, or if her daughter is happily married and living in a home made happy by the laughter of her own little children. If her son falls in bloody conflict, whether on the side of friend or foe, she forbids an overwhelming grief with a whispered repetition of her last words to him, "Brave sons must have brave mothers and I'll not fail you, my son." If her own are taken in sin, to her they are not lost, and if she could, she would wash away their sins with her own tears.

Why is the human soul so precious as to be accorded so much attention and concern? It is seemingly something more precious than the mere human body. The Lord enjoins us to "fear not them which kill the body, but are not able to kill the soul, but rather fear him which is able to destroy both soul and body in hell." (Matthew 10:28.) The "soul" of man we are told is a composite of both the human body and the eternal spirit. (Doc. and Cov. 88:15.)

God's Evaluation

Beyond the comprehension of mortal man, God has placed a supreme value upon a human soul when he says:

"Remember the worth of souls is great in the sight of God; for, behold, the Lord your Redeemer suffered death in the flesh; wherefore he suffered the pain of all men, that all men might repent and come unto him. And he hath risen again from the dead, that he might bring all men unto him, on conditions of repentance. And how great is his joy in the soul that repenteth." (Doc. and Cov. 18:10-13.)

"For God so loved the world" of men and women, young and old, "that he gave his only begotten Son" (John 3:16.) to open the way by which all might return to his heavenly realm. The plan for man's redemption was laid in heaven even before the earth was formed, and known even was the identity of him who was to make the atonement, who was to be as a "Lamb slain from the foundation of the world." (Revelation 13:8.) To prophets long before his advent upon the earth, the life and mission of the Savior was completely foretold. "He was wounded for our transgressions, he was bruised for our iniquities . . . and with his stripes are we healed . . . and he bare the sins of many and made intercession for the transgressor." (Isaiah 53.) The only thing the Savior expects from us in return for his suffering is that we repent of our sins and keep his commandments. Although his sufferings were so intense that he the Son of God was caused "to tremble because of pain and to bleed at every pore, and to suffer both body and spirit, and would that (he) might not drink the bitter cup, and shrink," (Doc. and Cov. 19:18.) yet he, as would a true mother, counts it all worthwhile if, at the end of the earth, mankind, for whom he died, might gain eternal life and become his sons and daughters eternally through the acceptance of his gospel, which is God's plan for man's salvation.

Preparation to Meet God

But after having had Jesus, our Savior, suffer all these things for us and all mankind that we might not suffer if we would repent, if we do not repent we must suffer even as he. (Doc. and Cov. 19:16-17.) For this purpose the Lord grants a span of years to the life of every soul in which he is given opportunity to "prepare to meet God."

That preparation to meet God is to commence with the beginning of life. In the early years of life your parents are held responsible in teaching you to pray, to walk uprightly before the Lord, to teach you the doctrine of repentance and to have you baptized when eight years old, which the Lord has said in revelation is the age when children "begin to become accountable before (him)." Up to this time Satan has no power to tempt little children, therefore they cannot sin. (Doc. and Cov. 29:46-47.) If one should die as a little child, he is redeemed from the foundation of the world by the atonement of the Savior and his reward in the celestial kingdom is certain. It is a solemn mockery before God, therefore, to baptize little children who know not the meaning of repentance and have no sins of which to repent. (Moroni 8.)

Baptism—A Preparation

Baptism by immersion for the remission of sins, however, is for those who have attained the age of accountability, a necessary preparation to meet our God. It is by this means that you become "the children of God by faith in Jesus Christ. For as many of you as have been baptized into Christ have put on Christ," (Galatians 3:26-27) or in other words through baptism have received "the power to become the sons and daughters of God." (Mosiah 5:7.) It is through this medium that you may receive forgiveness of your sins, and your hearts be purified. (Mosiah 4:2.) To be worthy of such a forgiveness after having been baptized, you must humble yourselves and call on the Lord daily and walk steadfastly in the light of the teachings of the gospel. By so doing you shall be filled with the love of God and will have no mind to injure one another but to live peaceably together. You will be unceasing in your care and teaching of your own little children, "you will succor those that stand in need of succor . . . and not suffer that the beggar putteth up his petition to you in vain, and turn him out to perish." (Mosiah 4:16.) You must, in a word, by not "leaving the principles of the doctrine of Christ . . . go on unto perfection." (Hebrews 6:1.) He who postpones the day of his repentance and baptism for the remission of his sins through the atonement of Jesus Christ will be heard to chant that doleful lament as the prophet said he would, "The harvest is past, the summer is ended, and we are not saved." (Jeremiah 8:20.)

A Vital Message

This message is so vital to every human soul, whose worth is so great in the sight of God, that he has commanded in every generation that it be preached to "every nation, kindred, tongue and people," by duly authorized messengers clothed with divine authority. One of the greatest of these missionaries, realizing the vital importance of his calling, declared: "And I, brethren, when I came to you came not with excellency of speech or of wisdom, declaring unto you the testimony of God. For I determined not to know anything among you, save Jesus Christ, and him crucified. . . . And my speech and my preaching was not with enticing words of man's wisdom, but in demonstration of the Spirit, and of power." (I Corinthians 2:1-4.) As in former dispensations so in our own day the commandment has been given to us to cry repentance unto the world with a wonderful promise from the Lord to those who heed that command:

If . . . "you should labor all your days in crying repentance unto this people, and bring, save it be one soul unto me, how great shall be your joy with him in the kingdom of my Father! And now, if your joy will be great with one soul that you have brought unto me into the kingdom of my Father, how great will be your joy if you should bring many souls unto me!" (Doc. and Cov. 18:15-16.)

Upon the youth of the Church principally for almost a hundred years has been placed the burden of responsibility of doing missionary work. According to records of the Church Missionary Department, nearly a quarter of a million men and women of the Church have served as missionaries since the organization of the Church in 1830.

Presently, about 17,000 missionaries are in the mission field at an average monthly expense of $125.00 or about $2,125,000 to the missionaries or their families. Not only these missionaries but every member of the Church who has been warned by the teachings of the gospel is required to warn his neighbor, that the neighbor may be left without excuse in the day of judgment. (Doc. and Cov. 88:81-82.)

"Saviors on Mt. Zion"

If the acceptance of the gospel is so essential to the welfare of man's eternal soul, you may well ask what is to become of the millions who have died without a knowledge of the gospel or the Lords' plan, by which the full effect of his atonement might be realized. If missionary work were to have been limited only to mortality, many souls would have been condemned without a hearing. Every one, good or bad, because of the atonement, will be resurrected, for "As in Adam all die, even so in Christ shall all be made alive." (I Cor. 15:22.) But only those who repent and are baptized for the remission of their sins will lay full claim to the redeeming blood of his atonement. In the plan of our Heavenly Father, justice and mercy are equally balanced. After the death of Jesus on the cross, during the three days while his body lay in the tomb, "quickened by the spirit . . . he went and preached (the gospel) unto the spirits in prison . . . that they might be judged according to men in the flesh, but live according to God in the Spirit." (I Peter 3:18-20; 4:6.) In so doing he kept his promise to the thief on the cross, "Today shalt thou be with me in paradise." (Luke 23:43.) He spoke of paradise as the place of departed spirits where the spirits of all who die must await the day of resurrection. To those who are righteous it is a place of peace and happiness but to those who are unrighteous it is a state of fearful anxiety for the judgments of God upon them. It was to the "disobedient in the days of Noah" who were in this spirit prison that the Master went and opened the door to the preaching of the gospel. Thus came a fulfillment of God's promise to his children of a benighted age that he would send one "To open the blind eyes . . . to proclaim liberty to the captive . . . to bring out the prisoners from the prison, and them that sit in darkness out of the prison house." (Isaiah 42:7; 61:1.) Baptism by immersion for the remission of sins, the only means by which man can accept the gospel, as an earthly ordinance, and so in the Plan of Salvation, our Father, with equal consideration for all his children, has provided a way for all members of his Church and Kingdom on the earth to be "saviors on Mt. Zion" by performing a vicarious work in behalf of those in the world of spirits, "the prison house," that they could not perform for themselves. This work for the dead performed in holy temples by members of the Church does in reality make of them who do this work "saviors" to those who have died without a knowledge of the gospel, for thereby they may claim the complete gift of the Savior promised to all mankind through his atonement. Reference to that service that may be rendered for those in the spirit world, as it was undoubtedly being performed by the saints in the days of the Apostle Paul and which we can now perform for our own dead, was given by him as an argument in proof of the resurrection. Said he: "Else what shall they do which are baptized for the dead, if the dead rise not at all? why are they then baptized for the dead?" (I Corinthians 15:29.) Temples in this day have been built in which this work so essential to the work of salvation might again be performed.

A True Appraisal

Now perhaps if you have given careful thought to

these sublime truths, you can begin to make a true appraisal of the worth of a human soul in a day when its destruction by war and sin has been so wanton. Those who have kept the faith and are innocent of wrongdoing, and whose lives were taken in the ruthless slaughter called war, have in a lesser sense given their lives as an atonement that freedom might live and that the full purposes of God might be realized. They shall not have died in vain; every drop of blood that has been shed must one day be repaid with mighty judgments upon the heads of men and nations responsible for this bloody carnage, for "the judgments of the Lord are true and righteous altogether." All guilty of such terrible crimes against humanity must suffer "even as they (our boys) have suffered." Who knows but that many of our choicest young men bearing the Holy Priesthood, whose lives have been taken in these terrible world conflicts, might not have been called to go to the spirit world while their bodies lie in the grave, as did the Savior's, to preach repentance to the millions of those who have died without a knowledge of the gospel. Those who accept of such missionary work and receive the gospel, as in the day of the Master's visitation, will be judged according to men in the flesh but live according to God in the Spirit, by having the hearts of their children on the earth turned unto their fathers in the spirit world. Friends or descendants here in mortality who have been so moved will search out these dead and labor in the House of the Lord in their behalf "lest the whole earth be smitten with a curse."

And so let these thoughts sober you with a true appreciation for the meaning of the Savior's comforting words to Martha and Mary "I am the resurrection and the life: he that believeth in me, though he were dead, yet shall he live." (John 11:25.) May this understanding stir you to new resolve to live worthy of the sacrifice made by Jesus the Savior of the world.

As our missionaries are sent to all nations, the Church

has available a full complement of youthful warriors of peace who have been tried in the furnace of adversity and temptation, to send out with a plan of peace, the acceptance of which will be the only effective block against war and bloodshed. This service the youth of this generation will perform with the memories of the past wars still ringing in their ears. To you young men who were in military service, who lost your buddies who were not members of the Church, through sacred ordinances in the temples of our God, you may be instrumental in bringing to them that which is more precious than mortal life, even the way to gain a fulness of eternal life in the presence of the Lord.

May you the youth of Zion be guided in making yourselves ready to answer that call "to go into the world" as such messengers in preparation for the winding up of God's great work for the salvation of human souls.

Unwelcome Wedding Guests

15

All of you have been in attendance at wedding ceremonies and the receptions which followed where members
of families and friends gather to offer congratulations
and blessings. Every effort is made to have everything
arranged in harmony with the wishes of those most
concerned. The place and the time, the flowers, the
refreshments and music, the serving, the gift room, and
the last and most important, the guest list of those to be
invited must be carefully checked. Nothing is done or
left undone to mar the occasion or to upset the feelings
of the bride and groom. What a blunder it would be if
someone in utter disregard of the wishes of the young
couple were to invite some guests whose presence would
be very distasteful to them. Happy anticipation might
then be overshadowed by the dreaded presence of the
unwanted guests.

Death—Separation

Despite all this care that these occasions should be
highlights in the lives of you young lovers, thousands of
you unwittingly, and I fear sometimes almost willingly
and of your own accord, invite in at your wedding parties
two of the most dreaded of all spectres on such occasions.
Their names were suggested by the civil ceremony which
many of you couples chose to have at the commencement
of your married life, but perhaps you didn't hear their
names. Listen carefully to the words of the civil ceremony

and the identity of these unwelcome guests will be revealed. The one officiating by authority of the law of the land pronounced you legally and lawfully husband and wife "Until death do you part." There they stand clearly before you—Death and Separation. You who are parties to a civil ceremony are to be married only during the period of your mortal lives. At death your marriage contract is to be dissolved and you are to be permanently separated or divorced from each other in the next life. Not only must this thought be a startling consideration, but if there be children and family life that too must end with death. According to the Lord's revelation, all manmade covenants, contracts, bonds, obligations, oaths, vows, performances, connections, associations or expectations . . . are of no efficacy, virtue or force in and after the resurrection from the dead . . . and have an end when men are dead." (Doc. and Cov. 132:7.)

Even though the legal officer or minister had declared you to be husband and wife for "time and all eternity," unless he had the authority so to speak, then that promise or contract would "not be valid, neither of force when they are out of the world." (Doc. and Cov. 132:18.) The Master told Peter and the other apostles of a power beyond that of man which he called the "keys to the kingdom of heaven," and by this power he said, "Whatsoever thou shalt bind on earth shall be bound in heaven." (Matt. 16:19.) That power and authority, by which holy ordinances are administered, is known as the holy priesthood and is always to be found in the Church of Jesus Christ in every dispensation of the gospel upon the earth.

A Heavenly Parentage

The holy order of marriage did not begin with life on this earth, neither was it intended that it should end with death. Let us take a brief glimpse of our premortal life as seen through the eyes of the prophets who have spoken. Through one of these prophets the Lord asks the

question: "Where wast thou when I laid the foundations
of the earth . . . when the morning stars sang together,
and all the sons of God shouted for joy?" (Job 38:4, 7.)
May I point that question at you young people for you
were the stars in the morning of God's first creation.
You were the sons and daughters of God in the pre-existent
world of spirits. Where were you? Another prophet
answers that question: "Now the Lord has shown unto
me, Abraham, the intelligences that were organized
before the world was . . . And God saw these souls that
they were good . . . for he stood among those that were
spirits." (Abraham 3:22-23.) Putting these two revelations
together then, we are to understand that spirits are
organized intelligences that were so prepared before
the foundations of the earth were laid, and that they
were organized by our Heavenly Father and dwelt
with him while the earth was being formed. But now may
I ask you a simple question: Could there have been a
Father in heaven without a Mother? With a similar
question in her mind the poetess penned this verse of
a well-known hymn:

> I had learned to call thee Father
> Through thy spirit from on high
> But until the key of knowledge
> Was restored I knew not why.
> In the heavens are parents single?
> No; the thought makes reason stare!
> Truth is reason, truth eternal,
> Tells me I've a mother there.
> —"Oh My Father"—Eliza R. Snow.

While still keeping that question in mind, think of
the significant statement contained in the scriptures describing the creation of man. "And God said, Let us make
man in our image, after our likeness . . . So God created
man in his own image, in the image of God created he
him, male and female created he them." (Genesis 1:26-27.)
If you consider carefully those in whose image and likeness male and female were created, I wonder if you will

not also discover the organizers of intelligences in the world of spirits.

First Earth Marriage

Now let us consider the first marriage that was performed after the earth was organized. Adam, the first man, had been created as well as the beasts and fowls and every living thing upon the earth. We then find this recorded: "And the Lord God said, It is not good that man should be alone; I will make him an help meet for him." After the Lord had formed Eve, he "brought her unto the man. And Adam said, This is now bone of my bones and flesh of my flesh; she shall be called Woman because she was taken out of Man. Therefore shall a man leave his father and his mother, and shall cleave unto his wife and they shall be one flesh." (Genesis 2:18, 22-24.) These words were undoubtedly just what they sound like. They were very likely the words spoken by Adam reciting the vows of the first marriage upon this earth. With the completion of that marriage the Lord commanded them to "be fruitful, and multiply and replenish the earth, and subdue it." (Genesis 1:28.) Here was a marriage performed by the Lord between two immortal beings, for until sin entered the world their bodies were not subject to death. He made them one, not merely for time, nor for any definite period; they were to be one throughout the eternal ages. If you were to say that because Adam and Eve transgressed and became subject to death that this eternal union was broken, then just remember that the purpose of the atonement by Jesus Christ was to restore that which was lost by the fall. Their restoration then to each other after the resurrection would not require a re-marriage, for death to them was not a divorce; it was only a temporary separation. Resurrection to immortality meant for them a reunion and an eternal bond never again to be severed. "For as in Adam all die, even so in Christ shall all be made alive." (I Corinthians 15:22.)

If you have carefully followed an explanation of this first marriage, you are prepared to understand the revelation given to the Church in our generation in these words:

"If a man marry a wife by my word, which is my law, and by the new and everlasting covenant, and it is sealed unto them by the Holy Spirit of promise, by him who is anointed, and unto whom I have appointed this power and the keys of this priesthood . . . it shall be done unto them in all things whatsoever my servant hath put upon them, in time, and through all eternity; and shall be of full force when they are out of the world; and they shall pass by the angels, and the gods, which are set there, to their exaltation and glory in all things, as hath been sealed upon their heads." (Doc. and Cov. 132:19.)

"If marriage then was for the purpose of the organising of spirits before the world was formed and for "multiplying and replenishing the earth" on which we now live, surely there must likewise be a divine purpose in its being continued after the resurrection. This purpose is declared by the Lord to be for "a continuation of the seeds forever and ever." (Doc. and Cov. 132: 19.) In other revelations he has told us also about his temporal or worldly creations: "Worlds without number have I created. . . . And as one earth shall pass away, and the heavens thereof even so shall another come; and there is no end to my works, neither to my words. For behold, this is my work and my glory—to bring to pass the immortality and eternal life of man." (Moses 1:33, 38-39.)

God's Many Creations

Go out into the darkness some bright, calm night and view the myriads of stars set in the heavens and contemplate the extent of God's creations; then you will understand the exclamation of the Lord as contained in his revelation to us: "Behold, all these are kingdoms, and any man who hath seen any or the least of these hath seen God moving in his majesty and power." (Doc. and Cov. 88:47.) This earth on which you stand "after it hath filled the measure of its creation" as the abode of mortal beings shall come to an end, and the heavens and the earth shall pass away "and there shall be a new heaven and a new earth." (Doc. and Cov. 29:23; Rev. 20:11.) Then "it shall be crowned with glory, even with the presence of God the Father," and those who are entitled to that heavenly glory shall "possess it forever and ever." (Doc. and Cov. 88:19-20.) Who is there to say that this is not the way by which our Heavenly Father's future kingdoms will be dealt with and prepared for the inheritance of his faithful children who because of their obedience to the Law of Celestial Marriage will make possible "a continuation of the seeds forever and ever"?

Marriage for time and for eternity is the "straight gate and the narrow way (spoken of in the scriptures) that leadeth unto the exaltation and continuation of the lives, and few there be that find it," but "broad is the gate, and wide the way that leadeth to the deaths; and many there are that go in thereat." (Doc. and Cov. 132:22, 25.) If Satan and his hosts can persuade you to take the broad highway of worldly marriage that ends with death, he has defeated you in your opportunity for the highest degree of eternal happiness through marriage and increase throughout eternity. It should now be clear to your reasoning why the Lord declared that in order to obtain the highest degree in the Celestial glory, a person must enter into the new and everlasting covenant of marriage. If he does not, he cannot obtain it. (Doc. and Cov. 131:1-3.) This was the apparent meaning of the words of the Apostle Paul to the Corinthians, when he said, "nevertheless, neither is the man without the woman, neither the woman without the man, in the Lord." (I Cor. 11:11.)

But now you have a flood of questions: You want to know why Jesus taught that there was no "marrying and giving in marriage" in the heavens of the hereafter. This statement by the Master was a rebuke to those who sought to entrap him with a question about the practice of marriage in the time of Moses. It was the law at that time that if a man married and died without children, it was the duty of his brother to take his widow and raise up seed. Supposing seven of these brothers had taken her as a wife in obedience to the law of Moses, to whom would she belong in the resurrection, since they had all been married to her? Jesus answered and said unto them, "Ye do err, not knowing the scriptures, nor the power of God." (Matthew 22:29.) They did not understand the principle of marriage for time and for eternity, although he had taught them plainly on another occasion: "Wherefore they are no more twain but one flesh. What therefore God hath joined together, let not man put asunder." (Matthew 19:6.) Marriage is not performed in the heavens hereafter. If you would be united for eternity as husband and wife and family, that sealing must be performed here upon this earth by the authority of the holy priesthood.

Knowing and believing this, no one of you should be content until you have prepared yourself to enter into this eternal relationship. Holy temples have been provided for this purpose and youth everywhere, in the Church or out of the Church, are invited to make their plans now by accepting the gospel and yielding obedience thereto in order to comply with this sacred law given by our Heavenly Father to fulfill his eternal purposes concerning us.

Should you marry in the Church? A statement of these great fundamental truths such as is given herein should supply a sufficient answer to all believers in the teachings of the gospel; but in addition to these teachings, writers of wisdom, regardless of their religious beliefs, and indeed all responsible leaders of all churches, have counseled that you marry someone of your own religious belief. Catholics should marry Catholics. Methodists should marry Methodists. Latter-day Saints should marry Latter-day Saints. If you disregard this counsel, you must be prepared to pay the price which is rather clearly set forth by an eminent authority on this subject. These are the words of Dr. Paul Popenoe:

"This price may be almost anything. It may be alienation from your own family or alienation of your bride from hers; it may be giving up your own church to join hers; it may be the abandonment by each of church affiliation, and living thenceforward without association with organized religion; it may be less than any of these, or much more. Count the price before you go ahead; and if you want to do so, pay it, in advance." (Popenoe— *Modern Marriage.*)

Some of you may decide to marry out of the Church with the secret hope of converting your companion to your religious views. Your chances for happiness in your married life are far greater if you make that conversion before marriage.

You young women advancing in years who have not yet accepted a proposal of marriage, if you make yourselves worthy and ready to go to the house of the Lord and have faith in this sacred principle, even though the privilege of marriage does not come to you now, the Lord will reward you in due time and no blessing will be denied you. You are not under obligation to accept a proposal from someone unworthy of you for fear you will fail of your blessings. Likewise you young men who may lose your lives in a terrible conflict before you have had an opportunity for marriage, the Lord knows the intents of your hearts and in his own time will reward you with opportunities made possible through temple ordinances instituted in the Church for that purpose. It is a significant thing to me that the statistics of the Church year after year reveal an almost equal number of males and females. For example a recent report showed 50.4 per cent of the Church population was male and 49.6 per cent female, a difference of only a few more males than females. Do you suppose that this is just a coincidence and a fact to be explained by scientific theory, or is it because of an anxious Providence who has ordained it so that all young men and young women who are Church members might find their companions within the Church and through eternal marriage be heirs to the promises of the fulness of his blessings?

To the end that man and woman might be brought together in this sacred marriage relationship, whereby earthly bodies are prepared as tabernacles for heavenly spirits, the Lord has placed within the breast of every young man and every young woman a desire for association with each other. These are sacred and holy impulses but tremendously powerful. Lest life be valued too cheaply or these life processes be prostituted to the mere gratification of human passions, God has placed foremost in the category of serious crimes against which we are warned in the Ten Commandments, first, murder, and second only to that, sexual impurity. "Thou shalt not kill! Thou shalt not commit adultery!" Satan in his diabolical cunning would have the girl in her youth by scanty or improper dress or by wanton look fan the flame of passion of her youthful boy companion to unholy bounds and likewise would prompt the lips of the young man to speak suggestive words or obscene tales and to take liberties with his girl companion that encourage the defiling of themselves before God by breaking his divine commandment. To the end that youth may not fall into the ways of unwisdom and thus become a prey to evil impulses, the Church counsels you to be modest in your dress and manner and to forbid the evil thoughts that would prompt your lips to obscenity and your conduct to be base and unseemly. To gain the highest bliss in holy wedlock, the fountains of life must be kept pure. The reward for you who keep yourselves clean and pure and embark upon the sea of matrimony in the Lord's appointed way is to enjoy a love and companionship in home and family that shall last forever. Death and Separation are not invited guests at the weddings of the righteous who marry according to the Lord's plan "for time and for all eternity."

May youth everywhere be guided to take the first steps today that will lead eventually to a holy marriage altar in the House of the Lord.

From the beginning of time the chosen people of the Lord in the various dispensations have, under his direction, designated sacred places and structures as temples of worship. Such temples have not been the usual meeting places for congregational worship. They have been structures "specially set apart for service regarded as sacred . . . and exclusively devoted to sacred rites and ceremonies."

During the exodus of the Israelites from Egypt, by command of the Lord, they carried with them a costly and elaborate structure which was constructed as the Lord directed. This structure was called the Tabernacle of the Congregation and was to them a temple of worship. At times during their journey the Tabernacle became the temporary abiding place of God, at which time "the glory of the Lord" filled the Tabernacle.

Temple of Herod

Some time after the arrival of the Israelites in the promised land, the Lord again commanded the building of a "house for the Lord God of Israel." Again specific and detailed revelations to the Lord's representatives directed them in the building and in the ordinances that were to be performed therein. Throughout successive periods of persecution, the Israelites built temples, the grandest of which, it is generally admitted, was the Temple of Herod, although its beauty and grandeur were, as described by one writer "in architectural excellence rather than in the sanctity of its worship," for at the time of the coming of the Savior in his ministry "its ritual and service were largely man-prescribed. . . . Devoid as it was of the divine accompaniments of earlier shrines accepted of God, and defiled as it was by priestly arrogance and usurpation . . . it was nevertheless recognized even by the Lord Jesus Christ as his Father's House." (*House of the Lord*, Talmage, p. 50.) It was here where the baby Jesus was presented. It was here where he frequently came to teach the people and where he declared his identity as the Son of God. It was from this place that he drove out the money-changers when they would have made his Father's House a den of thieves. When he was crucified on Calvary, the veil of the temple was torn in two by unseen hands, as though to indicate its rejection as a House of the Lord. From that day until the restoration of the gospel in the dispensation of the fulness of times through a prophet of the Lord, the only sanctuaries in which the sacred temple ordinances could be performed were those built on the Western Hemisphere and spoken of in the Book of Mormon, a record of that people. (2 Nephi 5:16; 3 Nephi 11:1.)

Temple Ordinances Restored

More than one hundred years ago, the Lord sent angelic messengers, as he had promised, to restore the keys of the authority to perform temple ordinances that had been lost by apostasy after the death of the apostles following the crucifixion of the Savior (Doc. and Cov. 110) when, as had been foretold, the Church was driven "into the wilderness." He then gave revelations to the Prophet Joseph Smith, as he had done to Moses and to Solomon as to where and how these temples were to be built and the nature of the ordinances to be performed therein. (Doc. and Cov. 124 and 128.)

The "Houses of the Lord," or these holy temples, now as in former days are open only to faithful Church members who are duly recommended as to their worthiness by designated Church officers. You may learn in the detail of the ordinances performed therein only if and when you are permitted to receive a recommend that accords you that privilege. Now because of these restrictions that forbid the presence of unbelievers and the unworthy, some of you have thought of this sacred place as a sort of secret order or oath-bound society, the like of which the Church throughout its history has consistently counseled its members to refrain from having membership in. Church members have been particularly advised against becoming "identified with any organization established for the benefit of any group which is antagonistic to the Church." This advice has been based upon the conviction that affiliation with "secret oath-bound societies" would cause members of the Church "to lose interest in Church activities or interfere with the performance of their duties." (General Handbook of Instructions No. 20, 1968. p. 165.) It was the Master himself who taught, "No servant can serve two masters: for either he will hate the one, and love the other; or else he will hold to the one, and despise the other." (Luke 16:13.) Throughout the history of the sacred scriptures the Lord has warned us against "all manner of secret works of darkness." (II Nephi 9:9.)

Secret Orders

Perhaps a brief history of some of these secret orders will be enlightening and will help you to distinguish between them and these holy temples established by revelation for the blessing of the Lord's work. Since the creation of the earth, there have been secret orders of one kind or another claiming origins that are all more or less obscure and established for purposes and motives variously expressed. Some of these are without question prompted by evil and sinister motives. Others may be for political or business advantage. Many no doubt through insurance plans and welfare activities strive for human betterment and accomplish much good.

The earliest "secret combination" recorded is that wherein Satan said to Cain, as he prepared him to kill his brother Abel: "Swear unto me by thy throat, and if thou tell it thou shalt die; and swear thy brethren by their heads, and by the living God, that they tell it not; for if they tell it, they shall surely die; and this that thy father may not know it. . . . And all these things were done in secret. And Cain said: Truly I am Mahan, the master of this great secret, that I may murder and get gain . . . and he glorified in his wickedness." (Moses 5:29-31.) We find that secret combination being perpetuated by an organization on the Western Hemisphere known as the Gadianton Robbers who administered "oaths which were given by them of old who also sought power, which had been handed down even from Cain." (Ether 8:15.) Proof that such secret societies existed among the ancient inhabitants of America and that the devil was recognized as the founder of them is that among their descendants, the Indian tribes, there has persisted even to this day the worship of the serpent which has ever been the symbol of the evil one, the tempter or the devil. They have their secret orders and rites and wherever such devil worship has prevailed, it has resulted in the degradation of the people who practiced it. (*Mormonism and Free Masonry*—Ivins, pp. 135-146.)

Ritual A Substitute

The secret orders of our day make various claims as to their origin. At the time of the construction of the Temple of Solomon we are told by a student of that period "the temple workmen numbered scores of thousands, and every department was in charge of master craftsmen. To serve on the great structure in any capacity was an honor; and labor acquired a dignity never before recognized. Masonry became a profession and the graded orders therein established have endured until this day." (*House of the Lord*, Talmage, pp. 5-6.)

Whatever may be the origin or the history of any or all of the so-called secret fraternal orders, one thing is certain, that within their teachings, rituals and brotherhood relationships there can be at best but a poor substitute for the fulness of the gospel with its rites, ordinances and sealings that have been given to the Church for the salvation of the children of men. I wonder if many who are affiliated with such orders have not become so largely for selfish motives and "to get gain," and at the neglect of the weightier matters of the gospel wherein they would have found treasures in heaven, "where moth and rust do not corrupt nor thieves break through and steal." (Matthew 6:19.)

Now let us consider these holy temples that are withheld from the gaze of the worldly. Is an institution that forbids the presence of unbelievers and the unworthy because of the sacredness of its ordinances to be considered similar to a secret oath-bound society to which we have made reference? Are there not other institutions whose business is kept from the public merely because of the nature of the business transacted rather than because of the necessity of secrecy? How is it with you young lovers? Even though you were to have no conversation about which you should be ashamed, would you choose to do your courting in a show window, with loud speaker connections for the public outside? Family pride would frown upon a broadcasting of the joys and sorrows, or the triumphs and failures of its individual members out of a sense of loyalty to each other. It would be an extremely unwise business man who would publish in the town newspaper a daily log of his institutional problems. His competitors would be most pleased, I am sure, to have such information to use in competition with him. If Church council decisions were not safeguarded until the proper time for action, gossip and rumor would well-nigh nullify the effectiveness of these decisions. It was the Master who said, "Give not that which is holy unto the dogs, neither cast ye your pearls before swine, lest they trample them under their feet, and turn again and rend you." (Matthew 7:6.) The ordinances, rites and ceremonies of the House of the Lord are sacred to faithful members of the Church, and to permit the gaze of the unholy would be to encourage the mockery of the scoffer and to invite the jeers of the enemies of righteousness.

Temple Ceremonies Sacred

There are many instances when, for reasons best known to himself, the Lord has revealed "his secret unto his servants the prophets" with a command that they keep such revelation from the world. The Apostle Paul tells of one such who "was caught up to the third heaven . . . and heard unspeakable words, which it is not lawful for a man to utter." (II Cor. 12:2-4.) The brother of Jared was commanded to write the words of a revelation in a strange language and seal them up, and the Lord would show them in his own due time to the children of men. (Ether 3:27.) The Apostle Paul spoke of a day "when God shall judge the secrets of men, by Jesus Christ, according to the gospel." (Rom. 2:16.) Members of the Church who have been admitted to the temple do not discuss even among themselves outside the temple these temple ceremonies because of their sacred character.

In one of the early revelations in this dispensation, it was made known by the Lord that it was his will that a holy House should be built with the promise that his glory would rest upon it and his presence would be here and he would come into it, and all the pure in heart that should come into it should see God on one condition. That condition was that they "do not suffer any unclean thing to come into it, that it be not defiled." (Doc. and Cov. 97:15-16.) Obedient to that instruction these holy temples are carefully safeguarded, not because of the necessity of secrecy but because of the sacredness of the work performed therein, by forbidding those who by the measure of the Lord's standards may be considered "unclean" in that they do not keep his commandments.

(Inscription at the entrance to the Alberta Temple
at Cardston, Alberta, Canada.)

> "Hearts must be pure to come within
> these walls,
> Where spreads a feast unknown to
> festive halls.
> Freely partake, for freely God hath
> given,
> And taste the holy joys that tell of
> heaven.
> Here learn of him who triumphed
> O'er the grave,
> And 'unto men the Keys, the King-
> dom gave:
> Joined here by powers that past and
> present bind,
> The living and the dead perfection
> find."
>
> —Orson F. Whitney.

Two Phases of Temple Work

In the two previous chapters I have described
two different phases of the work of the temples.[1] The
first referred to was the vicarious work for the dead,
who are in a similar position to those whom the Savior
visited in the spirit world while his body lay in the tomb.
To these who had not accepted the gospel while they
were in mortality and who were in the spirit world
awaiting resurrection, the Master preached the gospel
that they might "be judged according to men in the
flesh, but live according to God in the spirit." (I Peter
4:6.) As the Savior was empowered to perform a vicarious
work for all mankind by his atonement, so a merciful
and just God has made it possible that faithful members
of the Church might become "saviors on Mt. Zion" by
doing work for their kindred dead, by which the doors to
eternal salvation might be opened to them that thereby
they might receive the same privileges as though they
had been given the opportunity to receive the gospel while
they lived as mortal beings. We next considered the

sacred temple ceremony of marriage by which man and wife were joined together in holy wedlock for time and all eternity.

To aid you to understand more fully the nature and purpose of the complete temple ceremonies, may I take a moment to explain some important scriptures. To his disciples Jesus taught, "In my Father's house are many mansions . . . I go to prepare a place for you . . . that where I am, there ye may be also." (John 14:1-3.) Again in speaking of the resurrection of the dead, Jesus said concerning those who shall hear the voice of the Son of Man, "all shall come forth, they that have done good, unto the resurrection of the just and they that have done evil, unto the resurrection of the unjust." (John 5:29—Inspired Version.) The Apostle Paul enlarges upon these teachings of Jesus in his declaration that "There are also celestial bodies, and bodies terrestrial . . . There is one glory of the sun, and another glory of the moon, and another glory of the stars: for one star differeth from another star in glory. So also is the resurrection of the dead." (I Cor. 15:40-42.) In a glorious revelation to the Prophet Joseph Smith known as "The Vision," the Lord has told us in plainness about the Celestial glory provided for those who merit the highest honors of heaven; the Terrestrial glory, the next lower degree to be received by many whose works do not merit the highest reward; and finally the Telestial glory comprising those sinners of various types whose offenses are not those of utter perdition. We are given to understand that within each of these "glories," there are sub-divisions or gradations to fit the varying degrees of merit among mankind.

Highest Degree of Glory

To attain the highest degree of glory, or exaltation in the Celestial glory, there is required of each individual an attainment to the highest orders of the Holy Priesthood. It is with these ordinances, known as the holy temple endowment, by which the fulness of the blessings of the

Priesthood may be received, that the ceremonies for the living in the temples are directly associated. (Joseph Smith's Teachings, p. 237; D. H. C. 5:1-2.) One of the early prophets of this dispensation at the laying of the cornerstone of the Salt Lake Temple gave this definition of that temple endowment:

"Your endowment is to receive all those ordinances in the House of the Lord, which are necessary for you after you have departed this life, to enable you to walk back to the presence of the Father, passing the angels who stand as sentinels, being enabled to give them the key words, the signs and tokens, pertaining to the Holy Priesthood, and gain your eternal exaltation in spite of earth and hell." (Brigham Young, J. D. 2:31.)

Another of our leaders has defined the endowment as comprising "primarily a course of instruction" which includes a recital of events from the creation of the world through the various dispensations in order to impress upon the individual receiving the endowment the absolute necessity of personal purity and obedience to the Lord's commandments. (*House of the Lord*—Talmage, pp. 83-84.) The receiving of the endowment required the assuming of obligations by covenants which in reality are but an embodiment or an unfolding of the covenants each person should have assumed at baptism, as explained by the Prophet Alma to the effect that "Ye are desirous to come into the fold of God, and be called his people, and are willing to bear one another's burdens, that they may be light. Yea, and are willing to mourn with those that mourn; and comfort those that stand in need of comfort, and to stand as witnesses of God at all times and in all things, and in all places that ye may be in, even until death." (Mosiah 18:8-9.) Any person who is prepared to assume those obligations declared by Alma and "who humble themselves before God . . . and come forth with broken hearts and contrite spirits . . . and are willing to take upon them the name of Jesus Christ, having a determination to serve him to the end," (Doc. and Cov. 20:37.) need have no hesitancy in going to a holy temple and receiving in connection with the covenants taken promises of great blessings predicated upon compliance therewith.

Temple Ordinances Are Guide

The temple ceremonies are designed by a wise Heavenly Father who has revealed them to us in these last days as a guide and a protection throughout our lives that you and I might not fail of an exaltation in the Celestial kingdom where God and Christ dwell.

Youth should begin today to so order their lives that they will be found worthy at the proper time to go to the House of the Lord and be uplifted and sanctified by the temple ceremony which, as has been said, "contributes to covenants of morality, the consecration of yourselves to high ideals, devotion to truth, patriotism to nation, and allegiance to God." (*House of the Lord*— Talmage, pp. 83-84.)

When you enter a holy temple, you are by that course gaining fellowship with the saints in God's eternal Kingdom where time is no more. You have no time for man-made secret societies, if you do your duty as a faithful Church member. In the temples of your God you are endowed not with a rich legacy of worldly treasure, but with a wealth of eternal riches that are above price.

May you strive diligently and be guided to prepare yourselves to gain these priceless riches in the House of the Lord.

There is one question relative to the teachings of the Church which is the subject of frequent discussion among youth today. This question might be stated as follows: What activities may we engage in on Sunday that are in keeping with the law of the Sabbath? Before we discuss that question, may we examine for a moment the matter of law as it pertains to the teachings of the gospel.

Some teachings of the Church are based upon specific laws that have been laid down by divinely inspired pronouncements, which no man has a right to change or to modify except by God's command through revelation to his duly appointed leaders. Illustrative of these so-called laws are the Ten Commandments with their "Thou shalt not" declarations, included in which is to be found the Lord's revelation concerning the proper observance of the Sabbath Day. To persuade most of us to obey these laws it may only be necessary that we have a better understanding of their application to our own lives. Some may require a conversion as to the divine origin of the law in question before they are willing to comply. Others may require a conversion as to the importance and necessity of their compliance therewith.

World Governed By Law

We live in a world governed by law. The Lord declared that he had "given a law unto all things, by which they move in their times and seasons; and their courses are fixed, even the courses of the heavens and the earth, which comprehend the earth and all the planets . . . and any man who hath seen any or the least of these hath seen God moving in his majesty and power." (Doc. and Cov. 88:42-43, 47.) These laws of the universe we submit to daily without our being conscious of it. We know if we disregard the law of gravity, we may get seriously hurt. If we refuse to wear heavy clothing in sub-zero weather, we freeze. If we fail to plant in the springtime, there is no harvest for our winter's need. To get the benefit of things provided for our use, we must obey the laws that govern their operation. It wouldn't be necessary to argue with a pilot that he must provide gasoline and oil for his motors in sufficient amounts for his proposed flight. The young wife in her new kitchen could hardly expect her new electric range to give service unless it was connected with an electric power line, or a cake to be properly baked in it unless she regulated the intensity of the heat according to the requirements of her recipe. Traffic rules, health regulations or laws safeguarding life and liberty must be complied with or the violator meets disaster. Every soldier and sailor has been subjected to the stern discipline of a prescribed code of military practice. His failure to comply brings the punishment measured by the nature of the offense. Shall the Church of Jesus Christ ask less of a man individually in order that he may justify his claim to citizenship in the Kingdom of God?

"All kingdoms (including the Kingdom of God) have a law given . . . and unto every law there are certain bounds and conditions. All beings who abide not in those conditions are not justified." (Doc. and Cov. 88: 36-39.)

Now as you think about laws by which you live and move in the world about you, have you supposed that they are provided for your detriment? You have the option to disregard any or all of them if you choose, but if you do so be prepared to take the consequences, for "that which is governed by law is also preserved by law and perfected and sanctified by the same. That which breaketh a law, and abideth not by law, but seeketh to become a law unto itself, and willeth to abide in sin, and altogether abideth in sin, cannot be sanctified by law, neither by mercy, justice nor judgment. Therefore, they must remain filthy still." (Doc. and Cov. 88:34-35.)

Some General Principles

In this discussion, I desire only to lay down some broad general principles that will help you better to reach your own conclusions regarding this question of keeping the Sabbath Day holy and to find the answer to other questions of like nature.

Now in the first place in determining that which is right in the sight of God let us consider this question of your conscience that we talk so much about. The scriptures speak of an influence to be found throughout the universe that gives life and light to all things, which is called variously the Light of Truth, the Light of Christ, or the Spirit of God. "That (is) the true Light that lighteth every man that cometh into the world." (John 1:9.) It is that which "enlighteneth your eyes . . . and that quickeneth your understandings." (Doc. and Cov. 88:11.) Every one of you born into this world enjoys the blessing of this Light that shall never cease to strive with you until you are led to that further light from the gift of the Holy Ghost that may be received only upon condition of repentance and baptism into the Kingdom of God. That light or intelligence might be said to be the instinct in animals and the conscience or reason in man. The only thing that will dim that light in you will be your own sinning that may render you insensible to its promptings and warnings as to right and wrong. It is a true saying that prayer keeps one from sin and that sin keeps one from prayer, by which medium God's will might be made known.

Spirit A Counterpart

Now another thought: Within every one of you there dwells a spirit which is the exact counterpart of your full-grown physical body. To keep your physical body in vigor and health, food and drink must be provided at frequent intervals. Every germ cell of your bodies must have a nerve connection in order to maintain the vital life processes. Failure to maintain these nerve connections or to supply the required sustenance brings decay, stagnation, sickness and finally death to the physical body.

Your spiritual body needs nourishment at frequent intervals in order to assure its health and vigor. Earthly food does not satisfy this need. Food to satisfy your spiritual needs must come from spiritual sources. Principles of eternal truth, as contained in the gospel, and the proper exercise by engaging in spiritual activities are essential to the satisfying of your spiritual selves. Vital processes of the spirit are likewise maintained only by intelligent connection with spiritual fountains of truth. Spiritual sickness and death, which mean separation from the fountain of spiritual light, are sure to follow the severance of your connection with the spiritual nerve center, the Church of Jesus Christ.

Now after this brief statement of these great soul-stirring truths, let us return to a consideration of our first question: What activities may we engage in on Sunday that are in harmony with the law of the Sabbath?

Suppose first we examine the law as it has been in practice from ancient times and as it was clearly set forth in the Decalogue on Mt. Sinai:

"Remember the sabbath day to keep it holy. Six days shalt thou labor, and do all thy work. But the seventh day is the sabbath of the Lord thy God: in it thou shalt not do any work, thou, nor thy son, nor thy daughter, thy manservant, nor thy maidservant, nor thy cattle, nor the stranger that is within thy gates: For in six days the Lord made heaven and earth, the sea, and all that in them is, and rested the seventh day; wherefore the Lord blessed the sabbath day, and hallowed it." (Exodus 20:8-11.)

Since the resurrection of the Savior on the first day of the week, this day has been commemorated as the Lord's day, or the one day in seven on which man should rest from his labors.

But Sunday is more than a day of rest from the ordinary occupations of the week. It is not to be considered as merely a day of lazy indolence and idleness or for physical pleasures and indulgences. It is a feastday for your spirit bodies. The place of spiritual feasting is in the house of worship. Here you find fellowship with those who like yourselves are seeking spiritual nourishment. You are enjoined to sing and pray and pay your devotions to the Most High, and partake of the holy sacrament as a reminder of your obligations as a son or daughter of God here in mortality and in remembrance of the atonement of the Savior and to pledge again your loyalty to his name.

By the partaking of the sacrament you are participating in one of the most sacred ordinances of the Church. It has a similar significance to us today that the sacrifice of burnt offerings, given to Adam, had to the saints before the advent of the Savior upon the earth. When the sacrifice of burnt offerings was first given it was for the purpose of reminding Adam of the great atoning sacrifice of the Son of God that should transpire in the meridian of time, by which Adam and his posterity might be loosed from the bonds of death and if they were faithful to the gospel plan might partake of eternal life with our Heavenly Father in his kingdom. With the sacrifice of Jesus, by which he, "the just," suffered for "the unjust," the sacrifice of burnt offerings, as it had been observed up to that time, was fulfilled (3 Nephi 9:19-20.). In its place he instituted at the time of the Last Supper, before his crucifixion, the holy sacrament, by which the meaning of his great atoning sacrifice would be had in everlasting remembrance. The purpose and meaning of the sacrament and the seriousness that should accompany your partaking of it is clearly set forth in the Master's words as understood by the Apostle Paul: "This do ye . . . in remembrance of me. For as often as ye eat this bread, and drink this cup, ye do show the Lord's death till he come. Wherefore whosoever shall eat this bread, and drink this cup of the Lord, unworthily, shall be guilty of the body and blood of the Lord. But let a man examine himself, and so let him eat of the bread, and drink of that cup. For he that eateth and drinketh unworthily, eateth and drinketh damnation to himself, not discerning the Lord's body. For this cause many are weak and sickly among you, and many sleep." (I Corinthians 11:25-30.) All this is done for the one divine purpose, as declared by the Lord, "that thou mayest more fully keep thyself unspotted from the world." (Doc. and Cov. 59:9.)

You young men who have been in military service, if you have been faithful in meeting together and partaking of the sacrament, as you have been instructed, have been sanctified by your experience. I could only hope that now you have returned home you would remember the lessons of these experiences, and as the parents of tomorrow's youth see that no child in your home is left without the strength that comes from partaking of the sacrament in the weekly sacrament meeting.

Whether at home or in church, your thoughts and your conduct should be always in harmony with the spirit and purpose of the Sabbath. Places of amusement and recreation, while at proper times may serve a needed end, are not conducive of spiritual growth and such places will not keep you "unspotted from the world" but will rather deny you the "fulness of the earth" promised to those who comply with the law of the Sabbath. You who make the violation of the Sabbath a habit, by your failure to "keep it holy," are losing a soul full of joy in return for a thimble full of pleasure. You are giving too much attention to your physical desires at the expense of your spiritual health. The Sabbath breaker shows early the signs of his weakening in the faith by neglecting his daily family prayers, by fault-finding, by failing to pay his tithes and his offerings, and such a one whose mind begins to be darkened because of spiritual starvation soon begins also to have doubts and fears that make him unfit for spiritual learning or advancement in righteousness. These are the signs of spiritual decay and spiritual sickness that may only be cured by proper spiritual feeding.

A Day of Prayerful Study

May we not hope that in addition to our worshipful activities on the Lord's Day we might also on that day reduce the drudgery of the home to a minimum, and that outside the home only essential chores will be performed. Make this a day of prayerful, thoughtful study of the scriptures and other good books. While filled with the joy of the Sabbath, write a letter to your sweetheart or an absent loved one or a friend who may need your spiritual strength. Make your homes the places for the singing and playing of beautiful music in harmony with the spirit of the day. At evening's close as you gather at your fireside with the family alone or with friends, discuss the precious truths of the gospel and close with the benediction of family prayer. My experience has taught me that the prompting of the conscience to a faithful Church member is the safest indicator as to that which is contrary to the spirit of worship on the Sabbath Day.

But some of you ask, What of the man whose job depends on his working Sundays? Well, perhaps there is nothing else that he can do about it, but I have a friend in a nearby city who is occasionally required to work on Sunday. Always he makes a contribution of the earnings of that day to the work of the Lord inasmuch as that day belongs to the Lord. Perhaps if you did likewise you wouldn't find so many excuses to work on Sunday.

To the man who thinks the press of the harvest, or the threat of storm, or the shortage of labor all justify his working on Sunday, I would remind him of the first sermon preached by Brigham Young in the Salt Lake Valley on July 25, 1847, in which he told the brethren that they must not work on Sunday and that if they did they would lose "five times as much as they would gain by it."

Observance of Sabbath Not Sufficient

But do not suppose that a strict observance of the law of the Sabbath is alone sufficient to keep your spiritual bodies in good health. Every day of the week must give nourishment to your spiritual selves. Family and secret prayers, the reading of the scriptures, love in your homes and unselfish daily service to others are manna from heaven to feed your souls. Observance of the weekly Family Home Evening is another strong force for righteousness in the home. All that is contrary to the will of God is as poison to your spiritual life and must be shunned as you would avoid labeled poisons in your medicine cabinets at home.

I once read a suggested comparison of the body of each one of you with a fortress which is being defended against an everpresent enemy by a company of soldiers. The inmates of the fortress must be sustained against hunger by the maintenance of a supply train from a central source of supply. If in battle with the enemy, prisoners are taken, some of the soldiers are required to guard the prisoners and additional food is needed. If the supply and the number of defenders cannot be increased to carry the additional load, or if the supply line should be severed, the fortress is then under siege by the enemy and time alone is required to force a surrender.

The enemies of your own human "fortress" are both physical and spiritual, with perhaps the "enemies of the night" as the more to be feared. When you suffer an unexpected sorrow, a family disgrace, a shock in your finances, the perfidy of a supposed friend, or a secret sin against the laws of God, for example, you have a "prisoner" within your fortress that requires an additional supply from spiritual sources if you are able to take on the additional burden at least until you have transferred your "prisoner" to a prison camp behind the line of battle. If you have lost contact with the Church by carelessness and your faith in God has dwindled, if you have not understood by study and learning the way to a forgiveness of your transgression, or if you have not obtained through prayerful understanding the assurance of a future reward for sacrifices and pain, then you have cut your spiritual supply lines and the strength that your soul needs is sapped by the attention demanded by "your prisoners." You have been out-generaled by the enemy of spiritual light and unless you change your ways by a genuine repentance, and thus transfer your "prisoners" to a prison camp behind your lines, your fortress is doomed to certain capture by Satan's forces. You are then as the foolish man who built his house upon the sands and when the storms come great will be the fall thereof. (Matthew 7:24-27.)

And so I beg of you not to rob your spiritual bodies of that essential strength by breaking the Sabbath Day but sincerely urge you to live each day so that you might receive from the fountain of light nourishment and strength sufficient to every day's need. Take time to be holy each day of your lives. Let your conscience guide you from error in the future. Let your conduct be in compliance with eternal laws that have been given to you for your spiritual welfare.

The Rapture of the Moment or the Peace of Years

18

As the youth of today, you hear frequent admonitions and counsel from your Church leaders as to the kinds of recreational activities and entertainments that are considered either good or bad. Then you are often faced with the responsibility of planning the entertainment for socials or in choosing for yourselves amusements or entertainments that are in harmony with the counsel of the Church. In such a matter as this there may be no hard and fast rules, for under given conditions certain kinds of amusements or entertainments may be bad but under other conditions, these same entertainments might not be questioned. Let me illustrate this point with an old Chinese story that I read a few weeks ago.

One day a Chinese wheelwright, inclined to impudence, interrupted a mandarin at his studies with a question: "What is the mandarin doing?"

"I am reading the books wherein is contained the wisdom of the ages," the mandarin replied.

"Then the mandarin is wasting his time!"

"Very good," said the mandarin. "You will either prove your statement or you lose your head."

"Easily, sir," replied the wheelwright. "Now as a master wheelwright I can tell my son that if he shaves the spokes too much they will be loose and the wheel will be spoiled, and if he does not shave them enough, they will be too tight and the wheel will be spoiled. But I cannot tell him how much is too much or how little is too little. That he can only learn by experience."

Conscience the Judge

So it is with many situations with which you are confronted. The decision as to whether or not a thing is right or wrong must be left to the judgment of your own conscience, plus an understanding that comes with learning and experience. At best in all such matters the Church can teach you correct principles and you must learn to govern yourselves.

In previous discussions we have defined conscience as a power or influence that comes from our Heavenly Father which "enlighteneth every person that cometh into the world," that makes you blush at the obscene, that gives you a feeling of anxiety when things are wrong, that forewarns you of dangers that lie ahead and gives you a calm assurance in the presence of truth. One may not readily understand how he knows whether a thing is right or wrong, but there is no question in the minds of any of us who have had experience that if your life is pure, you may know of a surety as to whether or not a thing is right.

Statement of Great Truth

Now let me make a statement of a great truth, on which the answer to questions of right and wrong must hinge. Throughout the scriptures is to be found a significant phrase suggesting a standard of measurement if your lives would be in harmony with the purpose of our Heavenly Father concerning your mortal existence. Early in this dispensation of time, the Lord in a revelation said,

"Behold, blessed . . . are they who have come up to this land *with an eye single to my glory* according to my commandments. For those that live shall inherit the earth, and those that die shall rest from all their labors, and their works shall follow them: and they shall receive a crown in the mansions of my Father, which I have prepared for them." (Doc. and Cov. 59:1-2.) Now mark carefully the conditions under which you are to receive the fulfillment of that promise. To receive that blessing the Lord promises, you must keep his commandments "with an eye single to his glory." To understand that condition, then, we must first determine what the Lord's "glory" is and then ever to keep our "eye" fixed upon it as the ultimate goal of achievement in all that we do. To Moses the Lord declared that his work and his glory was "to bring to pass the immortality and eternal life of man." (Moses 1:39.)

To Abraham, God revealed that all spirits were "organized intelligences" before the world was created. With these, his spirit children, God made a covenant that those who were faithful, or even measurably so in the spirit world, would be given the privilege of mortal bodies and all those who kept the Lord's commandments here in the "second estate" on this earth would have "glory" added upon them, or in other words, "eternal life," after the resurrection in that celestial place where God and Christ dwell. Life then is granted to every soul as a proving ground with life eternal as the prize.

> "Isn't it strange that princes and kings
>   And clowns that caper in sawdust rings
> And common folks like you and me
>   Are builders for eternity?
> To each is given a bag of tools,
>   A shapeless mass, and a book of rules;
> And each must make ere life is flown,
>   A stumbling-block or a stepping stone."

And now as we consider for a few moments your problem as to what you may choose as proper recreational activities, let me remind you again of the purpose of your being on the earth. It is that you might obtain a fulness of joy. But remember as well the Lord has said that "in this world your joy is not full, but in (him) your joy is full." (Doc. and Cov. 101:36.) A heart full of happiness is an

evidence that you are building a heaven on earth that will
last for eternity. At one stage in the world's history, the
religious record tells the story of a people who had attained
to this heavenly joy of which the Lord spoke: "And there
were no envyings, nor strife, nor tumults, nor whoredoms,
nor lyings, nor murders, nor any manner of lasciviousness;
and surely there could not be a happier people among all
the people who had been created by the hand of God."
(IV Nephi 1:16.) The conclusion of this story is clear:
"Wickedness never was happiness!" (Alma 41:10.) Opposed
to God's plan of eternal happiness for every human soul is
Satan's plan that ends in remorse and awful remembrance
of all our guilt in that day of judgment.

Recreation A Diversion

I have never believed that in order to be righteous
one must be sad-faced and solemn. People approved of
the Lord have always been those who have laughed and
danced and sung as well as worshipped, but at all times
within proper bounds and not to excess. Recreation, as
a diversion, is as necessary to our temporal welfare as are
the more serious activities of life. One who keeps continually at a single pursuit of business or study will become as
a machine, and other traits or talents of his nature may
not receive proper development. You remember the old
saying, "All work and no play makes Jack a dull boy,"
but likewise don't forget either the wise counsel of one of
our leaders today that "all play and no work is likely to
make Jack a worthless boy." If you were to go to dances
three or four times a week, for instance, you would be
doing that which would be not only injurious· to your
health but to the stability of your character. And in your
laughter, may I suggest that you beware of the boisterous
laugh that reveals the vacant mind.

A Pleasure-Mad World

You are living in a pleasure-mad world that seems to
become more so as the final test of Satan's earthly power

over the souls of men draws near. His methods of conquest have not been greatly different than those he employed with our first parents in the Garden of Eden. He tempted Adam and Eve to partake of the fruit from the tree which had been forbidden. He told them with honeyed words that it was delicious to the taste and "good for food, and that it was pleasant to the eyes, and a tree to be desired to make one wise." (Genesis 3:6.) Thus because of an appeal to their appetites, physical senses, passions and vanities, they were tempted to partake of that which God had commanded they should not partake on pain of death and expulsion from the Garden of Eden.

In like manner since that time, Satan has been "going to and fro in the earth and walking up and down in it," (Job 1:7.) "to deceive and to blind men and to lead them captive at his will, even as many as would not hearken" unto the voice of the Lord, (Moses 4:4) nor to his servants, the prophets of the Lord. He is the master of deceit, adulteration and counterfeit. There is hardly a human appetite that he has not prostituted to his own evil designs; virtue he betrays into vice; and things invented and designed as benefactors to mankind he diverts to his own ends. No palace of art or temple of music was ever more glamorously decorated than the hell-holes of Satan that are labeled saloons, bars, road houses and gambling clubs. With blazing neon signs and lighted "white ways," the cheap and the tawdry are dressed in tinseled garb and with sensuous music from the nether regions issuing forth from such places, the passers-by are enticed to partake.

"Why not?" those who indulge may say. These things are "delicious to the taste, pleasant to the eyes" and will make you "wise," although albeit only in those things of which you should rather have been ignorant. All of these are sold to eager patrons under the false label of "Happiness."

Some pleasures bring happiness but certainly not all. You are concerned then to know at what point pleasure may lead to sin rather than to happiness. Pleasure may be said to be any mental gratification felt in attaining or anticipating the indulgence of any desire or appetite, and even sensual gratification. It is transitory and passes with the moment. It was Thomas Paine who said, "The mere man of pleasure is miserable in old age." Happiness is the state of being that springs from a possession of the good, and is more permanent and soul-satisfying and of larger measure and of a higher and more intellectual or moral nature. It is in fact a condition where pleasure predominates over either pain or evil. One of our writers has said: "True happiness is lived over and over again in memory, always with a renewal of the original good; a moment of unholy pleasure may leave a barbed sting, which, like a thorn in the flesh, is an ever-present source of anguish. . . . Happiness is not akin to levity, nor is it one with light-minded mirth. It springs from the deeper fountains of the soul and is not infrequently accompanied by tears. Have you never been so happy that you have had to weep?" (*Improvement Era*, Vol. 17, James E. Talmage.)

Invisible Forces at Work

If you have watched a little girl playing house with her dolls and dishes or a tiny boy building houses and barns and bridges in a sand-box, perhaps you have realized that guided by unseen Intelligence they are instinctively rehearsing the woman's or the man's part each is to play later in life. Attempt to reverse the objects of their play and you immediately find yourself working in contradiction to invisible forces at work in guiding their lives. Why shouldn't youth continue to "play" at that same game? There is in all youth that which is called the gregarious or gang instinct. The club, the class, the sorority, the institute, the lodge, the union or the fraternity are the growing-up expressions of that inward urge. If the majority of your associates in the club or fraternity are not maintaining high standards, you are paying too high a price for their friendship, and the gains derived from your association with them do not warrant a continuation of your membership. If a working majority are right, the small minority of contrary mind will likely yield to the pressure of the group, or might wish to join with other groups made up of their own kind. Wise teachers of youth do not try to break up these groups but rather try to effect a transfer of their energies from useless or destructive ends into a Boy Scout organization, a Gleaner Girl class, a Priesthood quorum or a community garden club, for example. It was under wise guidance of such impulses that our pioneer leaders conducted corn-husking and barn-raising parties, quilting bees and sewing circles and "sunshine" clubs to look after the sick. They made pleasure out of their work. Any recreational activity that satisfies this urge for social relationships should be fostered and sought for by youth. This social atmosphere can best satisfy this human need where large groups of your friends may be brought together in an enjoyable entertainment that promotes good fellowship and wholesome recreation. Dancing, skating and skiing parties, sleighriding, hiking, home entertainments, a dinner with your group at a canyon park or a roasting or toasting party over the grill in the backyard are certainly more to be desired than leisure activities that promote idleness or indolence or that cater to the appetites and passions rather than to one's social instincts. I could only wish in your dancing parties that you would encourage frequent changes of partners during the evening, as well as group dances, and faster dances of beauty and grace with music that makes an appeal to beauty and harmony rather than to boisterous performances that might well be confined to the circus or the vaudeville stage.

A Test in Choosing

Let me suggest a test in choosing the kinds of socials that you could wholeheartedly participate in "with an eye single to the glory of God." Ask yourself these questions: Is this the kind of a party or social that I in all good conscience could pray the Lord to bless with his Spirit? Would I be ashamed to have my mother or sister come to this place for their recreation? How would I feel if I were to see the Church leader for whom I have the greatest respect playing the kinds of games I am playing tonight? Your answers to that test should suggest several conclusions in making your selections.

First: Your socials should be characterized by wholesome environments. Second: Those who frequent these places of amusement should be of a good character. Third: Such amusement places should have the stamp of approval of your parents and your church leaders. Fourth: These social activities should be of such a nature as to be only incidental to your work or school and your obligations to home and family and should never be allowed to become the controlling forces in your lives.

Socials have another prime purpose. They bring you young men and women together during the mating time of your lives, for remember this, that one day you will more likely than not find your life's companion in the social atmosphere that you frequent most. The safest place where such companionships can be fostered is where parents and the Church have a guiding hand. The home that fosters entertainments for its youth within its walls and that church which provides socials commenced and ended with prayer, will have their reward in happy homes of the parents of tomorrow.

Idleness Should Be Shunned

Leisure-time activities that promote idleness should be shunned. For this reason principally card playing is discountenanced by the Church. There seems to be something so all-absorbing in this type of game that those who indulge make of it almost their ruling passion in life, with certainly little compensation in mental development in comparison with the time spent. Our leaders have advised us that "the same time expended in other enjoyable diversions, such as good music, good

literature, art, poetry, history or drama, would pay greater
dividends with the whole of life and its purposes in view."
(Restraints and Conventions, Clark, November. 1933 *Era.*)
These are the kinds of card games that seem to require
bets or prizes or other inducements to give them the
"proper" appeal. The kind of skill that is developed in
games of chance is the kind of skill that endangers the
moral qualities of the possessor and leads him on a questionable practice. If you could ride with me over the country
and view the curse of card playing among our young
people, that has ripened into gambling with all its trickery
and soul-destroying evils, you would agree with me, I am
sure, that homes and social groups who in their short-
sightedness were teachers of such a game to young boys,
have done grave harm to the characters of youth. Certainly
no leader worthy of a leadership in a home or in the
Church would knowingly become a party to activities
that would result in such practices. You young men must
realize that no reputable business executive or banker
would care to take a chance on an employee who gambles.
Lessons learned from such games make you less dependable
in places where honesty and integrity are requisite.

Peace of Years Lost

It was a wise man who said, "We lose the peace of
years when we hunt after the rapture of the moment."
(Bulwer Lytton.) You are a wise youth if you see in your
play not an end in itself but a means to a divine purpose
that conduces to the advancement of your eternal nature.
Avoid petting parties, drinking parties, or the use of nar-
cotics or harmful drugs to get a thrill. Shun ouija board performances or spiritual seances lest in an unguarded
moment, evil influences, thus invited to give you a new sen-
sation, might overtake you. Don't go "slumming"! The youth
who seeks constantly for a thrill in his pleasures is following
a dangerous road. He is hunting for the "rapture of the moment" and in so doing he may "lose the peace of years."
Tell me what you do when you don't have to do anything
and I'll tell you what you are.

"lose the peace of years." Tell me what you do when you don't have to do anything and I'll tell you what you are.

Be constantly guided by the light of truth, your own conscience, in all of your choices of entertainment, and thus advance along the road to happiness "with an eye single to the glory" of our Heavenly Father.

Youth of a Noble Birthright

19

We have heard much in the world community about so-called master races. The feeling of superiority in the minds of the leaders of these self-acclaimed superior groups who have campaigned for world domination has plunged the world into mighty and terrible world conflicts. The mystery of their fancied superiority has now been very largely exploded by the force of arms of the opposing nations they sought to conquer. The arrogance assumed by these master races, so called, has engendered the most 'bitter race prejudice in the world's history. There are other forces sweeping this and other countries that would break down all social barriers as between races and that would nullify existing laws prohibiting legal marriage between certain races. There are still others who place apparently erroneous interpretations on the declaration to be found in the opening paragraphs of the Declaration of Independence to the effect that "All men are created equal." It is well that you as the youth of our land have from the fountain of unfailing truth, the Church of Jesus Christ, the truths of the scriptures concerning these important problems that involve the relationship of human beings to each other and to God, our Heavenly Father.

Father of All Spirits

How many races are there? Most scientists have divided humanity into five groups: The white, the black, the brown, the yellow and the red races. Others have grouped the brown, yellow and red races as "subgroups" of a single race. The scriptures have taught us that God, our Heavenly Father, is the "Father of the spirits of all men" and that when we pass from this life our spirits "whether they be good or evil, are taken home to God who gave (us) life." (Ecclesiastes 12:7; Alma 40:11.) Thus, by the teachings of the scriptures, all mankind are made one great family. Furthermore, we are given to understand that all who live in mortality, if they would perfect their genealogical research, could trace their ancestry back to Adam and Eve, our first earthly parents in the Garden of Eden, through Noah and his family, who were the only living persons on the earth after the flood. Very few researchers in the genealogical field go far in their work until they find widely separated persons of varying nationalities with the same ancestors on the genealogical chart. All of this points unmistakably to the correctness of the scriptural teachings.

Some years ago there appeared in a leading magazine an interesting article on this subject written by a nationally known authority on sociology. Here is a quotation from that article:

"Practically all scientific students agree that all men who live, or ever have lived, were derived from some very early ancestral stock. . . . Where this parent stock had its abode we are not certain; but modern scientific opinion tends to believe that it was on the high central plateau of Asia." (May I pause to call your attention to the fact that it is the commonly accepted belief that Mt. Ararat, on which Noah's ark rested after the flood, was located in Western Asia.) "From this center, the great primary distribution of man as we know him took place. Driven by the pressure of increasing population, one contingent after another, made its way into one or another of the great habitation centers of the world. . . . The groups proceeded to develop different physical traits which were characteristic of each group respectively. . . . This result was due partly to the selective influence of their physical environment, and partly to the chance peculiarities of hereditary factors with which each group was endowed from the beginning. Thus were formed the five basic human faces recognized by the common man all over the world." (Henry Pratt Fairchild, *Harpers*, October, 1944.)

Scientists have done well in their studies to have arrived at such conclusions seemingly so much in harmony with the teachings of the scriptures, but there are other factors that affect the question of race and equality that only those who have faith in the revealed word of God may take into account.

"Known unto God are all his works from the beginning," (Acts 15:18.) but only by his revelation to us, such as the following to Abraham, may we know of these things: "Now the Lord had shown unto me, Abraham, the intelligences that were organized before the world was; and among all these there were many of the noble and great ones; and God saw these souls that they were good, and he stood in the midst of them, and he said: These I will make my rulers; for he stood among those that were spirits, and he saw that they were good; and he said unto me: Abraham, thou are one of them; thou wast chosen before thou wast born." (Abraham 3:22-23.)

No less a person than Peter who was so closely associated with the Master declared that Jesus also "was foreordained before the foundation of the world," (I Peter 1:20) even as Jesus himself prayed, "O Father, glorify thou me with . . . the glory which I had with thee before the world was." (John 17:5.)

The word of the Lord came also to Jeremiah the prophet saying that before he was born the Lord "sanctified (him) and ordained (him) a prophet unto the nations." (Jeremiah 1:5.) These and other similar scriptures make it plain that man existed in a spiritual condition before coming here to this earth and that in that pre-existence he had his free agency or right to choose. How could some of those spirits as seen by Abraham have become

noble and great except by faithfulness to God's cause? How
came God to choose Abraham or Jeremiah before they
were born? If we had the complete answer to these
questions, we would no doubt learn that they and others
stood up valiantly with Michael and his angels when "there
was war in heaven. . . . and Satan and his angels were
cast out" of heaven for rebellion. (Rev. 12:7-12.)

Now I bring you another truth declared by a revelation to Moses as recorded in the scriptures.

"Remember the days of old, consider the years of
many generations: . . . When the Most High divided to
the nations their inheritance, when he separated the sons
of Adam, he set the bounds of the people according to the
number of the children of Israel. For the Lord's portion
is his people; Jacob is the lot of his inheritance." (Deut.
32:7-9.)

Here several truths are clearly suggested. In the
first place, the extent of God's temporal creations was
determined by the number of spirits to come into mortality; the earth was to be divided into nations according
to the number of the children of Jacob, or Israel, before
she became a nation and a chosen lineage was to come
through Jacob's posterity. Logically then we also must
conclude that the end of this earth will not come until
all these spirits who were designated as worthy of mortal
bodies shall have been born into this world. In the
Apostle Paul's sermon to the Athenians, he declared also
that God "hath made of one blood all nations of men for
to dwell on all the face of the earth, and hath determined
the times before appointed, and the bounds of their
habitation." (Acts 17:26.) It was no doubt the prospect of
coming into mortal bodies and thus being "added upon"
that caused the stars of morning, or the spirit children of
God, as we are told in the scriptures, to sing together and
all the sons of God to shout for joy. (Job 38:4-7.)

There is no truth more plainly taught in the Gospel
than that our condition in the next world will depend
upon the kind of lives we live here. "All that are in the

graves shall hear his voice, and shall come forth; they that have done evil, unto the resurrection of damnation." (John 5:28-29.) Is it not just as reasonable to suppose that the conditions in which we now live have been determined by the kind of lives we lived in the pre-existent world of spirits? That the apostles understood this principle is indicated by their question to the Master when the man who was blind from his birth was healed of his blindness, "Master, who did sin, this man or his parents that he was born blind?" (John 9:2.) Now perhaps you will have a partial answer to some of your questions as to why, if God is a just Father, that some of his children are born of an enlightened race and in a time when the Gospel is upon the earth, while others are born of a heathen parentage in a benighted, backward country; and still others are born to parents who have the mark of a black skin with which the seed of Cain were cursed and whose descendants were to be denied the rights of the priesthood of God.

A Priceless Privilege

The privilege of obtaining a mortal body on this earth is seemingly so priceless that those in the spirit world, even though unfaithful or not valiant, were undoubtedly permitted to take mortal bodies although under penalty of racial or physical or nationalistic limitations. Between the extremes of the "noble and the great" spirits, whom God would make his rulers, and the disobedient and the rebellious, who were cast out with Satan, there were obviously many spirits with varying degrees of faithfulness. May we not assume from these teachings that the progress and development we made as spirits have brought privileges and blessings here according to our faithfulness in the spirit world? Now don't be too hasty in your conclusions as to what conditions in mortality constitute the greater privileges. That condition in life which gives the greatest experience and opportunity for development is the one to be most desired and any one so privileged is most favored of God. It has been said that "a smooth sea never made a skillful mariner, neither do uninterrupted prosperity and success qualify for usefulness and happiness. The storms of adversity, like those of the ocean, rouse the faculties and excite the invention, prudence, skill and fortitude of the voyager. The mariners of ancient times, in bracing their minds to outward calamaties, acquired a loftiness of purpose and a moral heroism worth a lifetime of softness and security."

All Are Equal

All are equal in that they are the spirit children of God, and also equal in their right to free agency, as well as in the fact that all are made innocent of previous wrongs committed as they enter this world through the atonement of the Lord Jesus Christ. The Lord has told us that "Every spirit of man was innocent in the beginning; and God having redeemed man from the fall, men became again, in their infant state, innocent before God." (Doc. and Cov. 93:38.) Who knows but that many of those with seeming inequalities in this life, if they do everything possible with their limited opportunities, may not receive greater blessings than some of those rewarded by having been born to a noble lineage and to superior social and spiritual opportunities who fail to live up to their great privileges! The history of the Lord's dealings with his children is filled with incidents that indicate that many of those who are the "elect according to the covenant," or that are of the "chosen" of God to be born through the chosen lineage of the House of Israel or the Lord's "portion" in the pre-existent world, will fail of their callings because of their sins. The descendants of Jacob or Israel, through his twelve sons, have been scattered far and wide among the nations as a punishment because of their transgressions, but in this instance the punishment of Israel has been a blessing to the nations who have thereby received the rights belonging to Israel. It was through the lineage of Judah, one of the sons of Jacob, that the Savior was born. Most of the prophets of every dispensation since the days

of Israel have been of the chosen lineage of Jacob through
his twelve sons, and we are led to believe by the prophets
of our own day that the vast majority of those who have
received the Gospel are of the tribe of Ephraim. The
Indians on the American continent are descendants of the
tribes of Ephraim, Judah, and Manasseh, we are told by
the Book of Mormon. (Omni 15-19; I Nephi 5:14-16.) Their
dark skin was a curse put upon them because of their
transgression, which in a day to come in their descendants
will be lifted and they will become white and delightsome
as they accept the Gospel and turn to the Lord.

Intermarriage With Other Races

Millions of souls have come into this world with the
mark that was put upon Cain's posterity and have been
denied the privileges of the priesthood and the fulness of
the blessings of the Gospel. Concerning them one of our
leaders has expressed this opinion: "I believe that race is
the one through which it is ordained those spirits that
were not valiant in the great rebellion in heaven should
come; who, through their indifference or lack of integrity
to righteousness, rendered themselves unworthy of the
priesthood and its powers, and hence it is withheld from
them to this day." (B. H. Roberts—*Contributor*, 6:297.) The
seed of Cain has been separated from the rest of mankind
from the beginning, but they are the children of God.
They may become Church members without the priesthood,
but a promise of hope has been given by a prophet in our
day in these words: "The day will come when all that
race will be redeemed and possess all the blessings which
we now have." (Quoted from President Brigham Young in
Wilford Woodruff, p. 351.)

We should manifest kindness and consideration for
these our brothers and sisters who have been born into
mortal bodies through the lineage of Cain, no doubt due
to some disqualifications resulting from their conduct in
the preexistence. Some of this race have become members
of the Church and are setting examples of faith and

devotion that all of us could well pattern after, despite the limitations of their privileges in the Church.

To impress the grave consequences and the seriousness of intermarriage as between those of different races and particularly with reference to intermarriage with the seed of Cain, President Brigham Young made this remark in an address before the legislature: ". . . that mark shall remain upon the seed of Cain until the seed of Abel shall be redeemed, and Cain shall not receive the priesthood until the time of that redemption. Any man having one drop of the seed of Cain in him cannot receive the priesthood. . . ." (*Wilford Woodruff*, page 351.) Surely no one of you who is an heir to a body of more favored lineage would knowingly intermarry with a race that would condemn your posterity to penalties that have been placed upon the seed of Cain by the judgments of God.

It might not be amiss likewise to urge upon you the most serious consideration of any question of your possible intermarriage with individuals of any other race than your own. No one of you with safety can defy the laws of heredity and the centuries of training that have developed strong racial characteristics and tendencies among the distinctive peoples of the earth and then expect to find a happy, congenial family relationship from such a union. The wisdom of experience fully demonstrates the importance of your marrying those of your own race and those with a similar background of customs and manners.

Foreordination

Now a further word about this matter of foreordination. The Prophet Joseph Smith taught that "Every man who has a calling to minister to the inhabitants of the world was ordained to that very purpose in the grand council of heaven before this world was." (*Joseph Smith's Teachings*, p. 365.) So likewise declared the Apostle Paul, "For whom he did foreknow . . . them he also called." (Romans 2:29-30.) But do not misunderstand that such a calling and such foreordination pre-determine what you must do. A prophet on this western continent has spoken plainly on this subject, "Being called and prepared from the foundation of the world, according to the foreknowledge of God on account of their exceeding faith and good works; in the first place being left to choose good or evil." (Alma 13:3.) This last passage makes the others preceding more understandable. God may have called and chosen men in the spirit world or in their first estate to do a certain work, but whether they will accept that calling here and magnify it by faithful service and good works while in mortality is a matter in which it is their right and privilege to exercise their free agency to choose good or evil.

But the Lord "requireth the heart and a willing mind; and the willing and obedient shall eat the good of the land of Zion in these last days." (Doc. and Cov. 64:34.) I fear there are many among us who because of their faithfulness in the spirit world were "called" to do a great work here, but like reckless spendthrifts they are exercising their free agency in riotous living and are losing their birthright and the blessings that were theirs had they proved faithful to their calling. Hence as the Lord has said, "there are many called but few are chosen," and then he gives us two reasons as to why his chosen and ordained fail of their blessings: First, because their hearts are set so much upon the things of this world, and second, they aspire so much to the honors of men that they do not learn that "the powers of heaven cannot be controlled nor handled only upon the principles of righteousness." (Doc. and Cov. 121:34-36.) All these have sinned "a very grievous sin, in that they are walking in darkness at noon-day." (Doc. and Cov. 95:5-6.)

You our youth of today are among the most illustrious spirits to be born into mortality in any age of the world. Yours is a noble heritage and a wonderful opportunity. May you join in the refrain of the rallying song of youth today:

"Holding aloft our colors, we march in the glorious dawn, O youth of the noble birthright, Carry on, Carry on, Carry on!" and be guided to fulfill your highest destiny.

Unfortunate indeed is the marriage that is built on a foundation of impressions and ideas obtained from the movies, television, billboards, cheap novels or "true story and confession" type magazines on the subject of marriage or love and romance that should have preceded it. I would like to present to you two definitions of love, one that comes as a summary from cheap "romance" stories and is labeled "bogus" from the opening sentence, and the other that breathes from the depths of a true love. Here is an example of the bogus romance: "Love is a mysterious visitation. It comes out of the nowhere into the here; unexpected, unannounced, perhaps uninvited. It is unpredictable, uncontrollable, undependable. No one knows whence it comes. All that anyone can possibly know is that it has come." (I might pause to say here that that last sentence is the only true statement in this whole summary.) I continue: "You are going down the street, pondering the future of the League of Nations. You turn a corner, or you step into an elevator, or an automobile crashes in your front yard. Your psychological moment steps out and looks you in the eye and then it is on. A moment ago it was not on; now it is; that is all there is to it. That is all you can ever know about it. . . . She seemed so ethereal, so incredible, so inaccessible that he simply did not dare to avow the emotion which overwhelmed him." (*Modern Marriage*—Popenoe.)

And I might add that even though such an attraction involves the breaking up of a home, some are ready to take even this rash step. If such impulses come, they issue from the nether regions, and such a conception of true love is an insult and an offense to that heaven-sent gift that is the highest attribute of God himself.

In contrast with the unreality of such trash, may I give you this:

> True love is but a humble low-born thing,
> And hath its food served up in earthen ware;
> It is a thing to walk with, hand in hand,
> Through the every dayness of this work-day world,
> Baring its tender feet to every flint,
> Yet letting not one heart-beat go astray
> From Beauty's law of plainness and content.
> A simple, fireside thing, whose quiety smile
> Can warm earth's poorest hovel to a home;
> Which when our autumn cometh as it must,
> And life in the chill'd wind shivers bare and leafless,
> Shall be blest with Indian summer youth
> In bleak November and with thankful heart,
> Smile on its ample stores of garnered fruit
> As full of sunshine to our aged eyes
> As when it nursed the blossoms of our spring.
> Such is true Love, which steals into the heart
> With feet as silent as the lightsome dawn;
> That kisses smooth the rough brows of the dark
> And hath its will through blissful gentleness
>
> —Lowell.

The first I have quoted in a false description of love is but an "infantile self-love" or just plain lust and is but as "sounding brass, or a tinkling cymbal" as compared with that divine attribute that "suffereth long, and is kind; (that) envieth not, (that) vaunteth not itself, is not puffed up, doth not behave itself unseemly, seeketh not her own, is not easily provoked, thinketh no evil." (I Cor. 13:4-5.)

Remember, young women, that no man loves the girl whom he would harm by thoughtless unseemly conduct that leads to a destruction and loss of that which is as precious as life itself. You young men must remember that following in the wake of the unholy embrace of a lewd woman, whose purposes and motives are evil, there can be nothing but the condemning thoughts of an offended and guilty conscience that will cast a shadow upon the happiness of your home of tomorrow, to say nothing of the shocking penalties that follow as a blight and a curse upon humanity when God's holy laws are broken. Youthful sweethearts, who are unfaithful in their conduct toward each other in failing to observe a strict moral code before marriage or who indulge in dishonest tactics or trickery, are only sowing seeds of mistrust and suspicion that become malignant growths, ofttimes requiring the only treatment society has yet discovered—the serious operation called divorce.

In youth the signs of an infatuation and a budding young love are early apparent. Mother now no longer must impress the necessity of soap and water as a cleanser for bodily extremities; the smile and daintiness of a beautiful girl have worked a most amazing transformation. The hair, the teeth, the shoes, the dress receive the most careful attention. Nothing must be overlooked in the young man's efforts to win the approval of the beautiful lady. He is in truth being sanctified by the companionship of "his girl." Our young lady, on the other hand, quite unbeknown to her "boy friend," has already made some hasty superficial calculations. If he is rather short of stature, she immediately develops an "attraction" for low-heeled shoes. If he is tall, then nothing will satisfy but extremely high heels. It is surprising how color choices are altered by the opinions of a certain young man, and how her interest in medics, engineering or music may be heightened by his attainments in these fields. Does she let him see her until her hair is tidied, her apron freshened or she has applied a dash of face powder or perfume just the way he likes it? Not if she can help it. Someone has sagely remarked that if you are in love with a girl, you should go to see her before eight o'clock in the morning, and if you still love her, marry her.

Refining Social Process

That refining social process which goes on almost unconsciously in your youthful days during the mating period of your lives is commonly called "courting." The thrill that comes from just being in each other's company, without the requirement of the physical embrace or the impassioned kiss, is the first evidence of sweet and holy companionship. Such a companionship brings an understanding and a mutual trust that do not require wordy and detailed explanations to prove constancy and fidelity. Silence while riding or walking together under such circumstances, is not to be mistaken for moodiness, but rather is an evidence of deep thought. A failure to appreciate the situation might be to the silent one an indication of a lack of understanding or of mutuality. That quiet or even unspoken trust that assures each of a genuine comradeship with the other is ofttimes that which provides strength and inspiration for life's highest attainments. As true comrades in times of sorrow, the one thinks and feels as sympathetically as the other who mourns. When you two as lovers can ascend to the heights of pure joy together and yet will never accept the acknowledgment of failure as defeat in each other, then you are becoming as one in preparation for that oneness that only a union in holy wedlock can bring.

Those who allow the marriage ceremony to terminate the days of "courtship" are making a well-nigh fatal mistake. If the new bride were to discover that her husband was just an actor before their marriage and now his quest is ended he stands revealed as a cheap counterfeit of his former self either in appearance or conduct, that would indeed be a shocking experience. Evidences and tokens of your love and a daily proof of your unselfishness toward her and your family will make love's flame burn more brightly with the years. Do you girls suppose that the same attention to personal details is less important after marriage? Surely the same qualities and traits in you that first attracted him are just as important in married life in keeping alive the flame of his affection and romantic desire.

Marriage—A Partnership

Marriage is a partnership. Someone has observed that in the Bible account of the creation woman was not formed from a part of man's head, suggesting that she might rule over him, nor from a part of a man's foot that she was to be trampled under his feet. Woman was taken from man's side as though to emphasize the fact that she was always to be by his side as a partner and companion. At the marriage altar you are pledged to each other from that day to pull the load together in double harness. The Apostle Paul with reference to marriage counseled: "Be ye not unequally yoked." (II Cor. 6:14.) While his counsel has to do more particularly with matters that pertain to an equality of religious interests and spiritual desires, yet the figure his statement suggests should not be overlooked. Like a yoke of oxen pulling a load along the highway, if one falters, becomes lazy and indolent or mean and stubborn, the load is wrecked and destruction follows. For similar reasons, some marriages fail when either or both who are parties thereto fail in carrying their responsibilities with each other. You young men must ever keep in mind that your lovely companion is possessed of finer sensibilities than you, and if your private conduct is brutal or beastly, bitterness and even disgust may drive out of her heart the affection and regard she once held for you. Both of you must remember that the prime purpose of your marriage under God's command is to build the bridge from the eternity of spirits to mortality, over which God's spirit children might come into mortal bodies. Your failure to remember that revealed truth will be your failure to attain the highest bliss in married life. Indeed, official statistics indicate that for a certain recent yearly period 57 per cent of divorces in the United States occurred in families where there were no children and another 21.2 per cent in families having but one child. Divorces in families having five or more children range from none to .7 of 1 per cent.

Spiritual Equality Important

But even more important than that you be "yoked equally" in physical matters, is that you be yoked equally in spiritual matters. Children born to parents of opposite and conflicting religious beliefs may "be the source of conflict rather than a bond." The instinct that prompts a parent to give to its offspring everything essential to its physical and spiritual welfare often widens the breach between a father and mother, devout in their own but opposing religious views. That the influence of The Church of Jesus Christ of Latter-day Saints does have a powerful effect in promoting the solidarity of the home is evidenced by the facts revealed in a compilation of figures for a given period that showed there were 7.4 divorces per every 100 marriages throughout the entire Church as compared with 17.3 divorces per 100 marriages in the United States as a whole. (*Mormon Village Family*, West.) There may be a tendency to overemphasize the value of the saving power of religion in marriage, but certain it is that any home and family established with the object of building them even into eternity and where children are welcomed as "a heritage from the Lord" have a much greater chance of survival because of the sacredness that thus attaches to the home and the family. The breaking of the sacred bonds of marriage by divorce is opposed by the "social heritage" of Church members who have received from the teachings of the Church a great religious faith to which I have made reference in a previous discussion. Indeed, a divorce where eternal temple covenants have been made which involves infidelity could result in loss of Church membership where true repentance does not occur. You, our youth, are urged to prepare to go to the House of the Lord to be married for time and all eternity, but if you are not so prepared then you should seek out an authorized Church leader to perform your marriage, that

your marriage might be accompanied by the most sacred
and solemn considerations possible under the circumstances.

Seek Divine Guidance

Young couples, if they are mindful of the counsel of
the Church, will kneel down in prayer together in their
first family prayer on the first night of their marriage to
express gratitude and thankfulness and to make supplications for divine guidance and blessing. Thereafter by themselves and later with their families, they are admonished
to begin the day with a supplication for aid and protection
for that day's need and at eventide to kneel again in thanksgiving and acknowledgment to ask a benediction upon the
home and family throughout the coming night. The Lord
has promised, "And if ye do this with a pure heart, in all
faithfulness, ye shall be blessed; you shall be blessed in
your flocks, and in your herds, and in your fields, and in
your houses, and in your families." (Doc. and Cov. 136:11.)
And again the Master has counseled: "Pray in your families unto the Father, always in my name, that your wives
and your children may be blessed. . . . I say unto you, ye
must watch and pray lest ye enter into temptation; for
Satan desireth to have you, that he may sift you as wheat.
Therefore ye must always pray unto the Father in my
name." (3 Nephi 18:18-21.)

Can you fancy any youth after participating in such
a family devotional going to a social entertainment with
an evil intent in his heart? I am reminded of the beautiful, simple faith of the daughter who never fails before
she leaves for a "date" with her boy friend to kneel in
prayer to ask that she will be blessed to help her companion to have a delightful and pleasurable time that
evening. Those who do not become her sweetheart always
remain her friends. I have thought of the great wisdom of
the devoted Scotch mother who would put her hands ten-
derly on the face of her manly son before he left to take a

young lady to an evenings' entertainment and say, "My son, you are taking out tonight a lovely daughter of a splendid family of our community. Be sure you return her to them as pure and clean as when you took her away." That son never failed her. It was this same sweet parent-child relationship that I heard expressed a few weeks ago at the conclusion of a marriage ceremony when as the father embraced his son, the stalwart son said with a look and a meaning that only he and his father understood, "Well, Dad, I made it." I fancied that there was something of a triumphal ring in his words and at the same time an acknowledgement of his father's counsel to become a man worthy of the father's name, worthy of a beautiful girl, worthy of the sanctified right to the privileges of a temple marriage. On Mother's Day each year as youth your attention is called to the importance of mother's place in the world. Make every day to you a Mother's Day and a Father's Day in which to remind yourselves of their worth as unfailing counselors and guides. From the harvest of their experience, you too may pluck from the "fruit of the tree of the knowledge of good and evil, that will make you wise" if you will only make them your confidants in the most intimate problems of your lives. Remember father had a lot of experience before he won your mother's affections and he has learned much about how it can be retained. Mother, too, has had invaluable experience out of which to teach her daughter the technique of that age-old secret of a successful home partnership thus expressed: "Let him think how well you manage him; but never let him know that you manage him."

Superficiality vs. Genuineness

Many of you have seen the film version of "Johnny Lingo" in which true love erases the drab, plain-looking appearance of the wife. To each other there was nothing but beauty in their life together because of the enchantment of a great love. Well, even if that play was a bit unreal, yet in it is a great thought: Faults and failings and the superficiality of mere physical attractions are as nothing compared with the genuineness of good character that endures and grows more beautiful with the years. You, too, may live in the enchantment of your happy homes long after the bloom of youth has faded if you but seek to find the pure diamond quality in each other that needs but the polishing of success and failure, adversity and happiness to bring luster and sparkle that will shine with brilliance even through the darkest night.

May you young husbands realize that the home is your wife's castle where from morning till night she toils to build in that home a lovely shrine at which her husband and her children might worship. For you to fail to appreciate her efforts or to disregard the sanctity of her home and its orderliness by your careless habits, would be to put into her mind the dangerous thought that her husband doesn't appreciate her efforts. You young wives must realize that as your companion comes home from his day's labor, he comes sometimes with nerves that are taut with the tensions of that day's efforts, hoping to find in you someone to give him the strength and the courage to go back inspired and better prepared to meet the problems of the next day. To nag and to scold and to fail to appreciate his problems is to fail in being the companion that he needs.

May the Lord bless you both and all youth everywhere that you may be guided to prepare yourselves by pure, clean lives for marriage and to live as companions in the home in such a way as to foster the love that will last always and bless you forever.

Out of the Shadows Into Life and Light

During World War II a young captain in the Air Force home on furlough, related his experiences as a squadron leader where as such he had flown fifty or more so-called "missions" over enemy lands. He was a Church member and had served as a missionary for the Church before the beginning of the war. He told of the many interesting discussions he had with the boys who were assigned to his squadron as they prepared themselves for their dangerous air flights over enemy territory. These flights nearly always resulted in some of their number either being reported missing or killed in action. One night they had been alerted for a particularly deadly mission and everyone surmised that the casualties would be high. There was the usual serious discussion in the captain's tent during which a young pilot of the group voiced the question that was probably in the mind of every man there. "If I should be shot down and killed over the target tomorrow, where will I be tomorrow night?"

A Glorious Promise

A similar question was asked by a young wife whose husband was reported "killed in action." Is there any assurance of reunion and a fulfilment of our dreams in the hereafter? That is the cry of a mother's grief as she lays away her infant child in death. Such is the whispered but often inaudible inquiry of the sick and the aged when life's sands are running fast. What strength and comfort must come to him in any of these circumstances, who hears the glorious promise of the Lord:

"Thy dead men shall live, together with my dead body shall they arise. Awake and sing, ye that dwell in dust: for thy dew is as the dew of herbs, and the earth shall cast out the dead." (Isaiah 26:19.)

The heavy hand of death becomes lighter, the pall of gloom is pierced and throbbing wounds are soothed as faith lifts us beyond the sordid trials and sorrows of mortal life and gives a vision of brighter days and more joyous prospect, as has been revealed, when "God shall wipe away all tears from their eyes; and there shall be no more death, neither sorrow, nor crying, neither shall there be any more pain: for the former things are passed away" (Rev. 21:4) through the atonement of the Lord Jesus Christ. With such faith and understanding you who may be called upon to mourn can sing as it has been written, "Death is swallowed up in victory. O death, where is thy sting? O grave, where is thy victory?" (I Cor. 15:54-55.)

Suppose we try to answer the pilot's question: If death overtakes him today, what becomes of him? The scriptures have answered, "Then shall the dust return to the earth as it was: and the spirit shall return unto God who gave it." (Ecclesiastes 12:7) A prophet in our own generation has made this teaching more understandable with this explanation:

"Where is the spirit world? It is right here. Do spirits go beyond the boundaries of the organized earth? No, they do not. They are brought forth upon this earth for the express purpose of inhabiting it to all eternity . . . When the spirits leave their bodies they are in the presence of our Father and God; they are prepared then to see, hear and understand spiritual things. If the Lord would permit it, and it was his will that it should be done, you could see the spirits that have departed from this world, as plainly as you now see bodies with your natural eyes." (Brigham Young J. D. 3:368-369.)

That place to which the spirit goes immediately upon mortal death is, to those that are righteous, "a state of happiness, which is called paradise, a state of rest, a state of peace, where they shall rest from all their troubles and from all care, and sorrow." Among the "spirits of the wicked, who are evil . . . there shall be weeping, and wailing, and gnashing of teeth," as these are cast out into outer darkness because of their iniquity. (Alma 40:11-13.) In the world of spirits all shall dwell either in a state of happiness or in awful anxiety, as the case may be, until the time of their resurrection (verse 14) which will reunite their spirits with their restored and immortal bodies of flesh and bones.

The spirit, if it could be seen with mortal eyes, would appear in bodily shape like a full-grown person with individual endowments that make it a counterpart of the body in which it tabernacles, "that which is temporal in the likeness of that which is spiritual." (Doc. and Cov. 77: 2.) It was that which came from God and entered at birth into the infant body prepared by its mortal parents. The spirit was of the "Lord from heaven." The physical body was "of the earth, earthy," (I Cor. 15:47.) or in other words, composed of the elements of which the things in the physical world are composed.

But what of the pilot's mortal body? Perhaps as he was shot down, his mutilated body fell into the ocean and was devoured by sea animals, or if blown to bits on foreign soil was given no hallowed burial ground. Is there nothing better for it then than to become transformed into parts of other bodies or of vegetation? Again the scriptures answer, "For since by (one) man (Adam) came death, by man (even Jesus Christ) came also the resurrection of the dead." (I Cor. 15:21.)

"Now, this restoration shall come to all, both old and young, both bond and free, both male and female, both the wicked and the righteous; and even there shall not so much as a hair of their heads be lost but every thing shall be restored to its perfect frame, as it is now, or in

the body." (Alma 11:44.) I suppose never in the history of
the world has there been a greater trial of the faith of our
young warriors on the battlefronts as they witnessed almost daily the horrible mutilation of human bodies and
then contemplated the restoration of each such body "to
its proper frame," as it was in mortal life before its destruction. The young pilot was only asking the question
which probably has been asked by every young man in
combat service and by loved ones at home who learned of
such ruthless slaughter.

Bodies Unchangeable

The Prophet Joseph Smith in a consideration of this
question made this statement: "There is no fundamental
principle belonging to a human system that ever goes into
another in this world or in the world to come. . . . If anyone supposes that any part of our bodies, that is, the fundamental parts thereof, ever goes into another body, he is
mistaken." (History of the Church, Vol. 5, p. 339.) A chemist
of renown gives what could be a definition of what Joseph
Smith termed "fundamental parts." Here are his words:
"Some biologists hold the view that there is an ultimate
molecule of life hidden in the protoplasm, which holds the
secret of the endless building up and breaking down."
(Outlines of Science, Vol. 3, p. 718, Arthur Thompson.)
This same scientist then makes this significant statement
in agreement with the Prophet: "The question may be asked,
Do not the particles that compose man's body, when they
return to mother earth, go to make or compose other
bodies? No, they do not. Some philosophers have asserted
that the human body changes every seven years. This is
not correct, for it never changes. That is, the substances
of which it is composed do not pass off and other particles
of matter come and take their places. Neither can the
particles which have comprised the bodies of men become
parts of the bodies of other men, beasts, fowl, fish, insects
or vegetables. They are governed by a divine law, and
though they may pass from the knowledge of the scientific
world that divine law still holds and governs them."

A Scientific Principle

In a discussion of this same subject, President John Taylor made this interesting comment: "It is true the body or the organization may be destroyed in various ways, but it is not true that the particles out of which it is created can be destroyed. They are eternal; they never were created. This is not only a principle associated with our religion . . . but also it is in accordance with acknowledged science. You may take, for instance, a handful of fine gold and scatter it in the street among the dust; again gather together the materials among which you have thrown the gold, and you can separate one from the other so thoroughly that your handful of gold can be returned to you; yes, every grain of it . . . every particle cleaving to its own element." (*The Gospel Kingdom*, p. 24.)

Now again we have a physician residing at Santa Monica, California, who makes this explanation: "We have bodies that are composed of bone, muscle, fat, blood, lymph, nerves and tissues. In all these tissues there is a building up and breaking down of complex chemical compounds. These substances are made into tissues. They give form and beauty to the body, and also supply energy. They are derived from the elements in food, drink and air. These are not the fundamental parts of the body, however for they are used and then discarded, and new substances come to take their place. This is not true of the fundamental parts. They never change. A person may fast for a certain period of time, and become very emaciated, 'lose flesh' we say. People may live on their own tissues until they become almost 'skin and bone,' yet they live and can, when fed again, regain their former form and weight. During the fast, the fundamental parts of the body are not lost, but only the tissues that are taken into the body temporarily." (Dr. Joseph A. Ammussen, *Improvement Era*, Vol. 30, page 701.)

Explanation of Scriptures

In these quotations from men of science and prophets in your own generation, you have explanations of that which has been written in the scriptures for nearly nineteen centuries, evidently intended to give an answer to a similar question being asked in that day. We find the Apostle Paul repeating that question, "But some will say, How are the dead raised up? and with what body do they come?" He then answers that question in these significant words: "Thou fool, that which thou sowest is not quickened, except it die: And that which thou sowest, thou sowest not that body that shall be, but bare grain, it may chance of wheat, or of some other grain: but God giveth it a body as it hath pleased him, and to every seed his own body." (I Cor. 15:35-38.) Here we have two or three things made plain by inference as we make the comparison of the resurrection to the sowing of a seed of grain, as suggested by the Apostle Paul. First, the death of the physical body must come before there can be a "quickening" to an immortal body. Second, there are fundamental parts given of the Lord or in other words "to every seed his own body," and third, although a seed of grain decomposes, in order to give new life, there remains sufficient of its fundamental element to give the new seeds the same look, size and shape, just as there will be retained those essential elements of our human bodies sufficient to give to each of us the same identity and personality our bodies possessed during our mortal lives. The great inventor, Thomas A. Edison, in answering a question as to whether he thought the soul was immortal replied, "Man is not the unit of life. . . . The unit (of life) consists of swarms of billions of highly organized entities which live in the cells. I believe at the time a man dies this swarm deserts the body, goes out into space, but keeps on earth and enters another or last cycle of life. The swarms of entities are immortal." While this is again but a theory there is suggested the core of truth that in each of us there are elements that are essential to our personalities and others that are not essential and that no part of any one of us necessary to a complete and perfect restoration "to our perfect frame as we are now in the body" will be lost in the resurrection. This of course is also a refutation of the false doctrine of reincarnation and bears out the teaching of another prophet who declared: "I say unto you that this mortal body is raised to an immortal body, that is from death, even from the first death unto life, that they can die no more, their spirits uniting with their bodies, *never to be divided*, thus the whole becoming spiritual and immortal, *that they can no more see corruption*." (Alma 11:45.)

First Fruits of Resurrection

Jesus was "the first fruits of the resurrection" or, in other words, the first one on this earth to be given power over death. He came forth with a tangible body of flesh and bones with the marks by which he was identified among his mortal associates. Just so, it is declared we shall all be changed "for our conversation is in heaven; from whence also we look for the Savior, the Lord Jesus Christ: who shall change our vile body, that it may be fashioned like unto his glorious body." (Philippians 3:20-21.) At his crucifixion and subsequent resurrection, "the graves were opened, and many bodies of the saints which slept arose, and came out of the graves . . . and went into the holy city, and appeared unto many." (Matt. 27:52-53.) This was a fulfillment of the vision and prophecies of the prophets of ancient Israel. Ezekiel in vision saw the gathering of Israel as a great army. As bones and flesh and skin came together in each individual and breath came upon them they lived as individual beings. (Ezekiel 37:1-14.) Isaiah and David and Daniel saw that great event and prophesied of it, and Job bore his marvelous testimony: "I know that my redeemer liveth and that he shall stand at the latter day upon the earth. And though after my skin worms destroy this body, yet in my flesh shall I see God." (Job 19:25-26.) When that day shall come, "when the Redeemer shall stand upon the earth" as Job prophesied, when the first trumpet shall sound "then cometh the redemption of those who are Christ's at his coming." This is referred to as the "first resurrection," in the final work of redeeming the dead, although the righteous who had lived before Christ were redeemed at the time of his resurrection. The rest of the dead who are under condemnation "live not again until the thousand years are ended, neither again, until the end of the earth." (Doc. and Cov. 88:98-101.)

Just Punishment Provided

We have not yet fully answered the pilot's question as to what becomes of him at death. After his sojourn in the world of spirits and finally his resurrection from the grave, what will then be his place? If he followed the ways of evil while he lived in mortality, he became the servant of the devil who had power over him. In the spirit world such a one will be "cast out into outer darkness" and will be denied the presence of the Lord until he pays the penalty of his misdeeds and repents of his sins through the acceptance of the gospel which will be preached to him there. If it was divinely understood that he would have accepted the gospel while in mortality had he been given the proper opportunity, such as he might yet be heirs even to the Celestial Kingdom of God. (History of Church, Vol. 2:380.) This separation or death as to things spiritual is termed "hell" by the writers of the scriptures (II Nephi 9:16.) and "is as a lake of fire and brimstone whose flame ascended up . . . and has no end." Each such soul is "filled with guilt and remorse having . . . a perfect remembrance of all (his) wickedness, yea, a remembrance that (he has) set at defiance the commandments of God." (Alma 5:18.) Hell, then, is to be understood to be both a place as well as a condition. Such a punishment is defined as being "eternal" and "endless" because God is eternal and endless. The prison remains eternally and endlessly as a place of punishment to sinners who merit that condition. Thus there is provided a just punishment for each person commensurate with the extent of his own sinning. Every one of you, including our young pilot, must stand before "the judgment seat of the Holy One of Israel . . . and then must . . . be judged according to the

holy judgment of God." (II Nephi 9:15.) And according to
the vision of John, "The books were opened: and another
book was opened, which is the book of life; and the dead
were judged out of those things which were written in
the books, according to their works." (Rev. 20:12.) The
"books" spoken of refer to the "records of your works
and which are kept on earth. . . . The book of life is the
record which is kept in heaven." (Doc. and Cov. 128:7.)
Those of you who have lived a righteous life and die without having become the servants of sin, or who have truly
repented of your sins, will enter into the "rest of the
Lord," which rest "is the fulness of the glory of the Lord."
(Doc. and Cov. 84:24.) To you whose lives may be taken
in war and to you who may mourn the loss of loved ones
so taken, may I bring you again the comfort of the words of
Moroni, the captain of the guard: "For the Lord suffereth
the righteous to be slain that his justice and judgment
may come upon the wicked; therefore ye need not suppose
that the righteous are lost because they are slain; but
behold, they do enter into the rest of the Lord." (Alma
60:13.)

Yes, "if you will take death and sin out of this earth,
I will take my heaven here and start in tomorrow morning."
Such was the remark of a young man who was asked where
heaven was located. How true are his words! Here upon
this earth, when it is cleansed from unrighteousness, will
be the eternal abode of you who are judged worthy of
celestial glory. Here you may dwell without sin and without death with the redeemed of your Father's house and
your posterity throughout eternity.

Youth of today, strive with all the strength at your
command to live worthy to inherit this better day. In the
years to come as you walk in the cities of the honored dead
to revere their memories, may each one of you be sobered
by a realization of the final state of man when each of you
shall take his chamber "in the silent halls of death."

May you be guided to live each day as though it were
your last on earth and be prepared for such a passing into
the presence of "that God who gave you life."

Jesus was being tried before Pilate on the charge of blasphemy. "Pilate therefore said unto him, Art thou a king then? Jesus answered, Thou sayest that I am a king. To this end was I born, and for this cause came I into the world, that I should bear witness unto the truth. Every one that is of the truth heareth my voice. Pilate saith unto him, What is truth?" (John 18:37-38.) To Adam and Eve, our first parents on this earth, God gave the commandment, "Be fruitful, and multiply, and replenish the earth, and subdue it and have dominion. . . ." (Genesis 1: 28.) Truth is the scepter of power, which if man possesses, will give him "dominion" and the ability to "subdue all things." It has been well said that "If you have truth on your side, you can pass through the dark valley of slander, misrepresentation and abuse, undaunted, as though you wore a magic suit of mail that no bullet could enter, no arrow could pierce. You can hold your head high, toss it fearlessly and defiantly, look every man calmly and un-flinchingly in the eye, as though you rode, a victorious king, returning at the head of your legions with banners waving and lances glistening, and bugles filling the air with music." (Wm. George Jordan) Is there any one of you who would not desire with all your heart to be thus equipped to meet the problems of life! Yours then should be a daily quest for truth, but in order that your search be fruitful, you must first know the answer to the question Pilate put to the Master, "What is truth?"

Definition of Truth

In a revelation given to the Church on May 6, 1833, the Lord gave us this definition of truth: "And truth is knowledge of things as they are, and as they were, and as they are to come." (Doc. and Cov. 93:24.) In the next statement the Lord gives us also the definition of untruth: "And whatsoever is more or less than this," meaning more or less than the knowledge of things present, past and future, "is the spirit of that wicked one who was a liar from the beginning." (verse 25) It was Jesus who declared to the believing Jews that "Ye shall know the truth, and the truth shall make you free . . . Whosoever committeth sin is the servant of sin." (John 8:32, 34.) To us in this day the Lord has said, "He that keepeth (God's) commandments receiveth truth and light, until he is glorified in truth and knoweth all things." (Doc. and Cov. 93:28.). And again we are told, "The glory of God is intelligence, or, in other words, light and truth." (verse 36.) Furthermore, the Master has impressed the vital necessity of a fulness of knowledge if we would gain eternal life, and likewise the supreme or the ultimate object of our quest for truth and indeed what it is that constitutes a fulness of truth. Ponder seriously these words, "And this is life eternal, that they might know thee the only true God, and Jesus Christ, whom thou hast sent." (John 17:3.) It is no small wonder that with the spread of truth thus so vital to the triumph of God's plan for the redemption and exaltation of the human soul that Satan, the master of lies, should seek to overthrow truth to the end that he might "lead captive at his will, even as many as would not hearken" unto the voice of the Lord by which a true knowledge of "things as they are, as they were, and as they are to come" would be revealed.

An Unfailing Guide

In order that the young, vigorous and inquiring minds of youth in all ages might have a standard and an unfailing guide by which to measure all learning and thus be able to sift the golden kernels of truth from the chaff of delusion and untruth, we have had the scriptures from the beginning which were given "by inspiration of God, and (are) profitable for doctrine, for reproof, for correction, for instruction in righteousness: That the man of God may be perfect, thoroughly furnished unto all good works." (II Timothy 3:16-17.) So the Master counseled us to search the scriptures, for in them we would find the way to eternal life, for they testify of the way men must travel to gain eternal life with him and with "the Father which hath sent (him)." (John 5:30.) This is the evident meaning of the Lord's statement to Pilate to which I made reference at the beginning of this discussion: "For this cause came I into the world, that I should bear witness unto the truth." So has it been the purpose of every prophet and teacher of righteousness to preserve the truth and to combat error for the salvation of every soul whose purity of life has made of him a fit vessel to receive truth when it should be made known to him.

You and I have been privileged to be born in a dispensation known in the scriptures as the "fulness of times," (Galatians 4:4) which is to precede the second coming of Jesus Christ, when there would be a "restitution of all things, which God hath spoken by the mouth of all his holy prophets since the world began." (Acts 3:21.) This is the day the prophet Ezekial foresaw when the "stick" or record of Judah, which is the Bible, and the "stick" or record of Joseph and Ephraim and his brethren, which is contained in the Book of Mormon, were to be joined together and were to become one in the hands of a man whom he would raise up. All of this has been done for a purpose explained by the Lord in revelation to us, "Behold . . . these commandments (contained in the fulness of the gospel) were given . . . that (his children) might come to understanding. And inasmuch as they erred, it might be made known; and inasmuch as they sought wisdom they might be instructed; and inasmuch as they sinned they might be chastened, that they might repent; and inasmuch as they were humble they might be made strong, and blessed

from on high and receive knowledge from time to time."
(Doc. and Cov. 1:24-28.)

The place of the Church in preserving truth in these
"the latter times" is thus pointed out when "some shall
depart from the faith, giving heed to seducing spirits, and
doctrines of devils; speaking lies in hypocrisy; having their
conscience seared with a hot iron, forbidding to marry and
commanding to abstain from meats . . ." (I Timothy 4:1-3.)
This, your day, was prophesied of as a day when "there
shall be false teachers among you, who privily shall bring
in damnable heresies, even denying the Lord that bought
them . . . and many shall follow their pernicious ways;
by reason of whom the ways of truth shall be evil spoken
of." (II Peter 2:1-2.) So the Church of Jesus Christ declares
with a boldness that is always characteristic of truth, "We
believe all that God has revealed, all that he does now
reveal, and we believe that he will yet reveal many great
and important things pertaining to the kingdom of
God." (Ninth Article of Faith) And again ". . . We believe
all things, we hope all things. . . . If there is anything
virtuous, lovely, or of good report or praiseworthy, we
seek after these things." (Thirteenth Article of Faith) Indeed the Church of Jesus Christ does not ask you to give
up any truth that you may learn from science or philosophy,
law or medicine. Rather is the Church commanded "that
you may be instructed more perfectly in theory, in principle, in doctrine, in the law of the gospel, in all things
that pertain unto the kingdom of God, that are expedient
for you to understand; of things both in heaven and in
the earth, and under the earth; things which have been,
things which are, things which must shortly come to pass,
things which are at home, things which are abroad; the
wars and the perplexities of the nations, and the judgments
which are on the land; and a knowledge also of countries
and of kingdoms." (Doc. and Cov. 88:78-79.)

Studies Outlined

If you will carefully analyze that commandment of
the Lord you will find broadly enumerated many of the

studies outlined in your scholastic courses: Astronomy, the physical sciences, mineralogy, history, current events, political science, law, medicine, world history, and so on through the entire school curriculum. The only thing the Church does ask of you in all your worldly studies is that you do two things:

First, that you measure every teaching to be found in the world of book-learning by the teachings of revealed truth as contained in the Gospel of Jesus Christ. If you find in your school texts claims that contradict the word of the Lord as pertaining to the creation of the world, the origin of man or the determination of what is right or wrong in the conduct of human souls, you may be certain such teachings are but the theories of men and as men improve their learning and experimentation, the nearer will their theories coincide with the truths that God has given to his Church. The second thing that the Church would have you keep in mind is that there is beyond the things that you can discern by the physical senses of "the natural man," things of a spiritual nature, "the things of God knoweth no man but the Spirit of God. . . . The natural man receiveth not the things of the Spirit of God; for they are foolishness unto him; neither can he know them, because they are spiritually discerned." (I Cor. 2:10-14.)

Within the limits of the natural man, you have your methods of experimentation pretty well established. With mortar and pestle, test tubes and Bunsen burners, with acids and materials to be analyzed, you proceed to your discovery of the component parts of water or to learn the various properties of phosphorus, for example. As a student of science you soon come to realize the limitations of your scientific research. When one climbs Pikes Peak he discovers that even from his vantage point the surrounding country is but a territory with receding horizons and yet other mountains to climb. So the naturalist stands in reverent awe as he contemplates how the delicate coloring, the fragrant odors and delicious tastes of nature's products are made by processes far beyond his grasp. The

great surgeon, by dissection and with scalpel and micro-
scope has learned much about the human body and how
it works, but he knows full well that beyond his reach is
the soul or intelligence in man that defies analysis with
the tools at his command. Every astronomer knows likewise that all he has been able to discern with the powerful telescope now provided for his use but leads him to
realize that there are worlds without number beyond his
present scientific sight. It was the great scientist Sir Isaac
Newton, in recognition of man's limitation, who declared:
"I do not know what I may appear to the world, but to
myself I seem to have been only like a boy playing on the
seashore and diverting myself in now and then finding a
smoother pebble or a prettier shell than ordinary, whilst
the great ocean of truth lay all undiscovered before me."
My association with men of great learning in science and
philosophy or in religion leads me to conclude that one's
faith in spiritual matters is disturbed by his scientific or
philosophical studies only because his knowledge in either
or both science and religion is deficient.

Methods Clearly Defined

In things of the spiritual world that can only be
spiritually discerned, the methods of finding truth are no
less clearly defined than in the physical laboratory. It was
the Master who, in reply to the question as to how his
hearers were to know whether his teachings were of God
or whether he spoke of himself, suggested a simple method
for perceiving spiritual truth. "If any man will do (God's)
will, he shall know." (John 7:17.) In numerous revelations
his will and the steps that must be taken by him who would
learn spiritual truths are made clear: "If you shall ask
(God) with a sincere heart, with real intent, having faith
in Christ, he will manifest the truth of it unto you, by
the power of the Holy Ghost. And by the power of the
Holy Ghost ye may know the truth of all things." (Moroni
10:4-5.) There must be first, desire, then study, then prayer,
and finally practice. "Prove me now herewith and see,"

the Lord constantly enjoins him who would know divine truth. You make a grave mistake that leads only to confusion when you presume to discover spiritual truths by the methods of the physical laboratory. I was greatly impressed when I heard one of the greatest scientists and scholars of our day, Dr. Robert A. Millikan, at a convention of scientists held at Fresno, California, counseled his listeners to be as scientific in proving religious teachings as they were in their studies in science. He declared that nothing spiritual should be discarded until it had been submitted to the most careful experimentation and testing to prove or disprove the whole matter. It has been said by some who speak loosely that "he who never doubted, never thought." Youth must understand that faith, not doubt, is the beginning of all learning, whether in science or religion. It is faith in the wisdom of ages past that leads to further study, experimentation and new discovery. It is faith that seeks for spiritual knowledge and power by studying out in your own mind the matter in question, by applying all possible human wisdom to the solution of your problem and then asking God if your conclusion is right. If it is right, your bosom shall burn within you and you shall "feel" that it is right, but if your conclusion is not right, you shall have a stupor of thought that shall cause you to forget the thing that is wrong. (Doc. and Cov. 9:8-9.)

An Expert Has Testimony

The expert in the scientific field is one who by his experimentation has come to know that an announced theory is true. An "expert," so-called, in the spiritual world is in the making when he, by humility and faith, knows that God hears and answers prayer. Such a one has "arrived" when he has an unshakable testimony that God is our Father and that through his son Jesus Christ all mankind may be saved by obedience to the laws and ordinances of the gospel. The Lord has given the inspired truth that "It is impossible for a man to be saved in ignorance." (Doc. and Cov. 131:6) Does this mean that one must be a college graduate or a man of letters to be saved? Not at all. Man cannot be saved in ignorance of those saving principles of the gospel of Jesus Christ if we were to have all the book learning in the world. We have been plainly taught by the leaders of this dispensation that "The principle of knowledge is the principle of salvation. . . . (and that) the principle of salvation is given us through the knowledge of Jesus Christ." (*Joseph Smith's Teachings*, p. 297.) "Reading the experience of others, or the revelation given to them can never give us a comprehensive view of our condition and true relation to God. Knowledge of these can only be obtained by experience through ordinances of God set forth for that purpose," (p. 324) But the Lord has encouraged us to strive diligently for knowledge and intelligence from every source. Here are the prophet's inspired words of counsel: "Whatever principle of intelligence we attain unto in this life, it will rise with us in the resurrection. And if a person gains more knowledge and intelligence in this life through his diligence and obedience than another, he will have so much the advantage in the world to come." (Doc. and Cov. 130:18-19.)

The individual preparation each of you must make in order to attain the fulness of knowledge, on which your eternal salvation rests, is suggested by the Apostle Peter in these words: "And beside this, giving all diligence, add to your faith virtue; and to virtue knowledge; and to knowledge temperance; and to temperance patience; and to patience godliness; and to godliness brotherly kindness; and to brotherly kindness charity. For if these things be in you, and abound, they make you that ye shall neither be barren nor unfruitful in the knowledge of our Lord Jesus Christ." (II Peter 1:5-8.) One who violates these fundamental human virtues cannot have the greatest truths of the spiritual world unfolded to him.

In a university publication sometime ago I read an article by a student entitled "Up from Heaven," suggesting that belief in the supernatural was childish and must eventually be overcome by advancement in intellectual studies.

You have no doubt known many like this young student, who, because of their "little learning," think they have outgrown the Church and religion. As a matter of fact, when you consider seriously the fact that the Church of Jesus Christ requires sacrifice of one's time and talents and means in order to qualify as a worthy citizen of the Kingdom, and that "pure religion and undefiled before God and the Father is this, to visit the fatherless and the widows in their affliction, and to keep himself unspotted from the world" (James 1:27.), you are led to this sure conclusion: That person who thinks he has outgrown his church and his religion has in reality proved himself too small to bear the responsibilities his membership entails and has shut himself up in his small intellectual world and the vast treasures in the unseen world of spiritual truths are closed to his understanding. "And if your eye be single to (God's) glory, your whole bodies shall be filled with light, and there shall be no darkness in you; and the body which is filled with light comprehendeth all things." (Doc. and Cov. 88:67.)

Many of you have attended your commencement exercises at the university or the high school, some of you have graduated to still higher schools of education, some of you have taken jobs, or have become married and have settled down to the serious problems of everyday living. Don't you be among those who are blinded to the wealth of learning beyond the understanding of the "natural man." You are standing on the threshold of the most profound of all schools of learning. "The University of Spirituality," if you will only keep God's commandments.

May you seek out of the best books "all that has been revealed," and be guided in your search for truth and seek just as earnestly to know "all that may yet be revealed," and thus make your lives balanced and complete.

Security is probably the most sought after thing in the world today. To the beggar it may be but a meal to ease the pangs of hunger and a crude bed at night sheltered from the cold. To the farmer, security is assured only when the season for planting and harvest is satisfactory for the maturing of the crops and when the labor supply and market conditions all conduce to an income sufficient for his needs with a safe margin for emergencies. The merchant must have goods to sell and customers to buy his goods, and the professional man enough patients or clients who pay their bills in order for him to be properly safeguarded. The banker depends upon the faith of the depositor in his institution and upon the integrity of the borrower.

As one grows older he is naturally concerned about the days ahead when his health may fail and his earning capacity may be greatly reduced, possibly to a point where he may not be able to sustain himself and those dependent upon him. In anticipation of such a possibility and to meet the sudden emergencies of life, we pay for protection or security through what we call insurance in order to cover losses that might occur from death, sickness, fire, theft or destruction from the elements. Each one, as he is able and endowed with wisdom, endeavors to make savings and investments that may become the back-log of safety for the future. These same desires for security are in the minds of you our youth of today as you face the hazards of an uncertain period during which time you hope to build happy homes as husbands and wives and become the parents of happy children.

False Philosophies

Among us today are purveyors of false philosophies and nostrums who, in various walks of life, are covertly seeking power and would lull you into quiescence through the fallacious thought that public gratuities can give you security through the work of others than yourselves and that you can then live upon the results of the efforts of your neighbors. Wise leaders among us have pointed out time and time again that if you needlessly accept from others such security as man can and should provide for himself, you become a dependent, and that as the proportion of dependents in a nation grows, the standard of living falls, opportunity and freedom disappear and the possibility of the realization of that "joy" for which men are created is greatly diminished.

One of our American educators in an address to youth at an eastern university has also pointed out another danger if we accept unsound theories. Here are his words: "While regimentation and enslavement may give men some meager requirements for living, the dictatorship inseparable from such conditions may toss them into the maelstrom of war at will and destroy the mirage of their fancied security." (Dr. Frank I. Kent, New York University, June, 1944.)

Youth of today, you must never forget that it is only through your own efforts and the joyous realization of work well done that you can give true satisfaction and have provided those factors which will make for real security for yourselves and others. The first step is taken to a genuine security in your own lives when you resolve that, God willing, you are determined to live by your own exertions and become independent of gratuitous public offerings. You must not overlook the fact that we are living in a material world and that no man nor group of men can surely make guarantees of permanent security, all of which may fail when new political theories replace the old. "Man proposes but God disposes," and it might be timely to remind you that he alone can guarantee safety amidst our mundane surroundings, and that the counsel of the Master is just as applicable to you today as it was to those who first heard his words: "Beware of covetousness: for a man's life consisteth not in the abundance of the things which he possesseth. . . . If then God so clothe the grass, which is today in the field, and tomorrow is cast into the oven, how much more will he clothe you, O ye of little faith? And seek not ye what ye shall eat, or what ye shall drink, neither be ye of doubtful mind. For all these things do the nations of the world seek after; and your Father knoweth that ye have need of these things. But rather seek ye the kingdom of God and all these things shall be added unto you. Fear not, little flock." (Luke 12: 15, 28-32.)

Your first consideration of those words of the Master may make them seem to be a bit idealistic and hardly applicable to present world needs, but before you dispose of his powerful and meaningful words, may I make some applications to your lives. Jesus is the central figure of that kingdom you are counseled to seek. The sacrifice of his life for the sins of all mankind, thus opening the way to a resurrection for all men to a newness of life according to their merit, is the core of the teaching of Christianity. You who would seek first "His Kingdom" must begin your search by applying that same fundamental principle of sacrifice and service for others. You who start out with a program of getting without giving are not following a course to give you the fulness of the Lord's bounty. A philosopher once said, "How prudently most men creep into nameless graves, while now and then one or two forget themselves into immortality." (Wendell Phillips.) Everyone is master of his own fortune. Whether he be an industrialist, a manufacturer, an inventor, a religious leader or a politician, his success has been largely determined by following a simple line of thought that stems from the words of the Master. His most valuable ideas have been those concerned with the needs of others.

When you begin to make service to meet others' needs your constant practice, you are beginning a program that will make you successful in your chosen field and your own needs will begin automatically to take care of themselves. This great idea in action has made great inventors, great statesmen, great business leaders.

A simply story has been told that perhaps will impress the meaning of this principle which points the way to material success and security.

"A certain woman found it necessary to dispose of her cat because she was leaving the community. She was concerned about seeing that it found a good home. Her small nephew was sent forth with the cat in his arms, and the idea that he carried with him was that poor kitty needed a home. No one was moved to compassion, so he returned sorrowfully with the cat. The older brother took the cat and strode forth confidently, calling at the nearby grocery store where the small boy had received his first refusal. He felt that this fine cat was not an object of pity but a useful animal. He reminded the grocer that just a few days before a package had been returned to the store because it had been damaged by mice. It was apparent that the grocer needed to get rid of the mice because they were costing him plenty of damage to his stock. The cat would soon pay for itself. The cat stayed, and the boy walked from the grocery store with a dollar in his pocket, not because he sensed the need of a dollar for himself, but because he sensed the grocer's need for a good cat." (Magazet.)

When you can lose yourselves in the unselfish service to others, you will unconsciously forget your own wants and they will be supplied most likely because of the reciprocal service or patronage of those whom you have thus served.

There is a story of a great Israelitish leader who applied another principle only upon which can there be a sure and certain foundation for temporal security. Israel had been overrun by the Persians and many had been taken captive. One of the captives, by name Nehemiah, had been appointed cup-bearer to the Persian king. With a constant ear for news from his captured homeland, he learned from recent captives that his people were greatly distressed and afflicted and the wall of Jerusalem had been broken down. Like a true patriot he wept tears and that night fasted and prayed and during the succeeding days sought by mourning and confession of his people's sins to gain from the Lord a blessing that would soften the heart of the king and prepare him to receive a plea for mercy that Nehemiah proposed to make in behalf of his people. His prayers were heard and answered insomuch that he was granted the privilege of returning to the city of his fathers' sepulchres, and was given the necessary passports and letters to governors of unfriendly states along the way, together with a military escort, and a timber permit to obtain building materials from the king's forests. News of his coming preceded him and some of the governors of the land were grieved when they heard "that a man was come to seek the welfare of the children of Israel." When he arrived in Jerusalem, he made a secret reconnaissance of the city to ascertain the extent of the destruction that had been suffered and the amount of the financial indebtedness of the people. He made his plans to rebuild the walls of the city and to help his people free themselves from the terrible bondage of indebtedness they were in. When his plans were ready he called a mass meeting of the people who agreed to follow his leadership. "Let us rise up and build," they said, "so they strengthened their hands for his good work." (Nehemiah 2:18.) He organized every man, woman and child into companies and gave them assigned duties commensurate with their abilities and physical condition. Here is a part of the record as told by this peerless leader: "Half of my servants wrought in the work, and the other half held both the spears, the shields and the bows and the coats of mail. . . . They which builded on the wall, and they that bare burdens with those that laded, every one with one of his hands wrought in the work, and with the other hand held a weapon. For the builders, every one had his sword girded by his side, and so builded. And he that sounded the trumpet was by me. . . . So we laboured in the work . . . from the rising of the morning till the stars appeared." (Nehemiah Chapter 4.)

Enemies Ridicule

Their enemies were not idle. They first sought to undermine them by ridiculing their building, saying that the rebuilt wall was so flimsy a fox walking on it would shake it down. The answer was a more fervent prayer to the Almighty for the unity of the people. Next the enemy resorted to intrigue and compromise and the leader, Nehemiah, refused their invitation for a conference with a reply that he was too busy with his important work. Then the enemy threatened to blackmail the workers by informing the king that a plan of rebellion was being fomented by the Israelites. Their final effort to block the work was to hire a traitor to endeavor to intimidate Nehemiah with threats upon his life. Despite these cunning plans of the enemy the work went forward under a great leader. Now the result of that kind of organization and team work and the secret of their success is declared in Nehemiah's own triumphal words, "So built we the wall; and all the wall was joined together unto the half thereof: for the people had a mind to work." (Nehemiah 4:6.)

You show me a people who "have a mind to work," to keep out of the bondage of indebtedness, and to work unitedly together in an unselfish service to attain a great objective, and I'll show you a people who have achieved the greatest possible security in the world of men and material things. The Lord has clearly marked the way by which the "saints" or members of his Church are to be provided: "This is the way that I, the Lord, have decreed to provide for my saints, that the poor shall be exalted,

in that the rich are made low. If any man shall take of the
abundance which I have made, and impart not his portion,
according to the law of my gospel, unto the poor and the
needy, he shall with the wicked, lift up his eyes in hell,
being in torment." (Doc. and Cov. 104:15-18.) I wish that
in all our dealings with the unfortunate and the needy that
we would take another lesson from the story of that cat
which I have related. When we begin to think of those
whom we would help as being useful for something
instead of being objects of pity, we will then begin to
plan ways by which the wisdom of the aged, the tenderness
and thriftiness of widowhood and the youthful vigor of
the able-bodied might be utilized toward the solving of
their own problems and for the blessing of the lives of
those less fortunate than they.

At the same time the Lord warns the poor, "Wo unto
you poor men, whose hearts are not broken, whose spirits
are not contrite, and whose bellies are not satisfied, and
whose hands are not stayed from laying hold upon other
men's goods, whose eyes are full of greediness, and who
will not labor with your own hands." (Doc. and Cov. 56:17.)
The promise of the Lord to the poor and the rich who heed
his counsel is that "the fatness of the earth shall be theirs."
(Doc. and Cov. 56:18.) The Prophet Joseph Smith declared:
"It has always been a cardinal teaching with the Latter-
day Saints that a religion that has not the power to save
people temporally and make them prosperous and happy
here cannot be depended upon to save them spiritually and exalt them in the life to come." Wise leaders
of the Church from the beginning have shown the
way to prosperity and happiness. Said Brigham Young:
"It is never any benefit to give out and out to man or woman,
money, food, clothing or anything else, if they are able-
bodied, and can work to earn what they need, when there
is anything on earth for them to do. . . . To pursue a contrary course would ruin any community in the world and
make them idlers. People trained in this way have no
interest in working. . . . Teach this girl to do housework

and that woman to sew and do other kinds of work . . . for the bone and sinew of men and women are the capital of the world." (Brigham Young, *J. D.*, 11:297.)

Church Welfare Program

In harmony with that counsel and obedient to the Lord's command, the Church in your day has developed a great movement known popularly or otherwise as the Church Welfare Services Program. Its purpose is to restore the unity, courage, faith and integrity of our pioneer fathers. We are like the ancient Israelites rebuilding the walls of our "fathers' sepulchres" that were broken down by the bondage of debt and public relief. In that task we have had powerful aid from wonderful friends not members of the Church who have given us, as it were, "safe journey across their lands and permits to cut timber from the king's forests." Some of the governors of the land "were grieved when they heard that a man was come to seek the welfare of these modern children if Israel." The faithful among our membership have said, "Let us rise up and build and be independent from public gratitudes." So they strengthened their hands for the good work. We have had enemies who have scorned and ridiculed our efforts, and those who have argued that we ought to compromise our standards of independence. Others have resorted to threats and blackmail and still others have been hired to become traitors to their own people by the lure of worldly honors or public offices. These were the same methods of the enemy in the days of the Master when he was betrayed by his own people. They were likewise employed when the saints were driven from Nauvoo and when Johnston's Army came to Utah in 1857 because of false rumors that had been carried to the president of the United States by traitors and blackmailers. Success has always crowned the efforts of the children of the Lord whenever "the people had a mind to work."

Probably as never before in American history or in the history of the Church, this is the time for every

youth and every citizen to take himself the old patriot's
oath, which was put on paper by Edward Everett Hale:

> "I am only one—
>   But I am one;
> I cannot do everything
>   But I can do something,
> And what I can do
>   That I ought to do;
> And what I ought to do
>   By the grace of God,
> I will do."

May youth forsake the path of idleness and depend-
ence that leads to regimentation and enslavement and gain
the independence that comes from service and sacrifice
and a struggle with necessity and honest toil.

During the Second World War, there came to my desk the report of a religious conference held by a group of one hundred forty young men who were members of the Church then engaged in military service in Italy. The announced theme for this unique Church gathering was significant and full of deep meaning. This was their theme: "We shall arise to the occasion of 1944 by the faith, courage and determination of the men of 1847." Thus they paid tribute to their pioneer fathers who braved the dangers of the unbroken paths that led to a home in the tops of the mountains in a country that was described by an orator on the floor of the United States Senate as a land "of savages and wild beasts, of deserts and shifting sands and whirlwinds of dust, cactus and prairie dogs" and of "endless mountain ranges, impenetrable and covered to the very base with snow."

It was in the valleys of these mountains that their grandfathers had built an empire and had made the desert to blossom as the rose and had bequeathed to these their grandsons a legacy far greater than mere worldly wealth. Their inheritance was the capacity to meet similar dangers, the will to triumph over seemingly insurmountable obstacles, and the determination to preserve the same principles of freedom and right to worship God that their forefathers would have given their lives to have maintained. The modern Moses who led that pioneer band of 1847 to the tops of the mountains has left the youth of today what might well have been a last will and testament of these pioneer virtues to the generations which were to follow after him. I quote Brigham Young's words from his last dictated entry before the saints were driven from their homes in Nauvoo, Illinois: "Our homes, gardens, orchards, farms, streets, bridges, mills, public halls, magnificent temple and other improvements, we leave as a monument to our patriotism, industry, economy, uprightness of purpose and integrity of heart, and as a living testimony of the falsehood and wickedness of those who charge us with idleness, dishonesty and disloyalty to the Constitution of our country."

Recount Blessings

If the departed spirits of those pioneers who have passed on could have attended the meeting of their grandsons on that far-off Italian battlefront, they would have thrilled with the discussions of that day. These young men, despite the horrors of war through which they were passing, recounted the blessings for which they were grateful,—that they were freed from certain worries about daily sustenance; that even from their meager earnings they could make substantial savings for the future; that there was great opportunity to read and study and think and plan for the vocations they would follow in the future; that they had opportunity to learn of foreign lands, peoples and customs; that they had fellowship with many men like themselves who were engaged in military service. They had learned how to endure other people's peculiarities and that Negroes, Jews, Indians, Westerners, Southerners and Easterners were all a part of America. They had learned to measure their growth through their responsibilities, hardships and rigid discipline. Most of all they had gained a greater appreciation for home, for loved ones, for God and for their great country. They sang again that old battle hymn of their pioneer fathers and no doubt with similar fervor.

And should we die before our journey's through,
    Happy day! All is well!
We then are free from toil and sorrow too,
    With the just we shall dwell!
But if our lives are spared again
    To see the saints their rest obtain,
O how we'll make this chorus swell—
    All is well! all is well!

All America could well be proud of the lofty ideal
to which these young warriors pledged themselves that
day. Here is that pledge:
    "As Church members we will never be among those
who clamor for personal gain and who will say, 'I served
my country. She owes me for it, and I aim to collect.'
Rather will we stand among the handful who regard
striving to uphold freedom and democracy and the dignity
of the human personality as a privilege that is its own
reward."
    This land will always continue to be a land of
freedom and opportunity so long as youth demonstrate
such lofty idealism and noble purpose.
    But always among those of such lofty ideals are to
be found some who count only their misfortunes. These
are the ones who say, "This army experience is time
wasted as far as I can see; it is just so much time taken
out of my life." Some have a feeling of defeatism, and
are being influenced by those who are clamoring for
a new social order. The dilemma in which youth find
themselves today, with respect to their future and the
social problems confronting them, is understandable.
You have seen strange flags of sedition raised and have listened to the attempts of men in high station trying to stir
up class hatreds that contradict the age-old constitutional
guarantee of free enterprise. Those of fearful mind remind
me of the story they tell of the employe of the United States
Patent Office in the eighties of the last century, who resigned
his position which he thought would soon terminate any-

way because practically everything in the way of inventions in America had been patented and there would soon be no further need for a continuation of the patent office. Little did he know that the next few years would usher in the greatest era of industrial and mechanical development in the history of the world.

Lamp of Faith

Someone has said, "He who carries the lamp will not despair no matter how dark the night. That lamp I call faith." (Myron C. Taylor.) I have faith in the future of this promised land of America and in its institutions of representative government, but more than that, I have faith in you, the youth of America, to build even more securely on the foundations laid by the faith and devotion of your pioneer fathers. That you as the youth of the Church would have an important part to play in preserving the ideals of this great country as quoted by one who was very close to him. I quote the words of Eliza R. Snow: "I heard the Prophet Joseph Smith say 'that the time would come when this nation would so far depart from its original purity, its glory, and its love of freedom and the protection of civil and religious rights, that the Constitution of our country would hang, as it were, by a thread.' He also said that this people, the sons of Zion, would rise up and save the Constitution and bear it off triumphantly.' " (Eliza R. Snow, 1870, *Women of Mormondom* by Tullidge.)

So today is no time for youth to whimper the refrain of the defeated and retire to the fancied security of the regimented state. Today is the day for youth to gird themselves with the armor of peace, having as their weapons "the shield of faith . . . and the sword of the Spirit, which is the word of God." (Ephesians 6:16-17.)

Prospects for Future Development

America holds much in prospect for future development. It has been well said that in times of adversity men begin to think. This is demonstrated by the fact that in times of war and great national stress, science and invention are greatly accelerated. Even in so-called "normal times" the technological developments are rapid today, and there is much more that awaits only the application of intelligent leadership to make for a development in the material world hitherto unheard of. Surely there is no one of you who thinks the "earth has been subdued" and that you have nothing left for you but to be a puppet of the universe and a dependent of the political state in which you live.

I want to say with all the sincerity within my soul that there is more guarantee of security in the intelligent will, initiative and determined independence of the American youth of today that in all the laws that Congress may make intended to provide us with insurance from the "cradle to the grave." Men who are dreaming of that kind of a security are not the kind that pioneered this country and explored the unknown. They are not the ones who built the world of today nor will they be the builders of the "new" world of tomorrow of which they speak. They are, as someone has siad, "only tenants in houses of other men's dreams." (George E. Sokolsky.) If you would be a builder in that world of tomorrow, you must make that pledge of those boys on the Italian battlefield and meet the problems of today with the faith, courage and determination of pioneers of 1847.

Now while men are talking about future security, the Lord has been directing through his prophets for over a hundred years a building program for temporal salvation of which he is the Master Architect. At the time of the early organization of his Church in this dispensation he gave this in a revelation to his people: "And thus shall my Church be called in the last days, even The Church of Jesus Christ of Latter-day Saints. Verily, I say unto you all . . . that the gathering together upon the land of Zion, and upon her stakes, may be for a defense, and for a refuge from the storm, and from wrath when it shall be poured out without mixture upon the whole earth." (D. & C. 115:4-6.)

Stakes of Zion Organized

Since that revelation was given, there have been organized more than 600 of those "stakes of Zion of which the Lord speaks. Each consists on an average of a membership of from 4,000 to 8,000 Church members presided over by successful men and women of faith and devotion and good judgment. Within each stake there are from eight to ten subdivisions called wards, led by men of good habits and wisdom, known as bishops, and who are to be as fathers to their people. They are assisted by men and women of superior attainments. In every ward or Church community, no matter how small, are smaller groups similar to fraternities, athletic or service clubs, and religious classes which are called priesthood quorums or auxiliary associations. There is one grand objective in all this great Church organization that now numbers more than three million persons. That objective is to provide for and to promote the spiritual, temporal and social salvation or welfare of every one who has membership in one of these priesthood or auxiliary groups, and if each such group is moved by the power and righteousness of the principles inherent therein, "they will have all the power necessary to meet every problem in this modern and changing world." (Brigham Young.) I want to give you something more to impress the importance of unselfish sacrifice as a principle of success in life, not only for your temporal but your spiritual salvation.

You who are home from military service and from school can bring to your Church group or priesthood quorum the lessons of leadership and team work that will stimulate unity of purpose and action in solving home problems. Apply in your private life and in the responsible assignments that may be given you after you return home, the rules of discipline that have made you successful warriors on the battlefront or on the football field. If your life is a bit messed up and your thinking is confused, don't forget to draw close to the bishop of your ward, whom the Lord has named as a father to his people. Make him your confidant and be guided by his counsel. Make yourself a useful member of your quorum or your group. Be willing to make additional sacrifices, if necessary, for the Church and for the welfare of others. Remember the truth of that fundamental teaching "that a religion that does not require the sacrifice of all things never has power sufficient to produce the faith necessary unto life and salvation." (Sixth Lecture on Faith, verse 7.)

Our greatest concern about you, our youth today, is not for your temporal needs. From plans now formulated you probably will receive some compensations that will aid your material well-being. That great pioneer colonizer and builder, Brigham Young, gave this prophetic counsel and warning to your grandfathers: "Take courage, brethren. . . . Plow your land, and sow wheat, plant your potatoes. . . . It is our duty to preach the gospel, gather Israel, pay our tithing and build temples. The worst fear I have about this people is that they will get rich in this country, forget God and his people, wax fat, and kick themselves out of the Church and go to hell. This people will stand mobbing, robbing, poverty and all manner of persecution and be true. But my greatest fear is that they cannot stand wealth." Many years of experience have proved that statement to be a prophecy that has been fulfilled.

May you who stand on the threshold of new opportunity accept the challenge of today's problems with a faith and courage worthy of your pioneer ancestry and as their noble sons and daughters, be guided to your destiny.

"Except the Lord Build the House"

_____ 25 _____

Several years ago I walked among ruins near Mexico City that bore mute witness of a civilization of culture and architecture that has long since disappeared. Some years before that I rode along the ancient irrigation canal systems in the vicinity of Mesa, Arizona, where a forgotten people of ages past performed a magnificent engineering feat in diverting the waters of the great Salt River to provide the life blood for that fertile land. Throughout Central and South America there are likewise silent witnesses in uncovered cities attesting to the existence of a superior civilization whose voices are now silent. What happened to the illustrious civilizations that have left these monuments of their culture? If the uncivilized Indian tribes found by early explorers are their descendants, why has there been such a decline and what caused their degradation? I would have you remember as well the ancient splendor of Rome and Greece and their contributions to the art and literature and laws of the western world, and recall again the history of the triumphs of such conquerors as Alexander and Cyrus the Great. Then I ask you also to seek the reason for the decay of these nations.

As we look back upon decades of war in which every nation in the world has been greatly affected, either directly or indirectly, it is well that we take stock of ourselves and see what lessons are to be learned from our terrible experiences.

Threats to Our Civilization

The greatest threats to our civilization today seem to be, first, from further war, with its increasing awfulness and devastating fury. Wars of the past seem just a prelude to the possible frightfulness of wars to come which "except those days should be shortened there should no flesh be saved." (Matthew 24:22.) We have seen the "vivid lightning flashes and the thunders" roar from the cannon's mouth. We have seen the "moon turned into blood and the stars fall from heaven," so it must have seemed, as nightly bombing excursions have rained hideous nocturnal destruction upon defenseless women and children in war-ridden countries. The tracer bullets and flares with anti-aircraft accompaniment have turned the nights into ghastly nightmares, when even bomb shelters proved pitifully inadequate to stay the physical torture, to say nothing of the mental hazards that have destroyed the normal sensibilities of hundreds of thousands.

The second threat we are faced with is the challenge of erasing the spectre of unemployment that seems to increase with greater industrial developments. But perhaps the most threatening of all is that imperceptible, insidious movement which seeks for a new order in our form of government with the inference that democracy has failed to meet the problems of our changing world.

With these sobering contemplations, it is well that we pause and ask ourselves these questions: Is our new power by force of arms really a culmination, or as someone has said "a prelude to decline"? Is our great nation to go the way of all other great civilizations which have attained similar heights?

At the conclusion of England's celebration of her most glorious era of prosperity and worldly attainments, her great poet-philosopher wrote:

> The tumult and the shouting dies—
>   The Captains and the Kings depart—
> Still stands Thine ancient sacrifice,
>   An humble and contrite heart.

Far-called, our navies melt away—
    On dune and headland sinks the fire—
Lo, all our pomp of yesterday
    Is one with Nineveh and Tyre!
Judge of the Nations, spare us yet,
    Lest we forget—lest we forget!
                    —Rudyard Kipling.

What is that which we must never forget? We must not forget that the message which heralded the coming of the Christ was "Peace and Good Will." The difference between peace through "Good Will" and peace through a security that comes by force is just the difference between God's plan for peace and man's. As I write to you now, I have two pictures before me. They are both labeled "Victory." One shows the victorious conqueror standing with drawn sword. His fallen foes are crushed and bleeding all about him. Destruction and terrible carnage are to be seen on every side. The other is the famous painting showing Jesus sitting at the seaside with old Zebedee and his two sons, James and John, teaching them the precious truths of the gospel. His one thought is how he can make the old man see the truth that is so vital to his own soul. He puts one hand on the old man's wrist, so that the learner may feel that in spite of his slowness of mind, he never once has lost his Teacher's kind regard. The first picture is man's way to victory by brute force. It can be at best only temporary and leaves in its wake smoldering fires of hatred and suspicion that burst into raging fires of war and bloodshed when and if the vanquished come again to strength and power, or when the conquerors, drunken with lust for power, contest with each other over the spoils. The second is the Lord's way to victory over men's souls. It is the only way to a permanent peace. It is the way of true representatives of Jesus Christ in the Church today.

World peace-planners will fail now as they have done in the past if they forget these inspired words written in

the burnished gold of pure truth: "The earth is the Lord's
and the fulness thereof, the world and they that dwell
therein." (Psalms 24:1.) "Except the Lord build the house,
they labor in vain that build it; except the Lord keep the
city, the watchman waketh but in vain." (Psalms 127:1.)

That was the burden of the message contained in the
prophetic utterance of a leader among the people of
ancient America concerning those who would inhabit this
promised land. These are the words of that prophecy:

"And this land shall be a land of liberty . . . and
there shall be no kings upon the land. . . . And I will
fortify this land against all other nations. And he that
fighteth against Zion shall perish, saith God. For he that
raiseth up a king against me shall perish, for I, the Lord,
the king of heaven, will be their king, and I will be a
light unto them forever, that hear my words." (2 Nephi
10:11-14.) But as with all of the Lord's promised blessings,
those promises of safety and security are predicated
upon obedience to divine law. This nation shall be free
from bondage, and from captivity, and from all other nations
under heaven, "if they will but serve the God of the land,
who is Jesus Christ." (Ether 2:12.)

To those of you who are striving to serve the God of
this land and thus realize the promised blessings of
national security, and yet who observe the flood of wickedness among the millions of this country who blaspheme
the name of Jesus Christ rather than serve him, the Lord
gives this comfort:

"Therefore, verily, thus saith the Lord, let Zion
rejoice, for this is Zion—the Pure in Heart; therefore, let
Zion rejoice, while all the wicked shall mourn. . . . The
Lord's scourge shall pass over by night and by day, and
the report thereof shall vex all people; yea, it shall not
be stayed until the Lord come. . . . Nevertheless, Zion
shall escape if she observe to do all things whatsoever I
have commanded her. But if she observe not to do whatsoever I have commanded her, I will visit her according
to all her works, with sore affliction, with pestilence,

with plague, with sword, with vengeance, with devouring fire." (Doc. and Cov. 97:21-26.)

Peace is that state or condition where conflict is absent. You who strive to "overcome the world" as did the Master can have an unsurpassed peace within yourselves, "not as the world giveth," but as the Lord alone can give. A community of such as you, who are of the pure in heart, who form membership in God's earthly kingdom, can institute principles of peace and liberty that will, by the aid of divine power, influence the state and the nation to build on the only secure foundation for world peace.

Youth must never forget that this the government of the United States was established "According to the laws and constitution of the people, which (God) has suffered to be established. . . . That every man may act in doctrine and principle . . . according to the moral agency which (God) has given unto him, that every man may be accountable for his own sins in the day of judgment. Therefore, it is not right that any man should be in bondage one to another." It was to accomplish this lofty purpose basic to all liberty that God "established the Constitution of this land by the hands of wise men whom (he) raised up unto this very purpose." (Doc. and Cov. 101:77-80.) Contained within the principles of that great heaven-inspired document is the message of this Church to the world in this fateful hour. Except the spirit of the Gospel of Jesus Christ and principles contained within the Constitution of the United States are inherent in world plans now being formulated, they are but building on sand and the Lord is not in that building.

It was a president of a great American university who said recently: "If we are to have world civilization, we must get the world to accept an ideal, to pursue it deliberately, and to pursue it as common to the whole world community." (President Robert Hutchins, University of Chicago.) Where is that ideal which the world must pursue in setting up a world community? That ideal was written more than nineteen centuries ago by the Prince of Peace in these words: "Thou shalt love the Lord thy God with all thy heart, and with all thy soul, and with all thy mind. This is the first and great commandment. And the second is like unto it, Thou shalt love thy neighbour as thyself. On these two commandments hang all the law and the prophets." (Matthew 22:37-40.)

But now I ask you, the youth of our land, what is that liberty about which we sing in our national anthem? It lies in the hearts of men and women. It is not the arrogance of the unbridled will and the freedom to do as one pleases. To follow such a course would be to deny yourselves of liberty and would lead to its overthrow among you. A society in which men recognize no check upon their freedom soon becomes a society where freedom is in possession of only a few who lust for power and domination. It was Abraham Lincoln who with uncanny foresight warned this nation against the logical results that could come from growing lawlessness where Caesars and Napoleons could be born to dictatorships within a democracy. Then as though he foresaw the probability of such an emergency, he points out our responsibilities in these solemn words: "And when such an one does (spring up among us), it will require the people to be united with each other, attached to the government and the laws, and generally intelligent, successfully to frustrate his design." (*Abraham Lincoln, Man of God*, page 74.)

May we fervently hope that the youth of today, as the statesmen and lawmakers of tomorrow, will safeguard these priceless liberties by the preservation of those fundamentals that are founded on the rock-bottom truths of obedience and sacrifice.

Fortifying One's Self for the Future

26

Thus far in this book I have tried to lead you to see and understand how the restored principles, powers and ordinances of our glorious gospel dispensation may be applied to the lives of the youth of today, both to those of you who have membership in the Church and to those of you who are not members of the Church but who are honestly seeking the truth. The priesthood of the Son of God or the power given to men to act in the name of the Lord in matters that pertain to the salvation of the souls of men is again among us. As one of those bearing that holy priesthood and called to be a special witness of the work of salvation in your day, I have written directly to you and about yourselves instead of writing to you about others. I have tried to impress upon you the part the Church must play in your lives if you would have the Lord as a partner in building for your eternal home. I have pointed out the awfulness of sin; that the wages of sin is death and that through the atonement of the Lord Jesus Christ, you who have sinned may by true repentance find forgiveness and the way to joy in this life and a fulness in the life to come. Your attention has been called to the teachings of the gospel of Jesus Christ as they apply to your courtship and marriage, to your temporal affairs and to your education. In our discussions we have found that way to solace and comfort in times of deep sorrow; how men must live if they would find everlasting peace, and how you and I must prepare ourselves that we might have the companionship of the Spirit of the

Lord and gain a living testimony of the reality of the existence of God and His Son Jesus Christ.

A Time of Momentous Happenings

You are standing today on the threshold of great opportunities. That is a cliche you will hear said more than once. Mark Twain said of his lovely 25 year old daughter, who died suddenly while he was in Europe on a lecture tour: "Susan died at the best time of life. She had lived her golden years, age 25. But after that there come the risks, the responsibilities, and the inevitable tragedies of life." You are now in the golden years of your life. To speak of those things sounds a long, long way off, but whether you like it or not, you are standing on the threshold of the things of life that will bring you risks and responsibilities and the inevitable tragedies of life.

Recently I met a young man, in a circumstance where I was the victim and he was the master, in a hospital bed where he was preparing me for an operation. "Could I ask you some questions?" he said. "I am very much worried about myself because in our ward we have had a couple in whom I had great confidence, who have recently been excommunicated from the Church because they have been living in sin, and it has frightened me and I want to know if you can tell me, how can I be fortified against the possibility of making a similar mistake? Where is that safety?"

As you observe the frightening events even on college campuses, you could be caught up in the maelstrom of mob psychology. Where is there safety? As I thought of his question I remembered some things which the Master said: "And fear not them which kill the body, but are not able to kill the soul: But rather fear him which is able to destroy both soul and body in hell." (Matthew, 10:28.)

Perhaps you may have read what the Apostle Paul said: "For we wrestle not against flesh and blood, but against principalities, against powers, against the rulers of the darkness of this world, against spiritual wickedness in high places." (Ephesians 6:12.)

The Apostle Paul put that statement in a meaningful way when he said: "For the good that I would I do not: but the evil which I would not, that I do." (Romans 7:19.)

"But I see another law in my members, warring against the law of my mind, and bringing me into captivity to the law of sin which is in my members." (Romans 7:23.)

You see those about you, some in important places, in the community or in the Church, who may have been called to account for misdeeds heretofore unsuspected, perhaps to be arrested before the law or to be excommunicated. Perhaps you have said, "If it could happen to him, it could happen to me. Can you tell me how I can avoid falling into sin or transgression?" So potent are the insidious forces of evil mastered by the ruler of darkness of that world, that it might well be said, as someone has put it, "Man is prone to do evil as sparks are to fly upward."

President Heber J. Grant used to tell us that in the later years of his administration he began to ponder if there was some outstanding thing the Lord would have him do. So he prayed earnestly about it and sought to have the answer. As he prayed, the startling answer as to the greatest thing that he could do was to teach this people to *keep the commandments!* And this is the most important thing for you to do—to keep the Lord's commandments.

The question, "What may I do to be safe?" recalls the Master's admonition and warning to the Nephites as he ministered among them. It also brings to mind that he has said to our generation in this day of conflict and frustration:

For I am no respecter of persons, and will that all men shall know that the day speedily cometh; the hour is not yet, but is nigh at hand, when peace shall be taken from the earth, and the devil shall have power over his own dominion." (D&C 1:35.)

That was said over 140 years ago. Today you are witnessing the fulfillment. Today is the day when the devil has power over his own dominion. But the promise of the Lord was, ". . . also the Lord shall have power over his saints and shall reign in their midst, and shall come down in judgment upon Idumea or the world." The Master said, "behold and lo, I am with you, but you will not see me." He could be near to every one of us in the midst of all the maelstrom of difficulties in which we find ourselves, if we keep His commandments.

The great writer James Russell Lowell put that in a great verse when he said:

> Truth forever on the scaffold,
> Wrong forever on the throne.
> Yet that scaffold sways the future
> And behind the dim unknown
> Standeth God within the shadows
> Keeping watch above his own.

How can you draw close to the Lord? The Master to the Nephites said: "Therefore blessed are ye if ye shall keep my commandments which the Father hath commanded that I should give you. Verily, verily, I say unto you, ye must watch and pray always, lest ye be tempted by the devil, and ye be led away captive by him." (3 Nephi 18:14-15.) We also read in The Doctrine and Covenants: "I, the Lord, am bound when ye do what I say; but when ye do not what I say, ye have no promise." (D&C 82:10.)

Moroni said it in a different way when he stated we should dispute not because ye see not, for we receive no witness until after the trial of our faith. Translated into plain English it means then: Watch and pray, be on guard always, lest Satan tempt you and you be led captive by him. Again the Master put it a little more plainly and repeating, "Behold, verily, verily, I say unto you, ye must watch and pray always lest ye enter into temptation; for Satan desireth to have you, that he may sift you as wheat. Therefore ye must always pray unto the Father in my name; And whatsoever ye shall ask the Father in my name, which is right (now that means, in other scriptures, which is expedient or what's good for you) believing that ye shall receive, behold it shall be given unto you." (3 Nephi 18:18-20.)

One man commented: "I can't get this through my wife's mind that the Lord always answers her prayers, even when he says 'No' he's answered her prayers." The Lord always answers your prayers—not always the way you would like to have him answer. But he says: "Pray in your families unto the Father, always in my name, that your wives and children may be blessed." He's always alert to sift you as wheat. In an early revelation the Lord said: "For behold the field is white already to harvest; and lo, he that thrusteth in his sickle with his might, the same layeth up in store that he perisheth not, but bringeth salvation to his soul." (D&C 4:4.)

The world is the field, the harvesters are the disciples of the Lord who keep his commandments and in interpretation of that parable the Lord said: "Therefore, let the wheat and tares grow together until the harvest is fully ripe; then ye shall first gather out the wheat from among the tares, and after the gathering of the wheat, behold and lo, the tares are bound in bundles, and the field remaineth to be burned." (D&C 86:7.) Pray in your families, the Lord has said, that your children may be blessed.

You sons and daughters, pray before you go out on a date—pray that you may have a good time and conduct yourselves according to Church standards that the Lord will help you to come home safely. Family prayer is a safeguard to the individual members of the family as they leave from the home each day and go out into the uncertainties of the world. The Master prayed: "I pray not that thou shouldest take them [the disciples] out of the world, but that thou shouldest keep them from the evil." (John 17:15.)

And that is the prayer we offer for you. We don't pray that you may be withdrawn into a "Shangrila" away from the evils of the world, because you are to be a leaven wherever you are, to bring about righteousness, but we are pleading with the Lord with all our might that while you are in the world, you may be kept from evil.

Some years ago I was in Japan visiting the servicemen

on the northern island of Hokkaido. A young man was called to speak in one of the services. He was a tall, handsome, curly haired young man and took the text that I have just quoted from the Master's prayer, "I pray that thou wilt keep us from evil." He delivered a great sermon on the subject of chastity. He closed by saying, "Rather than lose my virtue I would rather die and have my body sent home in a pine box and my dog tags follow after." Then he bore his testimony and as he started to walk away from the pulpit he staggered and fell over the pulpit in a dead faint. As we lifted him off the pulpit and worked over him, the mission president turned to me and said, "I wonder if he has a bad heart?" I said, "I think I detected something in that young man while he was speaking. There seemed to be something contending inside him against what he was saying." Later I said to him, "Young man, you've made a great impression upon us when you said that rather than lose your virtue you would rather die and have your body sent home in a pine box and your dog tags follow after. But son, the devil heard you just as well as we heard you, and if I don't miss my guess, you may almost have to give your life in order to keep yourself morally clean."

I learned that just before we came he had been tempted to go into the wicked city near one of the great air bases in the northern part of Hokkaido. Filthy women were plying their trade trying to trap these young men into their filthy clutches. He had succumbed and had made a date with one of those girls but his friends found it out and wouldn't let him go. They took him down to break the date and had kept him busy visiting the inactive boys in the camp until we came there to visit and then they assigned him to talk on the subject of chastity—a very excellent way to teach I submit.

Years later we were at the dedication of the Los Angeles Temple. I met again that young man from Camp Crawford in Hokkaido. He threw his arms around me as he said, "Just think, Brother Lee, I have been called to be a worker in the Los Angeles Temple." There was a lump in my throat—years before I had seen him over there at the crossroads, when in an unguarded moment he might have taken a path that would have led him far away from that which he was now qualified to do. The last time I saw him he was coming up the aisle with a lovely girl holding onto his arm and in his arms there was a bundle of loveliness—a beautiful new babe. Pride and joy shown in the faces of that young father and mother—thanksgiving no doubt—that pleased God. In the baby's veins there was no tainted blood because through the graces and mercies of good friends and the fact that a mother was praying for him, and that he had been taught to keep the commandments, he had now escaped the clutches of the power of evil.

The Master said: "Therefore hold up your light that it may shine unto the world." Then he said: "Behold I am the light which ye shall hold up—that which ye have seen me do. Behold ye see that I have prayed unto the Father, and ye all have witnessed." (3 Nephi 18:24.)

In that saying he set a standard for all who need direction—his light. The Apostle John wrote that the Savior was the true light "which lighteth every man that cometh into the world." (John 1:9.) He was a man sent from God. He was as a light that ". . . shineth in darkness; and the darkness comprehendeth it not." (John 1:5.) That's the light that you have. Every one of us has been born with that light, the light of Christ, that lights all of us who come into the world and it never ceases to strive with us, as long as we are keeping the commandments of God, to warn us and to guide us. You may call it conscience—you may call it the warning of the flesh. When you encounter obscene or filthy things may you be preserved never to lose the righteous blush of shame when you are confronted with these things.

A wise mother said to her son, "Never measure yourself by someone else's yardstick." But someone else said, "If you live long enough in the presence of an ideal you will grow to be like him." President McKay lifted this ideal to a high standard when he said, "We become what we love. Joseph Smith loved the Savior and became like him." Joseph Smith said, "I want to become as a smooth shaft in the quiver of the Almighty. My voice is always for peace."

We read a story a few years ago of a near serious accident of a young pilot who was making his first solo flight. He was up over the field and because of high tension he went momentarily blind. He shouted to the man in the control tower, "I've gone blind." Now was a time for a cool head and a steady voice. "Listen carefully—follow my direction and I will guide you down." He told him to reach out and which controls he should manipulate on the board—to circle the field and lose altitude and finally he was safely down. The real hero of that story was not the pilot. The real hero was the control operator. And so it is with the teacher—the parent—the one who steadies those about to go astray.

Sometimes as I go into the mission field I find a young man who says to me, "I don't have a testimony." My reply, "My boy, let me bear you my testimony, and for the time being suppose you cling to my testimony until you develop one for yourself." That is what I am saying to you young people today. Maybe you haven't developed to maturity your testimony. To give you that strength and resistance and until you develop one for yourself, then hold on to those of ours until you can develop one for yourselves. A young pilot we had installed as a counselor in a Boston stake presidency commented, "The most dangerous traffic guide in all the world is the lighthouse when the light's gone out, or a radar or control tower which fails to function."

The most dangerous leader in all the world or the most dangerous teacher is the leader that doesn't lead properly or the teacher that betrays his trust. If you don't follow that light which lights every person that comes into the world of which I have spoken, you will be led into temptation. I had this last admonition brought forcibly home to me a short while ago when a man in high station in the Church had fallen from his place and was excommunicated. The father of some children in the school where I was the principal implored, "Brother Lee, you won't fail will you? You won't fall like that." And I asked, "Why?" "Because if you do you might take some of my children out of the Church because of the respect they have for you." Many men fail and because they fail others have fallen because their ideal fell, but because men fail you must set your ideal higher than men, "Be ye therefore perfect, even as your Father which is in heaven is perfect." (Matthew 5:48.)

Now let me give you a few illustrations from the hearts of those who yearn for the strengthening hand of one who seeks earnestly to hold up the light of the Master for others to see. I was humbled by a letter I received from a new convert in Ohio, where I had just attended a stake conference. This was the letter:

"As you spoke an idea kept repeating itself in my mind—how life as a member of The Church of Jesus Christ of Latter-day Saints is like crossing a swinging bridge suspended between the points of birth by baptism and death into eternal life over the turbulent stream of worldliness and sin. As one starts onto the bridge, the nearness to baptism lends security and faith but as one becomes aware of the stream below and the vast expanse to be crossed, the sense of security gives way to spasmodic twinges of doubt and fear causing one to lose the rhythm of prayer, faith, love and work which makes one's progress smooth. The mists of doubt and apathy arise and corrode one's heart and mind impeding one's progress and restricting one's response to the magnetic force of love which streams across the bridge. It is then one breaks step and falls to one's knees and hangs on until the buffeting breaks loose the corrosion and the force of love restores faith and direction to the crossing.

"This is where the visits of the general authorities come in. It is as though the force of love calling us be-

comes vocal and adds impetus to our response to it—as a
voice calling us from farther along the bridge saying, 'Have
faith—this is the way for I can see ahead.' This is what
your visit did for many of us and we love you for this. It
restored our confidence in the goal by giving us guidance
and enabling us to feel the Divine Spirit which flowed
from our Heavenly Father through you. Thank you, and
God bless you and our Prophet (meaning President David
O. McKay) whom I have never met, (and I want you to get
this point) but have learned to know and love more dearly
because of you."

She might well have meant in the words that I have
quoted from the Master, "Because of your word of light
which you held up here I have come to love the Master
more because of you."

It doesn't always take words for people to be impressed. I had a letter from a sister up in Oregon some
years ago, who told of her husband who had been struggling to overcome the tobacco habit. As he sat in that conference session something happened to him. A feeling came
over him as if by some unseen contact and he said he
thought if he just tried once more he could stop the tobacco habit. Somehow the strength that was gained from that
unseen power gave him the strength to stop. Yes there is
a power beyond the sight of man that heals not only sick
bodies but sick souls.

I met a young man in Tokyo where we were holding
a servicemen's conference. He had his right arm in the
sling and as he was introduced he put out his left hand to
acknowledge the introduction: "I am not a member of the
Church" he said, "but I understand you are going to be
down in Manila in another few weeks and we are there
with the Seventh Fleet and I hope to be able to tell you
when you get there that I am now a member of the
Church." I had almost forgotten the incident until as we
held a conference out at Clark Field in Manila I spotted
the same man whom I had met in Tokyo. In an interview
we had with him a little later he said, "You noticed when

we met in Tokyo I had my arm in a sling. It was paining me terribly all through that service, but after we had shaken hands on the stand the throbbing pain seemed to stop and I took my arm out of the sling and began to flex it and there was no more pain. I went back to the ship, never needed any treatment, the infection seemed to have gone, and I sensed the fact that I had been in the presence of a power that had taken away the pain of my body, healed a sick body."

A girl cries out to some of the agonizing experiences contrary to these stories which I have told you, saying, "Why didn't I have the strength to resist temptation? How can I prevent falling again into sin?" I had written her but she expressed disappointment in what I had said. Then she said, "Now I know that knowing the truth does not give one the capacity to act in accordance with it. I think perhaps that loving the truth is the only thing that could give one this capacity. The scripture does not say if ye know me you will keep my commandments, but it says If you love me you will keep them. But I guess I have never loved him or loved the Church or loved the truth and it seems to me that in all things in life it is love not knowledge that directs our actions. How do you learn to love our Heavenly Father—to love the Church—the truth?"

Then she answers her own query, "I decided that you do it by giving yourself to it completely. Perhaps a mother does not give herself to her child because she loves it but she loves it because she gives herself to it." Then she added something that calls me back to King Benjamin's admonition.

These were the concluding words of her letter; "Besides I am sure half my problem stems with my over-concern about myself. (Listen to that you young people.) Perhaps this is one of the great evils which can come from psychology—to be constantly trying to analyze oneself or understand oneself or figure out oneself. Nothing could be further from the teachings of Christ." Perhaps the devil's workshop, but she says, "I think it ought to read, 'Idle mind or a mind preoccupied with self is the devil's workshop.' I think this has been my problem so I will try consciously to think of others when I begin to brood on my self and I guess when one can do that half the battle for goodness and happiness is won, perhaps even all the battle. This is the most reasonable plan that I can outline for myself at this time. Does it sound good or like the right one?"

Here again is this admonition, ". . . when ye are in the service of your fellow beings ye are only in the service of your God." (Mosiah 2:17.) But Patriarch Lehi said something else that is equally meaningful. "Think of your brethren like unto yourselves, and be familiar with all and free with your substance, that they may be rich like unto you." (Jacob 2:17.)

There's the secret of your happiness in life when you analyze it, to learn to live outside yourself in love.

I spoke at the Brigham Young University some years ago. A girl who was in the audience later wrote to me. She was filled with deep feelings of depression and disbelief in all things. It became so great that she stopped praying, she stopped going to church, she met with the wrong people and finally began to break the Word of Wisdom. She returned home for the summer and her father, the bishop of the ward and whom she dearly loved, "told me he was proud of me. The next week I received a letter saying I could not return to the BYU until I improved my grades. My world completely fell apart. I had not only let myself down but also my wonderful parents. It seemed after I received that letter things really fell down around me. I lost my job, I was unable to find another, met a non-member of the Church and became serious over him and I fought to keep my virtue. Everything I put my hand to seemed to fail. When I came back to school this semester my outlook on life was pretty low. The only reason I came back was to prove to a few important people that I wasn't stupid and did not need a psychiatrist. Upon hearing your talk my outlook changed. My testimony is strengthening, I am finding great consolation from prayer and have a true desire to repent of the wrongs I have done."

Her words portray a perfect description of the path which leads downward. This brings to mind that if you go down around the point of the mountain south of Salt Lake City, just before you go into Utah valley, you will see off to the right a highway sign "Utah Highway 187" and the legend reads, "The shortest highway in the State of Utah." Take that highway some time. It is only about a mile, curved, beautifully engineered as it winds down around the point of the mountain, but at the end of that mile you come to the gates of the Utah State Penitentiary. The shortest highway in the State of Utah.

So here was a girl who was a failure at school with depression, disbelief, who was breaking the Word of Wisdom, no church, wrong company, fighting to keep her virtue or from losing it, having lost her job, and so it goes. The greatest responsibility of Church members is to become truly converted, but more important, to stay converted. Here is the success story of the climb upward. She heard the gospel of Jesus Christ and her outlook changed. She got consolation in prayers, she repented of her wrongdoing, she now set her goals high, and she resolved anew, that "if I study hard and keep the commandments, I will succeed, and from now on the power of Satan no longer has any control over me."

A young man came into my office who was preparing to go on a mission. The next day he was to go to the temple for the first time. With a troubled look on his face, he said, "I made a mistake some years ago and I confessed it to my bishop, my stake president, and with an understanding of that and feeling that I was truly repentant they let me go on this mission. But somehow I can't go to the temple tomorrow until I have the assurance that the Lord has forgiven me of my sin. How can I know that I am forgiven?" That was an interesting question and searching for the answer I found it in another of King Benjamin's statements. He had been preaching with power to a group of people who were not converted, and we read: "And they had viewed themselves in their own carnal state, even less than the dust of the earth. And they all cried aloud with one vóice, saying: Oh have mercy, and apply the atoning blood of Christ that we may receive—forgiveness of our sins, and our hearts may be purified; for we believe in Jesus Christ, the son of God, who created heaven and earth, and all things; who shall come down among the children of men. And it came to pass that after they had spoken these words the Spirit of the Lord came upon them, and they were filled with joy, having received a remission of their sins, and having *peace of conscience,* because of the exceeding faith which they had in Jesus Christ who should come, according to the words which King Benjamin had spoken unto them." (Mosiah 4:2-3.)

I suppose the greatest expectation of any of you is to stand one day in the presence of the Lord. How can you prepare yourself for that day? In one great, meaningful statement, the Lord said this: "And if your eye be single to my glory, your whole bodies shall be filled with light, and there shall be no darkness in you; and that body which is filled with light comprehendeth all things. Therefore, sanctify yourselves that your minds become single to God, and the days will come that you shall see him; for he will unveil his face unto you, and it shall be in his own time, and in his own way, and according to his own will." (D&C 88:67-68.)

How are you sanctified to be made holy to live in the presence of the Lord? The Lord said it, ". . . verily I say unto you, that which is governed by law is also preserved by law and perfected and sanctified by the same." (D&C 88:34.) If there was no law given, as Alma said to his son Corianton, men would not be afraid to sin. (See alma 42: 20.) The law was given to make us afraid to sin. Well here is the formula by which we can sanctify ourselves. The Lord said, "It shall come to pass that every soul who forsaketh his sins and cometh unto me and calleth on my

name, and obeyeth my voice, and keepeth my commandments, shall see my face and know that I am." (D&C 93:1.)
There you are, you youth of Zion. If you will forsake your
sins, come unto him, call on his name, obey his voice and
keep his commandments, the promise is you will see his
face and you will know that he is. Peter also said, "And
beside this, giving all diligence, add to your faith virtue;
and to virtue knowledge; and to knowledge temperance;
and to temperance patience; and to patience godliness;
and to godliness brotherly kindness; and to brotherly kindness charity. For if these things be in you, and abound,
they make you that ye shall neither be barren nor unfruitful in the knowledge of our Lord Jesus Christ." (2 Peter
1:5-8.)

The message of the King of England just as the war
was being declared was a meaningful one when he said,
"Give me a light that I may tread safely into the unknown.
The man at the gate replied: Go out into the darkness
and put your hand in the hand of God: That will be better than a light and safer than the known way." And as
the Apostle Paul put it, "But as it is written, Eye hath not
seen, nor ear heard, neither have entered into the heart of
man, the things which God hath prepared for them that
love him." (I Cor. 2:9.)

"Beautiful roses don't grow on bushes unless the roots
of the parent bush have been planted in rich fertile soil,
nourished and cultivated, watered and pruned and cared
for. Just so beautiful flowers of virtue, sobriety, honesty,
and integrity are not found in an individual unless his feet
have been planted on a firm testimony of the Divine Mission of the Lord Jesus Christ." Remember that and you will
be on the way to safety.

You and I to be worthy of our places in God's kingdom must be defenders of the faith. As someone has written, "If you have no enemies, alas, my friend, the boast
is poor. He who has mingled in the fray of duty that the
brave endure, must have made foes. If you have none,
small is the work you have done. If you have hit no traitor

on the head, if you have dashed no cups from purged lips, if you have never turned a wrong to right, you have been a coward in the fight."

How I wish I could impress you who must daily walk out on the swaying bridge of worldliness and sin which flows as a turbulent stream below you, how I wish that when you have twinges of doubt and fear that cause you to lose the rhythm of prayer and faith and love, may you hear my voice as one calling to you from further along on life's bridge, "Have faith—this is the way—for I can see further ahead than you." I would fervently pray that you could feel the love flowing from my soul to yours, and know of my deep compassion toward each of you as you face your problems of the day. The time is here when every one of you must stand on your own feet. The time is here when no man and woman will endure on borrowed light. Each will have to be guided by the light within himself. If you do not have it, you will not stand.

Moreover, may the Lord bless you and clothe each of you with the armor of righteousness, that you might be able to withstand and stand steadfast through whatever trials may be yours in the days that lie ahead.

The Day in which We Live

27

(Remarks by President Harold B. Lee, given on Friday, October 6, 1972, as he was sustained President of the Church in solemn assembly.)

Today, at the greatest moment of my life, I find myself without words to express my deep and innermost feelings. What I may say, therefore, must be actuated by the Spirit of the Lord, that you, my beloved Saints of the Most High God, may feel the depths of my soul-searching on this momentous and historic occasion.

Order of the priesthood

As I have participated with you in this moving experience of a solemn assembly, there has been brought more forcibly than ever to my mind the significance of the great revelation of the Lord given to the Church in 1835. In this revelation the Lord gave specific instructions setting forth the order of the priesthood in the government of the church and kingdom of God.

In this revelation the Lord specified four requisites in the establishment of the First Presidency, or the presidency of the Melchizedek, or High, Priesthood of the Church, as the Lord speaks of it. (D&C 107:22.)

First, it was requisite that there be three presiding high priests.

Second, they were to be chosen by the body (which

has been construed to be the Quorum of the Twelve Apostles).

Third, they must be appointed and ordained by the same body—the Quorum of the Twelve.

Fourth, they must be upheld by the confidence, faith, and prayers of the Church.

All of these steps were taken in order that the quorum of the First Presidency could be formed to preside over the Church.

Those first steps were taken by action of the Twelve and they were attended to in a sacred meeting convened in the temple on July 7, 1972, where the First Presidency were named.

Upheld by membership

Today, as never before, have I more fully realized the importance of that last requirement: that this presidency, in the Lord's language, must be upheld by the confidence, the faith, and the prayers of the Church—which means, of course, the entire membership of the Church.

We witnessed a short while ago the outpouring of love and fellowship that was in evidence in the great regional conference of our wonderful Lamanite Saints from Central America and Mexico, assembled in Mexico City in August. Over 16,000 Saints were gathered together in a great auditorium, where they sustained their General Authorities.

Bonds of brotherhood

Again, in the mighty demonstration of this solemn assembly, I am moved with emotions beyond expression as I have felt the true love and bonds of brotherhood. There has been here an overwhelming spiritual endowment, attesting, no doubt, that in all likelihood we are in the presence of personages, seen and unseen, who are in attendance. Who knows but that even our Lord and Master would be near us on such an occasion as this; for we, and the world, must never forget that this is his church, and under his almighty direction we are to serve! Indeed, I would remind you what he declared in a similar conference of Saints in Fayette, New York, and undoubtedly would remind us again today. The Lord said: "Behold, verily, verily, I say unto you that mine eyes are upon you. I am in your midst and ye cannot see me." (D&C 38:7.)

Presidents of the Church

On the sacred occasion three months ago when I began to sense the magnitude of the overwhelming responsibility which I must now assume, I went to the holy temple. There, in prayerful meditation, I looked upon the paintings of those men of God—true, pure men, God's noblemen—who had preceded me in a similar calling.

A few days ago in the early morning hours, in my private study at home and all alone with my thoughts, I read the tributes paid to each of the Presidents by those who had been most closely associated with each of them.

Joseph Smith was the one whom the Lord raised up from boyhood and endowed with divine authority and taught the things necessary for him to know and to obtain the priesthood and to lay the foundation for God's kingdom in these latter days.

There was President Brigham Young, who was foreordained before this world was, for his divine calling to lead the persecuted Saints in fleeing from the wrath that threatened the Saints in those early gathering places in Missouri and Illinois and to pioneer the building of an inland commonwealth in the tops of these majestic mountains, to fulfill God's purposes.

To look upon the features of President John Taylor was to gain a realization that here was one, as President Joseph F. Smith spoke of him, "One of the purest men I ever knew. . . ."

As I saw the sainted face of President Wilford Woodruff, I was aware that here was a man like Nathanael of old, in whom there was no guile, and susceptible to the impressions of the Spirit of the Lord, by whose light he seemed to almost always walk "not knowing beforehand the thing he was to do."

While President Lorenzo Snow had but a brief administration, he had a special mission to establish his people on a more solid temporal foundation by the determined application of the law of sacrifice, to relieve the great burdens placed upon the Church because of mistakes and errors which had unwittingly crept in.

When I want to seek for a more clear definition of doctrinal subjects, I have usually turned to the writings and sermons of President Joseph F. Smith. As I looked upon his noble stature, I thought of the nine-year-old boy helping his widowed mother across the plains and the 15-year-old missionary on the slopes of Haleakala on the isle of Maui being strengthened by a heavenly vision with his uncle, Joseph Smith. It was he who presided during the stormy days when an antagonistic press maligned the Church, but his was the steady arm by the Lord's appointment to carry off the Church triumphantly.

I suppose I never drew closer to the meaning of a divine calling than when President Heber J. Grant placed his hands upon my shoulders and, with a deep feeling akin to mine, announced my calling to be an apostle of the Lord Jesus Christ. As his picture looked down upon me, there came again to my mind the prophetic words of his inspired blessing when I was ordained in the holy temple under his hands.

President George Albert Smith was a disciple of friendship and love. He was indeed a friend to everyone. My gaze at his likeness seemed to give me a warmth of that radiance which made every man his friend.

Tall and impressive was President David O. McKay, as he now looked at me with those piercing eyes, which always seemed to search my very soul. Never was I privileged to be in his presence but that I felt for a brief moment, as I had done on so many occasions, that I was a better man for having been in his company.

To him who sought no earthly honors, but whose whole soul delighted in the things of the spirit, President Joseph Fielding Smith was there with his smiling face, my beloved prophet-leader who made no compromise with truth. As "the finger of God touched him and he slept," he seemed in that brief moment to be passing to me, as it were, a sceptre of righteousness as though to say to me, "Go thou and do likewise."

Soul-searching thoughts

Now I stood alone with my thoughts. Somehow the impressions that came to me were, simply, that the only true record that will ever be made of my service in my new calling will be the record that I may have written in the hearts and lives of those with whom I have served and labored, within and without the Church.

The day after this appointment, following the passing of our beloved President Smith, my attention was called to a paragraph from a sermon delivered in 1853 in a general conference by Elder Orson Hyde, then a member of the Twelve. This provoked some soul-searching in me also.

The subject of his address was "The Man to Lead God's People," and I quote briefly from his sermon: ". . . it is invariably the case," he said, "that when an individual is ordained and appointed to lead the people, he has passed through tribulations and trials, and has proven himself before God, and before His people, that he is worthy of the situation which he holds. . . . that when a person has not been tried, that has not proved himself before God, and before His people, and before the councils of the Most High, to be worthy, he is not going to step in and lead the Church and people of God. It has never been so, but from the beginning some one that understands the Spirit and counsel of the Almighty, that knows the Church, and is known of her, is the character that will lead the Church." (*Journal of Discourses*, vol. 1, p. 123.)

As I have known of the lives of those who have preceded me, I have been made aware that each seemed to have had his special mission for his day and time.

A polished shaft

Then, with searching introspection, I thought of myself

and my experiences of which Orson Hyde's appraisal had made reference. Then I recalled the words of the Prophet Joseph's characterization of himself, which seemed somewhat analogous to myself. He said:

"I am like a huge rough stone rolling down from a high mountain; and the only polishing I get is when some corner gets rubbed off by coming in contact with something else, striking with accelerated force against religious bigotry, priestcraft, lawyer-craft, doctor-craft, lying editors, suborned judges and jurors, and the authority of perjured executives, backed by mobs, blasphemers, licentious and corrupt men and women—all hell knocking off a corner here and a corner there. Thus will I become a smooth and polished shaft in the quiver of the Almighty. . . ." (*Teachings of the Prophet Joseph Smith*, p. 304.)

These thoughts now running through my mind begin to give greater meaning to some of the experiences in my life, things that have happened which have been difficult for me to understand. At times it seemed as though I too was like a rough stone rolling down from a high mountainside, being buffeted and polished, I suppose, by experiences, that I too might overcome and become a polished shaft in the quiver of the Almighty.

Maybe it was necessary that I too must learn obedience by the things that I might have suffered—to give me experiences that were for my good, to see if I could pass some of the various tests of mortality.

In the selection of my noble counselors, President N. Eldon Tanner and President Marion G. Romney, I learned that I was not alone with a rich measure of the gift of prophecy. They too had passed the tests, and before the Lord they had not been found wanting. How grateful I am for these noble men of the First Presidency and the Twelve and the other General Authorities.

The morning after my call came, as I knelt with my dear companion in prayer, my heart and soul seemed to reach out to the total membership of the Church with a special kind of fellowship and love which was like the opening of the windows of heaven, to give me a brief feeling of belonging to the more than three million members of the Church in all parts of the world.

Prayers of the saints

I repeat what I have said on other occasions, that I most fervently seek to be upheld by the confidence, faith, and prayers of all the faithful Saints everywhere, and I pledge to you that as you pray for me, I will earnestly try to so live that the Lord can answer your prayers through me.

In these last months, there seem to have been awakened in me new wellsprings of spiritual understanding also. I know full well the truth of what the Prophet Joseph told the early missionaries to Great Britain: "The nearer a person approaches the Lord, a greater power will be manifested by the adversary to prevent the accomplishment of His purposes." (Orson F. Whitney, *Life of Heber C. Kimball* [Bookcraft, 1967], p. 131.)

There is no shadow of doubt in my mind that these things are as certain today as in that day, but also I am certain that, as the Lord said, "No weapon that is formed against you shall prosper; And if any man lift his voice against you he shall be confounded in mine own due time." (D&C 71:9-10.)

Solemn witness

How grateful I am for your loyalty and your sustaining vote! I bear you solemn witness as to the divine mission of the Savior and the certainty as to his guiding hand in the affairs of his church today, as in all dispensations of time.

I know, with a testimony more powerful than sight, that as the Lord declared, "The keys of the kingdom of God are committed unto man on the earth [from the Prophet Joseph Smith through his successors down to the present], and from thence shall the gospel roll forth unto the ends of the earth, as the stone which is cut out of the mountain without hands shall roll forth, until it has filled the whole earth.

"Wherefore, may the kingdom of God go forth, that the kingdom of heaven may come. . . ." (D&C 65:2, 6.)

I bear that testimony with all the conviction of my soul and leave my blessing upon the membership of the Church and the pure in heart everywhere, in the name of the Lord Jesus Christ. Amen.

Strengthening The Home

28

These are challenging times. Around the world there are influences which would strike at the home, at the sacred relationships of husband and wife, of parents and their children. The same destructive influences face our unmarried adult members of the Church.

How fortunate we are in the midst of all this to have the teachings of our Lord and Savior, Jesus the Christ, the head of the Church. His words, and those of his prophets, are ours to help us strengthen our homes and bring more peace and happiness into them.

There is no other people on the face of the earth, whom I know anything about, who have the lofty concepts of marriage and the sacredness of the home as do the Latter-day Saints. In a revelation given in our day the Lord said:

> . . . marriage is ordained of God unto man.
>
> Wherefore, it is lawful that he should have one wife, and they twain shall one flesh, and all this that the earth might answer the end of its creation.

(D. & C. 49:15-16.)

There are, however, unmistakable evidences that the same dangers that are abroad in the world are now among us and are seeking to destroy this God-given institution, the home. It has been my privilege through the years to visit, as have the other General Authorities, in some of the finest homes of our people, and it is from those visits that I have gleaned some things that I should like to mention to you, suggestive of the elements that build for strength and happiness in the home.

If I were to name the first thing that impresses me always in these fine Latter-day Saint homes, I would say it was a love for and a desire for children.

A few years ago I read some statistics taken from the Census Bureau which indicated that out of 180,000 divorces for that given year, 57 percent were in homes where there were no children; 21.2 percent where there was only one child; and in families with five or more children, divorces were less than one percent. Certainly it is true that parental love and oneness are a safe and sure guarantee to the happiness of any home.

Sometime ago I was privileged to hear something about the influence that had come from one of these homes in a letter written by a lovely daughter who had just given birth to her first baby. In the early hours of the morning her baby had come, and late in the afternoon she was in a reflective mood. In this reflective mood she had written home to her family, telling about her impressions and feelings at the miracle of motherhood, and how she had been privileged to be a participant in this wonderful creation, Then she wrote this:

> I wonder that we women are not required to undergo even more than labor pains to bring these little ones from another world into this one. It seems so right that we through pain are forced to slip for a few minutes, at least, half-way into another sphere, to sort of bring our baby by the hand into this new world.

I am reminded of the remark of a young man to his sweetheart, and her reply, when he planned to postpone their marriage because of finances. He said to her somewhat facetiously: "I think probably all I can promise you is a sagebrush home in Idaho." She replied: "Well, that is fine, then if we ever get anything, it will belong to both of us and not just you."

I am thinking of that mother blessed with a family of girls who knelt each night and prayed to God that somewhere there would be a mother rearing some sons worthy to become the husbands of her daughters. Then, when the daughters married, in talking with the mothers of the sons, she found that those mothers had been praying ever since their boys were born that somewhere God would be preparing some girls worthy to become the wives of their sons.

I say to you, brethren and sisters, that such lofty concepts of home, family, and the responsibilities of home and family, are certain guarantees to a happy and successful home.

Sometime ago I visited a mother who has reared an excellent family. We talked about the things that had helped to keep her family in line. She said:

> Brother Lee, I made it my practice and rule, when my children came along that I was going to make as many contacts with my children in the home as I possibly could. I was always there when they went to school; I planned to give up everything else, if necessary, to be there when they came home; I was there when they had their parties and their friends in the home; and I always waited up after the evening parties in order to greet my children when they came home from dates, because I found that at such moments I was able to encourage a frankness between us, and it permitted me to enjoy their confidences that over the years builded a comradeship which kept them safe in times of difficulty.

What a blessing is such a wise mother! Such children, so taught, with whom mothers and fathers have made such comrades, will, in times of stress and storm, turn to mother and father as the ship laboring in the storm to the port for safety.

Ours is the responsibility as parents to teach our children chastity, to enter marriage pure from sexual transgression.

The Apostle Paul, apparently because of the importance that he saw of love in the home, made this statement:

> Husbands, love your wives, even as Christ also loved the church, and gave himself for it; . . .
> So ought men to love their wives as their own bodies. (Eph. 5:25, 28.)

Still another prophet condemned the infidelity of men and their unfaithfulness to their companions, those who had failed in their parental responsibilities, in these words:

> For behold, I, the Lord, have seen the sorrow and heard the mourning of the daughters of my people in the land of Jerusalem, yea and in all the lands of my people, because of the wickedness and abominations of their husbands.
>
> . . . Ye have broken the hearts of your tender wives, and lost the confidence of your children, because of your bad examples before them and the sobbings of their hearts ascend up to God, against you. And because of the strictness of the word of God, which cometh down against you, many hearts died, pierced with deep wounds. (Book of Mormon, Jacob 2:31, 35.)

Husbands, be true to your wives. Wives, be true to your husbands. Guard against the great sin of Sodom and Gomorrah. It has been labeled as a sin second only in seriousness to the sin of murder.

I speak of the sin of adultery, which as you know, is the name used by the Master as he referred to unlicensed sexual sins of fornication, adultery and besides this, the equally grievious sin of homosexuality which seems to be gaining momentum with social acceptance in the Babylon of today's world, and with which Church members must not be a party. While we are in the world we must not be of the world. Any attempts being made by the schools or places of entertainment to flaunt sexual perversions, which can do nothing but excite to experimentation, must find among the priesthood in this Church a vigorous and unrelenting foe through every lawful means which can be employed.

The common judges of Israel, our bishops, branch presidents, stake, and district presidents, must not stand by and fail to apply disciplinary measures within their jurisdiction as set forth plainly in the laws of the Lord. The procedures are set forth in plain and simple instructions that cannot be misunderstood. Never must we allow supposed mercy to the unrepentant sinner to rob the justice by which true repentance from sinful practices is predicated.

May I say here that we in the Church are unalterably

opposed to abortion. The only exception would be in cases where doctors find it necessary to perform an abortion to save the life of the mother. We reaffirm that the first purpose of marriage is to bring children into the world and they ought to be welcomed.

Now some of you have made mistakes and have no doubt sinned. Satan, that master of lies, would try to make you believe that because you have made a mistake, all is lost. He will try to persuade you to continue to live the life of sin. This is a great falsehood. All sins, except the unpardonable sin, which is the sin against the Holy Ghost, can be repented of and through the power of redemption and the gospel of Jesus Christ, all sins may be remitted, but they cannot be remitted until we who have sinned, as the prophets have taught, have done all we can to make right that which we have done which was wrong in the sight of God.

In one sentence, repentance means turning from that which you have done wrong in the sight of the Lord, and never repeating that mistake again. Then we can have the miracle of forgiveness. "But how can I know that the Lord has forgiven me of my sin?" you may ask. Here is one example from the Book of Mormon which gives you an answer. In the time of the great Prophet King Benjamin, as spoken of in the Book of Mosiah, he had preached with such power that these people were pricked in their hearts and desired to have the atoning blood of the Savior by which their sins could be washed away, and they said as they cried out, "We know that our sins have been forgiven because we have a peace of conscience." If you fully repent, you too can enjoy this peace of conscience.

Much of what I know about parenthood is that which I have learned over the years from the laboratory of my own home.

Recently, I came across a talk which had been given by one of my own daughters to a group of mothers and daughters, in which she related an experience with her first-born son. In this talk she related this experience, and I quote:

"Many years ago when our oldest son was a very little boy I found myself, one warm summer night after supper, frantically, trying to finish canning some apricots. I am sure that you all know the scene, you young mothers. Everything has happened during the day to keep you from getting to that project and finishing it. And now with the baby settled for the night and your husband off to his meeting on time, your little three-and four-year-olds are all but finished getting their pajamas on and getting ready for bed; you think well, now, I will get to those apricots. You realize that they are ripening fast and you realize that they are just not going to last until morning.

"This was the situation I found myself in that night, so I was beginning to pit them when my two little boys appeared in the kitchen and announced that they were ready to say their prayers. In desperation and not wanting to be interrupted for the umpteenth time, I said to them, very quickly, 'Now boys, why don't you just run in and say your prayers alone tonight and mother will just keep working with these apricots.'

"But David, the older of the two, planted his little feet firmly in front of me and asked, not unkindly, 'But mommy, which is more important, prayers or apricots?' Little did I realize then as a young mother and a busy wife, that in my life ahead there would be many such dilemmas that I would be faced with, large and small, as I carried out this role as wife and mother in my home, and that my success in these responsibilities would be measured by the manner in which I was able to solve problems. This was my challenge then, and this, as I see it is your challenge as wives and mothers today. How do we meet that challenge is the big question of our lives."

What a lesson in priorities that little boy taught his mother. Prayers should come before apricots!

Now, you husbands, remember that the most important of the Lord's work that you will ever do will be the work you do within the walls of your own home. Home Teaching, bishopric's work, and other Church duties are all important, but the most important work is within the walls of your home.

And you wives, may I plead with you to try to understand us, stubborn, strong-willed, sometimes careless, thoughtless men that we are. Will you sometimes try to reach under that gruffness and that outside veneer and keep on saying to us that you understand us, you want to help, and you want to be a part of our lives? Do not let your man say, and say it honestly, "My wife doesn't appreciate what I do. She doesn't care." And likewise, husbands, don't let your companion say that she gets no expressions of commendation for all her sacrifice and service. Such a feeling of resentment in your hearts could one day explode. So I beg of you to lay the foundations of the home on a solid, firm foundation of love, trust, and faith. Start the day with family prayer. Kneel together before you retire. There may have been some rough edges through the day and a good way to smooth them out is by kneeling together in prayer. See to it.

Some of you do not now have a companion in your home. Some of you have lost your wife or husband or you may not yet have found a companion. In your ranks are some of the noblest members of the Church—faithful, valiant, striving to live the Lord's commandments, to help build the kingdom on earth, and to serve your fellow men.

Life holds so much for you. Take strength in meeting your challenges. There are so many ways to find fulfillment, in serving those who are dear to you, in doing well the tasks that are before you in your employment or in the home. The Church offers so much opportunity for you to help souls, beginning with your own, to find the joy of eternal life.

Do not let self pity or despair beckon you from the course you know is right. Turn your thoughts to helping others. To you the words of the Master have special meaning: "He that findeth his life shall lose it: and he that loseth his life for my sake shall find it." (Matthew 10:39.)

Also appropriate are the words of King Benjamin: "And behold, I tell you these things that ye may learn wisdom:

that ye may learn that when ye are in the service of your fellow beings you are only in the service of your God." (Mosiah 2:17.)

God grant that the homes of the Latter-day Saints may be blessed and that there shall come into them happiness here and the foundation for exaltation in the celestial kingdom in the world to come.

Conclusion

And now as I close this book of talks under the general subject heading, *Decisions for Successful Living*, I have but one prayer in my heart and that is that out of your experience in the world of chaos and confusion, out of the hopeless depths of great world calamity, there will come new convictions and greater appreciation for the finer things of life.

May you dedicate your lives to a new resolve and be guided to become leaders in that not-too-far-distant glorious millennial day of universal peace when Christ himself shall reign as King of Kings and Lord of Lords, I pray in the name of the Lord Jesus Christ. Amen.

INDEX

Theories of men compared with truths of Gospel, 192.

Thompson, Arthur, quoted on ultimate molecule of life, 182.

Thoughts will condemn us, our, 90.

Threats to Our Civilization, 214.

Thrill-seeking youth on dangerous road, 159.

Time of Momentous Happenings, A, 220.

Tobacco abstain from, 77; help given in overcoming the, habit, 228.

"Transgressors is hard, the way of", 98.

Treasures on earth and in heaven, 8.

True Appraisal, A 119.

Trust, betrayal of, 31.

Truth, Gospel is divine, 8; ultimate triumph of, 16; "shall make you free", 34; sacrifice for, 42; giving life for defense of, 62; the light of, 144; statement of a great, 152; your search for, 188; Pilate asks what is,? 188; is scepter of power to give man dominion, 188; William George Jordan quoted on, 188; definition of, 189; shall make you free, 189; vital to the triumph of God's plan, 189; Satan seeks to overthrow, 189; purpose of prophet is to preserve, 190; place of Church in preserving, 191; not asked to give up any, 191; methods of finding spiritual, defined, 193; of all things made known by power of Holy Ghost, 193; spiritual, not discovered by methods of physical laboratory, 194; poem on, by Lowell, 222.

Truths of God are spiritually discerned, 192; theories of men compared to revealed, 192.

Twain, Mark, writes of deceased daughter, 220.

U.

Unemployment, the challenge of, 214.

United Order, the, 109.

United States Constitution inspired by God, 217.

Universe, harnessing power of, 73.

University of Spirituality, the, 196.

Untruth, definition of, 189.

Unwelcome Wedding Guests, 122.

Utah Highway 187 leads to state prison, 231.

V.

Valiant, mortal bodies of those not, 165.

Values born of stern necessity, true sense of, 14.

Vanities, Satan appeals to, 155.

Vicarious work for the dead, 119; 138.

"Vice is a monster", 88.

Vices of film luminaries, dangers of parading, 27.

Victory is by brute force, man's way to, 215; the Lord's way to, 215; two pictures of, 215.

Virgins, don't be as the foolish, 80.

Virtue, Gospel is a defense of, 7; fruits of, 93; beautiful flowers of, 233.

Virtues, greater publicity to men's, 27.

Vision, Joseph Smith tells reality of, 50; The, revelation given Joseph Smith, 139.

W.

War, those whose lives are taken in, 187.

Wards, subdivisions of stakes, 211.

Warning, a revelation of, 111.

Wars to come, frightfulness of, 214.

Weak, pursuit of easy things makes men, 15.

Wealth, Brigham Young quoted on fear of, 212.

Webster, Daniel, quoted on working on souls, 20.

Wedding Guests, Unwelcome, 122.

Welfare program, Church, 204.

Whitney, Orson F., author of Alberta Temple inscription, 138.

"Wicked are as a troubled sea," 89; fate of, before resurrection, 186.

"Wickedness never was happiness," 154; the flood of, 216.

Widowhood, the thriftiness of, 203.

Witnesses, faith based on testimony of, 75.

Woman, Bible account of creation of, 174.

Women to be denied no blessing, faithful, 129.

Woodruff, Wilford, gives Manifesto, 108; like Nathanael of old, 237.

Word of Wisdom given as God's law of health, 77; a challenge to the world, 77; rewards of, 78.

Words will condemn us, our, 90.

Work our pleasure, make, 23; to the man required to, on Sabbath, 148; with a mind to, 197; "have a mind to," 202; most important is within walls of your own home, 248.

World governed by law, 142.